The White House

The White House

An Architectural History

By

William Ryan
and
Desmond Guinness

McGraw-Hill Book Company

New York   St. Louis   San Francisco   Auckland   Bogota
Hamburg   Johannesburg   London   Madrid   Mexico
Montreal   New Delhi   Panama   Paris   Toronto
Sydney   Tokyo   Sao Paulo
Singapore

DF BT

Library of Congress Cataloging in Publication Data

Ryan, William, date.
The White House: an architectural history.
Bibliography: p.   1. Washington, D.C. White House.
I. Guinness, Desmond, joint author.   II. Title.
NA4443.W3R9   725′.17′09753   80-10135
ISBN 0-07-054352-6

*The editors for this book were Jeremy Robinson and Joseph Williams,
the designer was Naomi Auerbach, and the production supervisor
was Teresa F. Leaden. It was set in Korinna
by York Graphic Services.*

Printed and bound by Halliday Lithograph, Inc.

Contents

c. 1

Foreword

Because the White House was a creation of the government, an unusually large and comprehensive body of records relating to its design and construction has been preserved. Not all are in the National Archives, as Thomas Jefferson extracted some architectural drawings from the government holdings for personal study. These were later collected from Jefferson descendants by Thomas Jefferson Coolidge, Jr., and deposited in the Massachusetts Historical Society. Other drawings were placed in the hands of B. Henry Latrobe, whose son subsequently donated them to the Maryland Historical Society.

To encourage students of the White House to consult original records, references to the dates and authors of documents are frequently incorporated in the text; additional references appear in the notes. The bibliographical material also indicates the principal National Archives classifications in which White House documents can be found.

We are much indebted to the many people who provided historical material for this book, or who assisted us in locating it, including: Gray D. Boone, Editor, *Antique Monthly;* Charles E. Brownell, Assistant Editor for Architectural History, The Papers of Benjamin Henry Latrobe; Clement E. Conger, Curator, and Betty C. Monkman, Registrar, the White House; Malcolm Freiberg, Editor of Publications, Winifred Collins, Curator, and Robert Sparks, Assistant Librarian, Massachusetts Historical Society; Wilhelmina S. Harris, Superintendent, Adams National Historic Site; Mrs. George C. Homans; Mary M. Ison and Jerry Kearns, Reference Librarians, Prints and Photographs Division, Library of Congress; Isabel Barrett Lowry, Executive Secretary, The Dunlap Society; Dorothy Provine, Civil Records, James Harwood, Fiscal Branch, Sara Strom, Reference Librarian, William H. Leary and Paul White, Still Pictures, National Archives; Richard J. Simpson, Public Services Librarian, Fine Arts Library, and Christopher Hall, Assistant Librarian, Frances Loeb Library, Harvard University; Raymond Teichman, Audiovisual Archivist, Franklin D. Roosevelt Library; Hillory A. Tolson, Executive Director, White House Historical Association; and Martin I. Yoelson, Chief of Interpretation, Independence National Historical Park.

We thank Academy Editions, London, for permission to reproduce an illustration from their publication *Architectural Principles in the Age of Humanism* by Rudolf Wittkower, as our figure 67; Mrs. Aristotle Onassis for kindly permitting quotation of a letter; The Carolina Art Association, Mary M. Muller, Administrator, for permission to quote the problem solved by Hoban, published in The *Architects of Charleston* by Beatrice St. Julien Ravenel; and The Papers of Benjamin Henry Latrobe, Edward C. Carter II, Editor, for permission to quote from Latrobe letters belonging to the Maryland Historical Society. We also thank the Maryland Historical Society, Romaine S. Somerville, Director, for allowing us to photograph their drawings of the President's House competition; and the Columbia Historical Society, Perry G. Fisher, Librarian, and Robert Truax, for permitting us to photograph engravings in the Society's collections.

We are particularly grateful to John Harris, Betty Monkman, and Charles E. Brownell for their advice and comments on various parts of the manuscript.

The assistance of R. Jackson Smith, who made photographic prints for several of the illustrations, and Elizabeth Barclay, who expertly typed the manuscript, is much appreciated.

The White House

One

Political Prologue

The building and rebuilding of the White House—and the decision to place it upon a ridge overlooking the Potomac River—began with the state of mind of the delegates to the Second Continental Congress in 1783. A treaty of peace had just been signed in Paris ending the American Revolution, and General George Washington intended to retire to Mount Vernon as soon as the army could be demobilized. He alone had held the states together for the past seven years, replacing George III as the symbol of unity. Now a new order in the central government was necessary to broaden the meager powers granted by the independent, sovereign states to carry on the war. With the integrating effect of the conflict with Great Britain subsiding, and Washington no longer active, the concept of a national identity had to be strengthened.

Until the states showed confidence in the federation by establishing a capital, the credibility of a peacetime association was in doubt. During the war, delegates to Congress, like roving ambassadors, could meet at any agreed place or time. Six different towns were host to the national legislature as British forces chased it up and down the eastern seaboard. With this annoyance past, it was time to build a permanent house for the Congress and the federal executive services in a prestigious and convenient place. Individually, most of the delegates favored Philadelphia, the country's largest city, for its easy access, agreeable climate, plentiful boarding houses, and pleasant social life.

But the states had other ideas. There was a long tradition, born in colonial times, of competition and distrust. Some states had been founded by dissidents from another, such as Rhode Island from Massachusetts. Others had been operated by large trading companies and had long enjoyed almost complete political autonomy. Puritan New England and Anglican Virginia had quite different social patterns. The interests of the mercantile north often opposed those of the agrarian south. Small states feared domination by the large. Having risked their lives and fortunes to rid themselves of oppressive external control, most of the citizens were slow to admit the need for a more highly organized central authority, especially one located in an already influential state.

Accordingly, Congressional debate on a permanent seat opened with no consensus, and a long general discussion of the project took place over several months. Three attributes were considered essential: a central and convenient location, legal control vested in the national government, and use of a navigable river with access to the lands of the interior as well as to the sea.

Location was at first regarded only in the geographical sense; travel was arduous, and the capital should be accessible. As choices narrowed, the political and economic advantages of nearness to central power became apparent. States soon arranged themselves into groups; the North (then known as the "east") solidified against the South, with the central states, from New Jersey to Virginia, switching about as the exact site brightened or dimmed their future prospects.

The most favored rivers were the Susquehanna, Delaware, and Potomac. The last two eventually became the chief competitors, as they were closer to the center of population.

Federal jurisdiction was never a problem; most of the early offers from the states freely provided for "exempt" districts. But in June 1783, while Congress was still debating the residence issue, an incident occurred showing that ultimate police power in the national capital must be exercisable by an agency of the national government, thus ruling out the use of any existing large city.

Soldiers barracked at Lancaster, Pennsylvania, sent a petition to Congress on June 13 requesting back pay which had become long overdue. The "mutinous memorial" excited much indignation and was sent to the Secretary of War. Because neither the Secretary nor the Congress had any money, the soldiers did not receive a satisfactory reply.

On June 19 word was received that 80 soldiers were on their way to Philadelphia to lay their case before Congress, with intimations that, unless satisfied, they would attempt to seize the federal bank. The State executive felt that the militia, being civilian, would not be willing to restrain the soldiers unless provoked by an actual outrage, and the authority of the government might be risked in an attempt to order them to do so. Congress was much displeased, and felt that if the state and the city governments could not protect them, it was high time to remove to some other place.

Two days later, the soldiers presented themselves, drawn up in the street before the State House, where Congress was assembled. President Dickinson (of the Council of the State) was called in, but repeated that without some injury to persons or property, nothing could be done.

The soldiers remained in position, picketing, in effect, without offering any violence. Individuals occasionally shouted offensive words, and wantonly pointed their muskets at the windows of the hall. No danger of premeditated violence was considered likely, but it was observed that spirituous drink from the tippling houses nearby began to be liberally served out to the soldiers and might lead to some accidental excesses. No incident occurred, however, and at the usual hour Congress adjourned. The soldiers, "tho in some instances offering a mock obstruction," permitted the members to pass through their ranks. They themselves retired soon after to the barracks.

In the evening Congress again met and delivered an ultimatum to the state government; if the mutiny were not suppressed, Congress would move to Trenton

or Princeton. The local executive produced nothing but a repetition of doubts.

Reports from the barracks were "in constant vibration. At one moment the mutineers were penitent and preparing submissions; the next they were meditating more violent measures. Sometimes the bank was their object; then the seizure of members of Congress with whom they imagined an indemnity for their offence might be stipulated."

On June 24, word from the barracks being unfavorable, Congress determined to meet at Princeton, and left. After their departure, the mutineers submitted, and most of them accepted furloughs under a resolution Congress had passed. At the same time they "betrayed their leaders, the chief of whom proved to be a Mr. Carberry a deranged officer, and a Mr. Sullivan a Lieutenant of Horse, both of whom made their escape. Some of the most active Sergeants also ran off."

Congress reconvened at Princeton, in a room at Nassau Hall, on June 26. By that time, it dawned on the Philadelphians what their indecision and weakness had cost them, as the total revenue from the sitting Congress was at least $100,000 per year. In July, Congress was asked to return, but declined because of the insult suffered not only from the soldiers but from the State Executive Council in failing to protect them. In spite of the relative triviality of the action, the principle of a safe residence for Congress and all offices of the national government, with adequate police

Fig. 1 Pennsylvania State House, seat of the Continental Congress in 1783.

powers, was established. The Continental Congress never returned to Philadelphia, completing its interrupted session in Princeton. In November of that year, the next session of Congress was held at Annapolis; in 1784 it sat at Trenton for sixty days and then moved to New York, where it remained until replaced by the new Congress devised by the Constitution in 1789.

Washington had been informed of the "mutiny" in Philadelphia, and he advised Congress that the bitter feelings generated and the inconvenience of Princeton, causing low attendance and a lack of a voting majority, made it impossible to get agreement among the states on a permanent seat. Desultory actions followed in October 1783, but the momentum was lost and no further action was taken until the new Constitution later settled the matter.

Serious defects in the Articles of Confederation became apparent during this critical period, and the sentiment of the country slowly moved toward modification of the Articles to provide for the regulation of commerce and restoration of order to the economy. The Confederation Congress passed a resolution on February 21, 1787, calling for a convention of delegates to revise the Articles. By May 14, twelve states were represented at the State House in Philadelphia.

Here an astounding event happened. Two months after hearing the first proposals, the Constitutional Convention arrived at a series of brilliant compromises and judgments which have stood to this day as the basic law of the land. They resolved most differences among the states by providing a bicameral Congress; adopted a suggestion in the Virginia Resolutions that the Chief Executive should consist of "a single person"; established federal courts; and sandwiched into a list of broad powers of Congress the right "to exercise exclusive legislation in all cases whatsoever, over such district (not exceeding ten miles square) as may, by cession of particular States, and the acceptance of Congress, become the seat of the government of the United States."

The Constitution, submitted to the states in the autumn of 1787, was ratified on June 21, 1788, by nine states, enabling it to go into effect. On September 13, the old Confederation Congress provided a procedure for the election of the President, and in the process, terminated itself.

The act had called for the assembly of the electors in February 1789, but bad weather prevented a quorum of Congress from counting the votes until April. George Washington, elected President unanimously, took the oath of office in New York on April 30, 1789.

The new Congress took up the question of residence in September, but adjourned without resolving it. In late May of the following term, legislation on residence was debated about the same time as the matter of funding the old bond issues of the states. The Secretary of the Treasury, Alexander Hamilton, proposed that the federal government assume the debt at face value, although at adjusted rates of interest. Differences on "Assumption" and "Residence" became the cause of so much antagonism that Washington and Hamilton, remembering the slender margins by which the Constitution was ratified and that North Carolina and Rhode Island were still outside the Union, became alarmed about the continuation of the new government. Jefferson, who had been in France as minister during the framing of the Constitution, doubtful about the wisdom of many of its provisions, had been persuaded by Washington to become Secretary of State. Although no friend of Hamilton, he agreed to intervene.

Jefferson described the subsequent events in his *anas:*

> This measure [Assumption] produced the most bitter & angry contests ever known in Congress, before or since the union of the States. . . . The great and trying question however was lost in the H. of Representatives. So high were the feuds excited by this subject, that on it's rejection, business was suspended. . . . The Eastern members, particularly, who . . . were the principal gamblers in these scenes, threatened a secession and dissolution. Hamilton was in despair. As I was going to the President's one day, I met him in the street. He walked me backwards & forwards before the President's door for half an hour. He painted pathetically the temper into which the legislature had been wrought, the disgust of those who were called the Creditor states, the danger of the secession of their members, and the separation of the States. He observed that the members of the administration ought to act in concert, that tho' this question was not of my department, yet a common duty should make it a common concern . . . ; and that the question having been lost by a small majority only, it was probable that an appeal from me to the judgment and discretion of some of my friends might effect a change in the vote, and the machine of government, now suspended, might be again set into motion. I told him that I was really a stranger to the whole subject. . . . ; that undoubtedly if it's rejection endangered a dissolution of our union at this incipient stage, I should deem that the most unfortunate of all consequences, to avert which all partial and temporary evils should be yielded. I proposed to him however, to dine with me the next day, and I would invite another friend or two, bring them into conference together, and I thought it impossible that reasonable men, consulting together coolly, could fail, by some mutual sacrifices of opinion, to form a compromise which was to save the union. The discussion took place. I could take no part in it, but an exhortatory one, because I was a stranger to the circumstances which should govern it. But it was finally agreed that . . . it would be better that the vote of rejection should be rescinded, to effect which some members should change their votes. But it was observed that this pill would be peculiarly bitter to the Southern States, and that some concomitant measure should be adopted to sweeten it a little to them. There had before been propositions to fix the seat of government either at Philadelphia, or at Georgetown on the Potomac; and it was thought that by giving it to Philadelphia for ten years, and to Georgetown permanently afterwards, this might, as an anodyne, calm in some degree the ferment which might be excited by the other measure alone. So two of the Potomac members (White & Lee, but White with a revulsion of stomach almost convulsive) agree to change their votes, & Hamilton undertook to carry the other point. In doing this the influence he had established over the Eastern members, with the agency of Robert Morris with those of the middle states, effected his side of the engagement, and so the assumption was passed, and 20 millions of stock divided among favored states, and thrown in as pabulum to the stock-jobbing herd.

As a result, three Southerners changed their votes for Assumption: Richard Bland Lee (Virginia); Daniel Carroll (Maryland), later one of the original Commissioners of the District of Columbia; and Alexander White (Virginia), who succeeded him in that post in 1795. On the strength of this compromise, the Residence and Assumption bills became law on July 16 and August 9, 1790, respectively.

For the next ten years, the national offices would return to Philadelphia; and on the first Monday in December 1800 they would be transferred to the new district on the Potomac, accepted for the permanent seat of the government of the United States.

Fig. 2 Congress Hall, Philadelphia. Originally built as a courthouse, this building housed Congress from 1790 to 1800.

Two

Selecting the Site

During the congressional recess in the fall of 1790, Washington returned to Mount Vernon, Jefferson to Monticello, and the government offices were moved from New York to Philadelphia. Left behind was the elegant building converted for the use of the federal government by New York under the direction of Major Pierre Charles L'Enfant only a year earlier. The city had hoped, by quickly providing adequate accommodations, to encourage the capital to remain permanently, but the provision in the Constitution for a separate federal district was by now broadly accepted, and Philadelphia lay ready and waiting.

George Washington had refrained from active participation in the selection of the federal seat. Recognizing his obvious bias toward a location only a few miles from his home, perhaps he wished to avoid offending more distant states by putting himself in a seemingly partisan position. Once the issue was settled, however, the President began promptly to implement the law. On October 16, 1790, he traveled from Mount Vernon to Georgetown "in order to fix on a proper selection for the Grand Columbian Federal City," which he intended to locate at the fork of the Potomac River and its eastern branch, later known as the Anacostia River. He had previously opened negotiations with the local landowners. With Jefferson, a plan was prepared for acquiring title to the land needed for public purposes and dividing the city lots between the government and the former owners.

When government operations resumed in Philadelphia in the winter of 1790–1791, activity on the Potomac site quickened. Jefferson prepared a memorandum concerning the federal district on November 29, 1790, suggesting most of the ground rules eventually adopted by the President. As Jefferson often mentioned, the streets were to be laid out at right angles as in Philadelphia, forming squares of about 8 acres each. And, "for the President's house, . . . 2 squares should be consolidated. for the Capitol & offices one square. for the Market one square. for the Public walks 9. squares consolidated." Here is the first reference anywhere to the concept of a great park—the Mall—connecting the principal public buildings.

Jefferson also proposed that the district commissioners should have some taste in architecture, as they might have to decide among different plans; but final approval of plans for the public buildings was left to the President.

Fig. 3 Federal Hall, New York City. Charles Pierre L'Enfant hurriedly enlarged the old City Hall for the use of Congress, 1788–1789.

Three commissioners for preparing the federal seat were appointed: General Thomas Johnson of Frederick, Maryland, sixty years of age, former governor, then State Chief Justice, and soon to become a justice of the first U.S. Supreme Court; the Honorable Daniel Carroll, sixty-one years old, a congressman and uncle of Daniel Carroll of Duddington, owner of the largest parcel of land within the federal city; and Dr. David Stuart, physician, plantation owner, personal friend of Washington, and husband of the widow of Mrs. Washington's son, John Parke Custis. The commissioners did not meet formally until the middle of March, by which time Carroll's term in Congress had expired.

Major Pierre L'Enfant, military engineer and architect, and Major Andrew Ellicott, astronomer and surveyor, were requested to make studies of the area adjacent to Georgetown. The initial directives from the President and the Secretary of State clearly distinguished between their related but quite different responsibilities. Jefferson notified the Commissioners, January 29, 1791, that

> the President having thought Major L'Enfant peculiarly qualified to make such a draught of the ground as will enable himself to fix on the spot for the public buildings, he has been written to for that purpose, and will be sent on if he chuses to undertake it.

Jefferson wrote to Ellicott four days later:

> Sir: You are desired to proceed by the first stage to the Federal territory on the Potomac, for the purpose of making a survey of it. The first object will be to run the two first lines mentioned in the enclosed proclamation. . . . A plat of the whole on which ultimate directions for the rest of the work shall be sent to you, as soon as they can be prepared. Till these shall be received by you, you can be employed in ascertaining a true Meridian, and the latitude of the place, and running the meanderings of the Eastern branch, and of the River itself, and other waters which will merit an exact place in the map of the Territory.

Ellicott also was a "peculiarly qualified" person for his job; in fact, he was one of only two men in America with the means to "ascertain a true Meridian" with great accuracy. Ellicott had built a transit-instrument (an astronomical telescope mounted on a tilting and rotating base marked in degrees, minutes, and seconds much like a theodolite) for observing the movement of celestial bodies. The only other such instrument in the country belonged to David Rittenhouse of Philadelphia. L'Enfant having accepted, Jefferson wrote to him in March:

> You are desired to proceed to Georgetown, where you will find Mr. Ellicot employed in making a survey and map of the Federal territory. The special object of asking your aid is to have drawings of the particular grounds most likely to be approved for the site of the federal town and buildings. You will therefore be pleased to begin on the eastern branch, and proceed from thence upwards, laying down the hills, valleys, morasses, and waters between that, the Potomac, the Tyber, and the road leading from Georgetown to the eastern branch, and connecting the whole with certain fixed points of the map Mr. Ellicot is preparing. Some idea of the height of the hills above the base on which they stand, would be desirable.

The stream called the "Tyber" in this letter was a creek formed from the confluence of three small brooks which joined just north of present Pennsylvania

Avenue and broadened into a shallow basin south of the location of the President's House. In the previous century the land adjoining it had been the plantation held by the family of Thomas Pope. He or one of his descendants had named the homestead "Rome," and the muddy little rivulet the "Tiber." It was also commonly called "Goose Creek." The two names were used interchangeably for the stream until its total obliteration in the mid-nineteenth century.

Jefferson was keenly interested in participating in the design of a plan for the city as well as in its execution, but his visualization of the nation's immediate need and ultimate destiny was modest, in consonance with his agrarian philosophy. The President, believing that the United States would expand to equality with the European nations, thought of the capital city as eventually becoming another London or Paris, which then had populations of 800,000 and 600,000, respectively.

As Secretary of State, Jefferson had drafted a proclamation for the President amending the bounds of the federal district, primarily to include Alexandria, on March 30, 1791. In a paragraph later deleted, the draft proclamation stated "that the highest summit of lands in the town heretofore called Hamburg, . . . shall be appropriated for a Capitol . . . and such other lands between Georgetown . . . and the stream heretofore called the Tyber . . . as shall be found convenient . . . shall be appropriated for the accommodation of the President of the U.S. for the time being, and for the public offices of the government of the U.S."

This has been interpreted previously as reversing the final sites of the Capitol and the President's House, but according to a sketch prepared by Jefferson to illustrate his scheme, the description in the proclamation is not quite correct. Jacob Funk, a previous owner, had laid out a town named "Hamburgh" in 1768. It extended approximately from 19th Street to a line beyond 23d Street, and from H Street south to Constitution Avenue in the present city. The locus of old Hamburgh is shown on Jefferson's sketch by the solid lines around the area marked "President." The site marked for the Capitol was far to the east of Hamburgh, in an area known as "Beall's Levels"; in today's city, this is a block or two beyond the Treasury, in the vicinity of Garfinckel's department store. The President's House would have been near the intersection of present-day Virginia Avenue and F Street. All the land south of these locations to the water line (now Constitution Avenue) was intended for "public walks" connecting the legislative and executive seats.

This was a tiny capital indeed compared to the one envisioned by Washington. Before seeing this plan L'Enfant had criticized regular squares and right-angled street layouts as being ill-suited to the rolling terrain. On March 26, he prepared a memorandum on the Potomac site for Washington, in which he cautioned that such a pattern of parallel and uniform streets would absolutely annihilate the advantages of the most desirable locations. Regular plans, he said, may be seducing to the eye on paper, but when applied to the ground become tiresome and insipid, a mere contrivance of some cool imagination wanting a sense of the grand and the truly beautiful.

In this lengthy report to the President, L'Enfant for the first time described the locations proposed for the President's House, the Capitol, and the other public buildings. On a long ridge running northwesterly from Jenkins Hill, parallel to the Potomac, these edifices would rear with a majestic aspect over the country, and could be seen 20 miles off. While conveniently near the first settlements, in ages to come they would stand in the center of the capital city, with a grand prospect of the land and waters below.

The ridge referred to is that beginning at sites of the House Office Buildings and the Capitol (Jenkins Hill), circling under the old City Hall and the old Patent Office (now the National Collection of Fine Arts) to the area of the White House. While newer government buildings have spread over lower ground, those built between 1792 and 1840 were all in the high location selected by the farsighted L'Enfant.

The President came to Georgetown on March 28 to confer with the newly assembled Commissioners, Mr. Ellicott, and Major L'Enfant, who presented the report he had written. Two days later Washington left for Mount Vernon, after giving "some directions . . . to the Commissioners, the Surveyor and Engineer with respect to the mode of laying out the district. . . ." The President confirmed this in a letter to

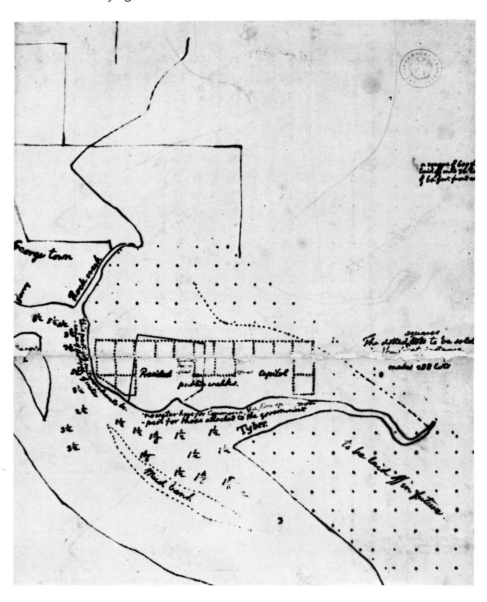

Fig. 4 Jefferson's plan for the Federal City, 1791.

Jefferson on March 31, mentioning that "the whole shall be surveyed and laid off as a city (which Major L'Enfant is now directed to do). . . ."

At Mount Vernon, word was received that Pennsylvania had introduced a bill in the state House of Representatives "to provide funds for a Congress-hall, a house for the President, et ca" in Philadelphia, obviously hoping to forestall further development of the new federal city. Washington promptly wrote his agents to complete the negotiations with the proprietors in the district in a "speedy effectual manner" so that "the consequent arrangements may take place without delay." Notwithstanding his own convictions, the President forwarded several suggestions for the Federal City to L'Enfant, including the Jefferson scheme. He writes on April 4:

> Although I do not conceive that you will derive any material advantage from an examination of the enclosed papers, yet as they have been drawn under different circumstances, and by different persons, they may be compared with your own ideas of a proper plan for the Federal City, under the prospect which it now presents itself.—For this purpose I commit them to your private inspection until my return from the tour I am about to make.—The rough sketch by Mr. Jefferson, was done under an idea that no offer, worthy of consideration, would come from the Landholders in the vicinity of Carrolsburgh from the backwardness which appeared in them,—and therefore was accommodated to the grounds about Georgetown.—The other, is taken up upon a larger scale, without reference to any described spot.

Also on April 4, L'Enfant requested Jefferson to send him any city maps he might have within reach, not for the purpose of copying, but to study details such as the placement of public buildings, arsenals, shipyards, markets, and the like.

Jefferson immediately sent plans of "Frankfort on the Mayne, Carlsruhe, Amsterdam, Strasburg, Paris, Orleans, Bordeaux, Lyons, Montpelier, Marseilles, Turin and Milan," truly an astonishing collection to have had on hand. On April 10 he reported his action to Washington, adding, "They are none of them however comparable to the old Babylon, revived in Philadelphia, & exemplified."

L'Enfant's plan, one of the last great baroque city plans, did not in the end closely resemble any of those sent to him by Jefferson. The grid of Philadelphia was basic, as Jefferson wanted, but overlaid with monumental avenues connecting the principal centers of activity in the city. By modern standards, it had many faults, primarily the awkward intersections, some of which L'Enfant might have corrected if his employment had been continued. But other reasonable devices, such as curved or winding streets to adjust the plan more comfortably to the terrain, to lead to nearby towns, or simply to break the monotony of a long avenue, would not have occurred to him. The geometric city, drawing its parts to a focus at the seat of power, was then, as it is now, an anachronism in a republic. It is an imperial concept, and L'Enfant repeatedly referred to his creation as the seat of a "vast Empire."

The grand design provided ample and appropriate space for the government buildings, and elegance suitable for a national capital. It was on a very large scale, far too large in the eyes of many, but it satisfied the President and conformed to his vision of the country's future. Jean de Ternant, appointed French minister after the war, remarked that "the President shows the greatest interest in this new Salente, which is to bear his name." Ternant may have made a most astute observation in linking Salente, a Utopian city in Francois de Fénelon's *Télémaque,* with the city of

Washington. Fénelon's book, translated into English by Hawkesworth in 1769, was in Washington's library. Mentor, friend and teacher of Telemachus, describes in Chapter XII the government and construction of Salentum, which closely resembled the circumstances of the project on the Potomac. Fénelon's ideas, intended to instruct the grandson of Louis XIV, would be equally useful to a President. Washington referred to the book in a letter to Lafayette regarding the visit to America by his son George Washington Lafayette and a tutor, M. Frestel: "M. Frestel has been a true Mentor to George. No parent could have been more attentive to a favorite son; and he rightly merits all that can be said of his virtues, of his good sense, and his prudence."

L'Enfant's remarkable plan has been described as a deliberate imitation of Versailles. But William T. Partridge has found that L'Enfant's analysis was far more careful than this superficial attribution implies. The topography was the fundamental consideration; siting of the major buildings, communication, visual impact, and routing of principal avenues and squares along contour lines were parts of a complex concept. Small wonder that the scheme should resemble the best-planned cities of L'Enfant's day and be scaled to the grandeur befitting the capital of a new nation.

Cities with radial and diagonal avenues had existed since the rebuilding of Rome by Paul III; the trident array of streets invented there had become a widely used baroque device. The L-shaped arrangement of grounds connecting the Capitol and the President's House at Washington appears in other guises at Versailles, in Paris as it was in 1790, and at Williamsburg, Virginia. The proportions of the major axes and the relation of the several intermediate points to the main termini are almost identical in all four of these cities.

L'Enfant had prepared a preliminary plan of the capital city and a report dated June 22, 1791, prior to the return of the President from his tour of the Southern states. On June 28, Washington was again at Georgetown, where he examined the ground with Ellicott and L'Enfant in order "to decide finally on the spots on which to place the public buildings." The following day he laid a plat before the proprietors, showing the proposed sites of the Capitol and the President's House, and conveying general ideas of the city plan. They were told some changes would be made—a reduction in the number of diagonal avenues, for one—and the relocation of the President's House more westerly for the advantage of higher ground. The plan met with the general approval of the subscribers, which Washington noted with much pleasure.

L'Enfant returned to the drawing board and by August 19 had prepared a second plan which he presented to Washington, with a letter beginning:

> The heig[ht] of my Ambition [is] Gratified in having met with your approbation in the project of the Plan which I now have the Honor of presenting to you altered agreeable to your direction. . . .
> The inspection of the anexed map of doted lines being sufficiently explanatory of the progress made in the work will I hope leave you satisfied how much more has been done than may have been expected from hands less desirous of meriting your applause. . . .

These paragraphs confirm that L'Enfant made numerous changes in his first plan as Washington desired in their previous meeting, and the notation "map of doted

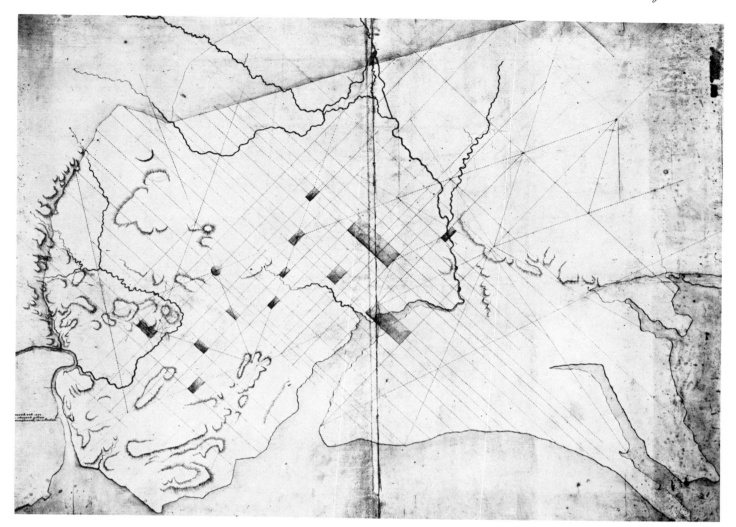

lines'' definitely relates this letter to the earliest existing L'Enfant plan. L'Enfant noted further that ''the spots assigned for the Federal House & for the President palace in exibiting the most sumpteous aspect and claiming already the suffrage of a crowd of daily visitors both natives and foreigners will serve to give a grand idea of the whole. . . .'' Contours are indicated on this map, showing that the President's House is on the easterly edge of a ridge, complying with Washington's earlier directions to move the site westward to higher ground.

The final plan of the city was placed before Congress on December 13, 1791. Just when L'Enfant delivered it to the President is uncertain, but in a speech to Congress on October 25 Washington stated that ''a city had also been laid out agreeably to a plan which will be placed before Congress. . . .''

Now on the edge of achieving a great artistic and engineering triumph, and destined for still greater fame as the architect of the public buildings, L'Enfant became involved in a series of arrogant and politically inept quarrels with the Commissioners.

Fig. 5 L'Enfant's plan of dotted lines, accompanying his report to President Washington, August 19, 1791.

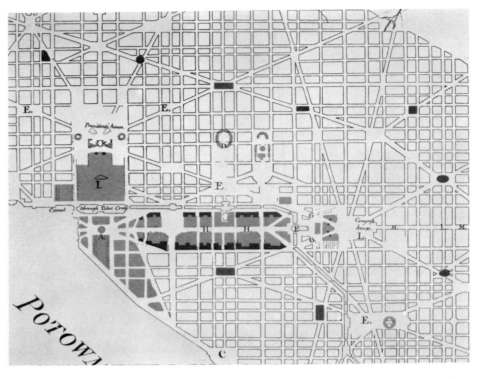

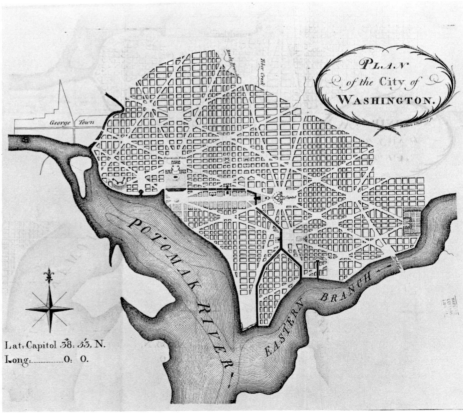

Fig. 6 Center section of L'Enfant's plan of Washington. From a copy prepared by the Coast and Geodetic Survey, 1887.

Fig. 7 The first published map of Washington, March 1792.

The troubles began with L'Enfant's demolition of a house being built by Daniel Carroll of Duddington, a brother-in-law of Commissioner Daniel Carroll. The building had been started in 1790, long before L'Enfant arrived on the scene. It stood on an eminence near a spring, a spot which L'Enfant later chose as a public square to be ornamented with a fountain. In an early exchange of correspondence, Carroll had assured L'Enfant that the house would be taken down whenever it should be deemed an obstruction in consequence of building in that part of the city. The impatient Major, however, arbitrarily determined to remove it at once, without consulting the Commissioners. While this caused no little consternation, it was only the beginning of a battle of wills between L'Enfant and his superiors, who were strongly supported by the President.

L'Enfant begged Washington to appoint him "Director General," independent of the established chain of responsibility, answerable only to the President. Washington declined, and from that time (January 1792) L'Enfant refused the use of his plan. Jefferson privately advised Daniel Carroll to post a watch over the survey stakes to prevent a whole summer's work being lost through vandalism. Elisha O. Williams was given this duty.

Jefferson now had no alternative; Major Ellicott was requested to prepare the official plan for engraving. L'Enfant's ace had been trumped, and his dream of making a fortune from the sale of his plan evaporated.

In cordial but firm letters, both Washington and Jefferson attempted to persuade L'Enfant to cooperate with the commissioners, but his inordinate pride and ambition prevented a reconciliation. On February 27, 1792, convinced that any further delay in the planning of the city was severely detrimental, Jefferson sent L'Enfant a succinct note:

Sir

From your letter received yesterday in answer to my last, & your declarations in conversation with Mr. Lear, it is understood that you absolutely decline acting under the authority of the present Commissioners. If this understanding of your meaning be right I am instructed by the President to inform you that notwithstanding the desire he has entertained to preserve your agency in the business the condition upon which it is to be done is inadmissible, & your services must be at an end.

I have the honor to be Sir &c.

Th: Jefferson.

Andrew Ellicott wrote to the Commissioners from Philadelphia on February 23, 1792:

On my arrival at this city, I found no preparation was made for an engraving of the City of Washington.—Upon the representation being made to the President and Secretary of State, I was directed to furnish one for an engraver, which with the aid of my Brother, was compleated last Monday, and handed to the President—In this business we met with difficulties of a very serious nature—Major L'Enfant refused us the use of the *Original!* What his motives were, God knows.—the plan which we have furnished, I believe will be found to answer the ground better, than the large one in the Major's hands.—I have engaged two good artists (both Americans) to execute the engraving, and who will begin work as soon as the President comes to a determination respecting some small alterations. In several conferences with the President and Secretary of State, I have constantly mentioned the necessity of system in the execution of the business, without which there can be neither economy, certainty, nor decision. The Major has both a *lively fancy* and *decision;* but unfortunately no system, which renders the other qualifications less valuable and in some cases useless.—I suspect that measures are now taking, which will reduce the Major to the necessity of submitting to the legal arrangements, or deserting the City.

Another letter to the Commissioners of March 7 ended:

As Mr. Jefferson is now waiting for a small sketch of the City, I am under the necessity of closing this before I intended.

An engraving of the long-awaited plan of the City of Washington was published for the first time in the March 1792 issue of the *Universal Asylum and Columbia Magazine* of Philadelphia.

Three

L'Enfant, Jefferson, and Washington: First Architects of the President's House

Pierre Charles L'Enfant was educated at the Academie Royale de Peinture et Sculpture in Paris from September 1771, studying at times under his father, a painter of battle scenes at Versailles and a designer for the Gobelins factory. It is not known how long his training lasted, but he was not among the prizewinners who were given advanced instruction at the School in the Louvre. At the age of twenty-two, in 1776 he applied for service in America, and was sent under the aegis of the fictitious trading house of "Rodriguez Hortales et Cie.," devised by Beaumarchais to supply the American Army. Some 25,000 guns of various kinds, as well as powder, tents, and clothing, supposedly destined for the West Indies, were actually delivered to American ports, together with a large number of French officers and men.

L'Enfant distinguished himself in the Revolution, and left the American Army with the rank of major. Establishing himself in New York, he developed an active architectural practice. A dozen or more buildings were built or altered by him from 1783 to 1789. In that year the Congress under the new Constitution was sitting in New York. L'Enfant learned of the government's intention to locate the capital city in the wilderness on the Potomac. He applied to President Washington in a letter dated September 11, 1789, for an appointment as Engineer to the United States. Since the government was at that moment housed in a building designed by him, it is not surprising that L'Enfant's application was accepted when the need for an engineer-designer arose in 1791.

At a later time, Washington wrote:

> Since my first knowledge of the gentleman's abilities in the line of his profession, I have received him not only as a scientific man, but one who added considerable taste to his professional knowledge; and that, for such employment as he is now engaged in, for prosecuting public works, and carrying them into effect, he was better qualified than any one, who had come within my knowledge in this country, or indeed in any other, the probability of obtaining whom could be counted upon.

Washington and Jefferson intended from the beginning to entrust the design of the public buildings to L'Enfant. The President confirmed this in a letter of February 28, 1792, reproaching L'Enfant for his behavior:

> . . . five months have elapsed and are lost, by the compliment which was intended to be paid you in depending alone upon your plans for the public buildings instead of advertising a premium to the person who should present the best (which would have included yourself equally). . . .

The "five months" refers to a letter Washington had written Jefferson on August 29, 1791, about several basic aspects of the progress in the Federal City. "When ought the public buildings to be begun, and in what manner had the materials best be provided?" was one of the questions raised. Jefferson promptly held a meeting (September 8) with the Commissioners and James Madison in Georgetown, where the decision was made to advertise "a medal or other reward for the best plan," and in any case to begin "the digging of the earth for brick" in the fall, with provision of other materials to depend on funds available. The President held the design competition in abeyance, expecting L'Enfant to provide suitable plans.

L'Enfant had something in mind for the President's House by the time his plan of the city was completed late in 1791, as an outline of a building is shown in the President's square. No indication of a corresponding building appears in the space allotted to the "Congress House." The area of the original plan around the site of the President's House is now almost obliterated, but the 1887 copy by the Coast and Geodetic Survey shows an elaborate central structure with extensive wings and courtyards. The L-shaped buildings were possibly intended for the executive offices.

Other evidence indicates that L'Enfant had at least a general plan of the President's House to support this sketch. Jefferson had written him on April 10:

> Whenever it is proposed to prepare plans for the Capitol, I should prefer the adoption of some one of the models of antiquity, which have had the approbation of thousands of years, and for the President's House I should prefer the celebrated fronts of modern buildings, which have already received the approbation of all good judges. Such are the Galerie du Louvre, the Gardes meubles, and two fronts of the Hotel de Salm. But of this it is yet time enough to consider, in the mean time I am with great esteem Sir &c.

The outline on the map does not accord with any "fronts" of the buildings mentioned by Jefferson. The court formed at each side by the auxiliary buildings may be construed as a deferential bow to Jefferson's preference for the courts at either side and in front of the Hotel de Salm facing the Rue de Lille in Paris. There is no sign of a semicircle on L'Enfant's outline; the curved front of the Hotel de Salm, containing the circular salon, was evidently disregarded. The proposed building, like the city plan, appears to be an original concept.

Fig. 8 Outline of L'Enfant's plan for the President's House. The structure would have been 700 feet long.

Fig. 9 View of L'Enfant's President's House from Pennsylvania Avenue. A visualization by Elbert Peets.

Fig. 10 Castle Howard, Yorkshire.

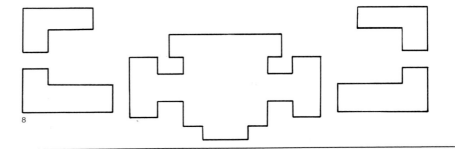

8

9

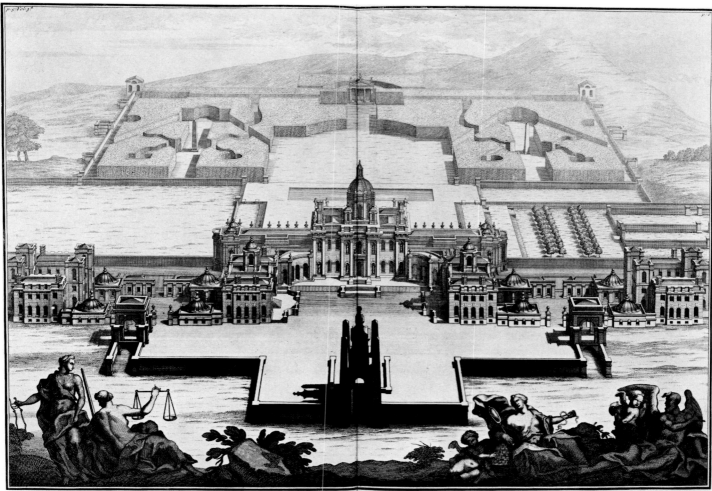

10

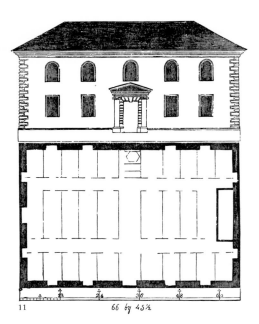

11   66 by 45½

12

Elbert Peets, who made a careful analysis of L'Enfant's materials, believed he intended the "President's Palace" to have a cupola. In size and configuration, it was to resemble Castle Howard.

By late 1791 L'Enfant had begun a huge excavation at the site of the President's House for the foundations and cellar of the building and for drainage.

L'Enfant was now in deep trouble, not only with the Commissioners, but also with the President and the Secretary of State. On January 22, 1792, he wrote a final appeal directly to Washington, outlining some ideas for financing the development of the city, listing the projects to be undertaken during the coming season, and reiterating his belief that the work should be under the authority of a single director. The activities at the President's House would consist of:

1. "continuing the cleaning of the cellar" and laying the foundations so that they would be safe from injury the next winter;
2. "planting" the wall of the terrace supporting the building;
3. wharfing the edge of the river to bring in supplies;
4. reducing the slope of the two streets at the side of the President's park and garden to a proper gradation, using the removed earth for fill at the wharf;
5. constructing various shops and equipment for the stoneworkers, ironmongers, etc., and storage sheds for protecting materials.

At the time, he did not know that Washington was already looking for someone to replace him; the person the President had in mind was Major Ellicott. While L'Enfant awaited a response from the President, he did little to further construction in the city, but in February he had shown "different views" of building plans to Mr. Trumbull, according to information received by the President from George Walker of Georgetown. On February 27 L'Enfant was dismissed. Eight days later, Jefferson wrote that "Majr L'Enfant had no plans prepared for the Capitol or government house, he said he had them in his head. I do not believe he will produce them for concurrence." Jefferson's specific reference to the Capitol leaves open the possibility that L'Enfant had begun an architectural study for the President's House first, as was strongly indicated by his city plan.

George Washington repeatedly disclaimed any knowledge of the rules of architecture, but he was not without some skill in that art. His large library contained a few books on architecture, building design and construction, as well as numerous engravings and periodicals. As a young man he had been trained in surveying and drawing, and he owned instruments for both to the end of his life.

Shortly after 1764, Washington drew a plan and elevation for a new brick building to replace the wornout structure of Truro parish church at Pohick, near Mount Vernon. On a new site about two miles from the old, a new church was erected by 1773 essentially according to his design.

Before the Revolution, he began to enlarge the substantial house at Mount Vernon built by his half-brother, Lawrence, to nearly three times its size, by extensions added at both ends. He revised the interior and added dormers, a pediment, and an observatory on the roof, as well as the famous tall verandah. Curved Palladian colonnades connected the main house to buildings housing the kitchen and other household offices on either side of the entrance court.

Washington was not an architect in the usual sense, but he could and did draw plans. From the many letters he sent to Lund Washington during the war it is clear

Fig. 11 George Washington's plan and elevation for Pohick Church. An engraved copy by Benson J. Lossing.

Fig. 12 Side view of Pohick Church, near Mount Vernon. The building closely follows Washington's drawing.

Fig. 13 Elevation of Mount Vernon, drawn by George Washington.

Fig. 14 Landward facade of Mount Vernon.

13

14

that he knew exactly what he wanted accomplished at Mount Vernon. Lossing says he "drew every plan and specification for the workmen with his own hand." He relied on the "workmen," however, for the designs for the decorative elements, which they in turn took from standard pattern books. The contractor-builder was Going Lanphier. One Sears probably did the chimneypieces and trim; an unknown "stucco-man" decorated the ceilings.

After his retirement from the Presidency, he drew plans for two speculative houses in Washington, which he built more to enhance the city and encourage others than for profit. He consulted Thornton on the possibility of adding a portico to these buildings, but abandoned the idea for the sake of economy. Photographs of the houses before their destruction to make room for the 1908 House Office building show them to be quite plain, practical structures.

In a letter to the Commissioners, March 8, 1792, he presented an idea which became a tenet of the building program:

> For the President's house, I would design a building which should also look forward but execute no more of it at present than might suit the circumstances of this country, when it shall be first wanted. A Plan comprehending more may be executed at a future period when the wealth, population and importance of it shall stand upon much higher ground than they do at present.

Washington is not known to have ordered or prepared plans for any specific features of the public buildings, but he frequently offered guidelines and criticism which tended to shape the final design. His remarks on Judge Turner's plan for the Capitol are illustrative of this influence:

> The Dome, which is suggested as an addition to the center of the edifice, would, in my opinion, give beauty & grandeur to the pile; and might be useful for the reception of a Clock—Bell—&c.—The Pilastrade too, in my judgement ought (if the plan is adopted) to be carried around the semi-circular projection at the end, but whether it is necessary to have the elevation of the upper storey 41 feet is questionable; unless it be to preserve exactness in the proportion of the several parts of the building;—in that case, the smaller rooms in that storey would be elevated sufficiently if cut in two, and lighted. This would add to the number of Committee rooms of which there appears to be a deficiency; and query, would not the section B in the North division of plan No. 2. be more usefully applied as a library than for the purpose it is designated?—
>
> Could such a plan as Judge Turner's be surrounded with Columns and a Colonade like that which was presented to you by Monsr. Hallet (the roof of Hallet's I must confess does not hit my taste)—without departing from the principles of Architecture—and would not be too expensive for our means, it would in my judgment, be a noble & desirable structure.—But, I would have it understood in this instance, and always—when I am hazarding a sentiment on these buildings, that I profess to have no knowledge in Architecture, and think we should (to avoid criticisms) be governed by the established rules which are laid down by the professors of this art.

In another context Washington mentioned that "some difficulty arises with respect to Mr. Hallet, who you know was in some degree led into his plan by ideas we all expressed to him. . . . his feelings should be saved and soothed as much as possible."

It is clear that the President and others offered advice to several of the contending architects—at least Hallet, Thornton, and Blodget—for the Capitol, prior to selection of the winning entry. No record exists of consultation between Washington and the entrants for the President's House competition except for two—James Hoban, who visited him just prior to beginning work on his plan; and, of course, Thomas Jefferson, who submitted an anonymous composition.

Hoban must have been an attentive and responsive listener. In their conversation, Washington expanded upon his basic concept for the President's House, as he mentioned in a letter in 1793:

> It was always my idea (and, if I am not mistaken, Mr. Hoben coincided in the propriety & practicability of it) that the building should be so arranged that only a part of it should be erected at present; but upon such a plan as to make the part so erected an entire building, and to admit of an addition in future as circumstances might render proper, without hurting, but rather adding to the beauty & magnificence of the whole as an original plan.—I was led to this idea by considering that a House which would be very proper for a President of the United States for some years to come, might not be considered as corresponding with other circumstances at a more distant period:—and, therefore, to avoid the inconveniences which might arise hereafter on that subject, I wished the building to be upon the plan I have mentioned.

This, plus his well-known preferences expressed in his critique of the Turner plan, would have given the de facto architect a good idea of what the building should look like. Hoban's plan incorporated everything Washington desired.

During the planning stage of the Federal City and its public buildings, there were frequent conferences and correspondence among the President, Jefferson, and L'Enfant.

Many references exist to alterations and improvements of L'Enfant's plan of the city given him by Washington. Before L'Enfant dug a cellar hole for the President's House, some decision by the President also would have been made, even though plans were not yet developed; the excavation went on for some time, and neither Washington nor the Commissioners attempted to stop it.

Of the three original planners of the Federal City and buildings, Jefferson was by far the best fitted to undertake the major architectural responsibility. Washington had a limited but adequate education in a parish school; L'Enfant had training in the arts of painting and sculpture. Jefferson not only had a full academic education at the College of William and Mary, but had surrounded himself for years with the best works on architecture available. He was a diligent student, clever and original in many ways; yet his final writings and his architectural designs are nearly always traceable to the work of an earlier genius. This paradoxical combination of inventor and copyist is first shown by Monticello. The plan of the early version of the building, drawn about 1771, was taken from one of the standard pattern books of the time, and the elevation was adapted from Palladio. A few years later, while governor of Virginia, he was involved in the removal of the capital from Williamsburg to Richmond. The new capitol was as close a copy of the Maison Carrée at Nîmes as its proposed use would permit. Jefferson enlisted the help of Charles-Louis Clérisseau, who had published a monograph on the temples at Nîmes, in making the adaptation. His plan for the new governor's house, never realized, was the first of several based on Palladio's La Rotonda.

Thus, by 1791, Washington and Jefferson had each created his own residence and furnished the basic design for one public building. Washington, however, had little intrinsic interest in architecture. Jefferson loved it, as his letters, his many sketches, and his extensive collection of architectural books and prints so clearly show. During his five-year residence in Paris he was violently smitten with French architecture, especially the Hotel de Salm, then under construction. He used to go almost daily to look at it; "sitting on the parapet, and twisting my neck round to see the object of my admiration, I generally left with a *torti-colli*," he confided to the Comtesse de Tessé. See Plate 2.

Jefferson was concerned from the beginning in the architectural designs for the Federal City. Ellicott's hurried version of L'Enfant's plan had left many acute corners and slim triangles where radial avenues crossed the rigid grid of streets. With more study, these could have been reduced, as Le Nôtre had done in the area of the Avenue de St. Cloud and the Avenue de Sceaux at Versailles. When the Commissioners mentioned this problem in February 1792, Jefferson counseled,

> the angular buildings at the commencement of the avenues may probably be offensive to the eye, if not well managed. I have seen this deformity obviated by terminating the house at that end by a bow-window, or with a semi-circular portico, & other fancies.

A semicircular bow was subsequently used by Thornton at the Tayloe (Octagon) house in 1800, at one of these problem corners. It appears again in 1937 at the apex of the Federal Triangle.

Although he suggested to L'Enfant that the President's House be based on the Louvre, the Garde-meubles, and the Hotel de Salm, Jefferson either did not wait for L'Enfant to prepare such a design or, seeing the dismissal of the arrogant Frenchman as inevitable, made sketches of the idea himself.

Fig. 15 Octagon House, Washington, built in 1800. President Monroe lived here after the President's House was burned in 1814.

15

16

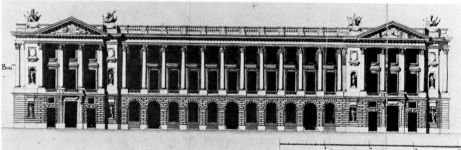

17a

17b

Fig. 16 Perrault's facade of the Louvre, one of the "fronts" recommended to L'Enfant by Jefferson as a model for the President's House.

Fig. 17a Facade for the Garde Meubles, Paris; drawing by Ange-Jacques Gabriel, 1765.

Fig. 17b The Garde Meubles building, now the Ministère de la Marine, Place de la Concorde, Paris.

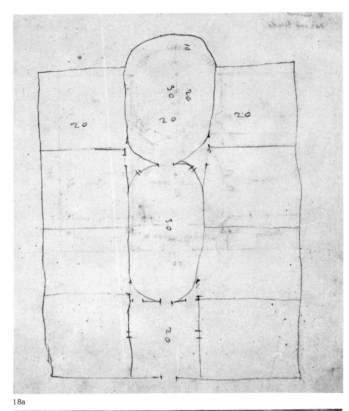

18a

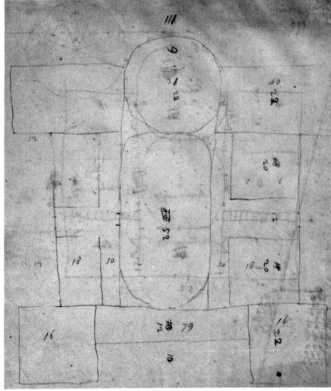

18b

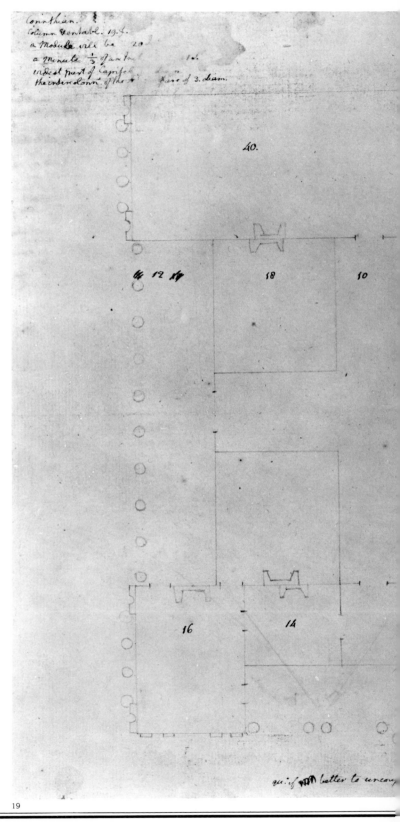

19

Fig. 18a Floor plan by Thomas Jefferson, based on the Hotel de Langeac, Figure 20a. It appears to be a preliminary sketch for his first plan for the President's House.

Fig. 18b A refinement of Figure 18a, adapting the room arrangement to Jefferson's idea for using the fronts of three famous Parisian buildings.

Fig. 19 Jefferson's final scheme for the President's House.

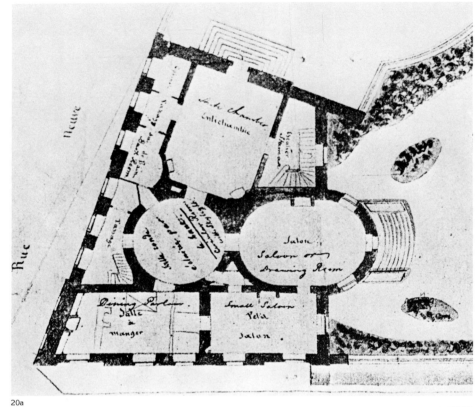

20a

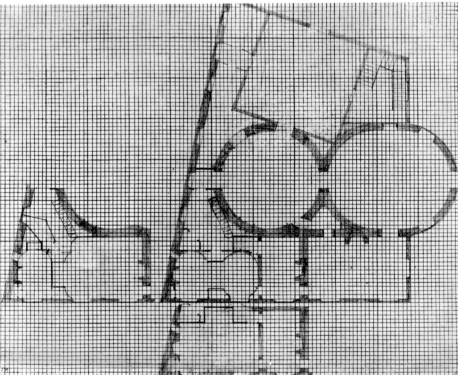

Fig. 20a Plan of the Hotel de Langeac in Jefferson's time. English notations were added in 1817.

Fig. 20b Jefferson's sketch of the ground-floor plan of the Hotel de Langeac, with minor changes in stairways and an alcove bedroom.

20b

The design shows how deeply the architecture of Paris had affected him. Not only are the favored fronts represented, but the arrangement of a circular salon adjoining a larger one having straight sides and rounded ends, peculiar to the Hotel de Langeac, forms the central theme of the floor plan.

This suite created a massive obstruction preventing easy access to the other rooms, resulting in an extensive maze of connecting corridors. Only four of the twelve rooms were large enough to accommodate the normal functions of a President's House. The remaining six were about the size of modern suburban living rooms, varying from 12 feet by 14 feet to 16 feet by 22 feet.

The overall dimensions of the building were 111 feet by 96 feet, larger in floor area than Hoban's original design but smaller than the President's House as built. More than 40 percent of the floor area was taken up by recessed porches, corridors, and similar nonproductive space. A total of 58 columns decorated the exterior.

In a personal memorandum drawn for his later anonymous entry in the competition—based on a completely different design—Jefferson estimated the number and size of rooms for the President's House in detail. The principal room floor areas, converted from Jefferson's units into square feet, were as follows:

	Square feet
Antichamber	1,000
Audience Room	1,500
Parlour	1,500
Parlour	1,500
Dining Room	1,000

If the estimated space were really necessary, then this early plan would have been somewhat cramped, although the total floor space more efficiently arranged was ample. The exterior compressed the decoration of monumental buildings, on three of its sides, to bandbox proportions.

Since nothing is recorded in correspondence or proceedings about this sentimental dream of French architectural charm, Jefferson may have recognized it as impractical. He did not submit it to the Commissioners for consideration.

With L'Enfant gone, Jefferson unable to translate his ideas into substantive form, Washington too busy with larger affairs, and Ellicott engaged elsewhere, the Commissioners' building program came to a halt. For a brief moment, James Hoban came close to filling the void. On March 14, 1792, the Commissioners write Jefferson:

> The President on his return from Charlestown last Summer, mentioned to us an Architect who had been highly recommended to him by some of the first Characters in the place. If he still approves of him and we can be informed of his name we will endeavor to engage him.

On March 21, Jefferson replied that "the President is not able to give you any satisfactory information regarding the Charleston architect." The plan for an open competition was then well along, and no further follow-up of Hoban's qualifications was made.

Four

The Competition for the President's House

"The advance of the season begins to require that the plans for the buildings and other public works at the Federal City should be in readiness," wrote Jefferson on February 22, 1792. Five days later, he dismissed the man who was preparing these, and the machinery of the city was in almost total confusion. Fully aware of the divisive political effects of trouble on the Potomac, Washington and Jefferson moved promptly to remedy the situation.

In Philadelphia, Ellicott finished the alterations of his new plan as the President wished, primarily reducing the number of avenues, and sent it to Thackara and Vallance for engraving. At the time his employment abruptly ended, L'Enfant had not verified the compatibility of some of his schemes to the actual topography. By survey, Ellicott had found squares under the waters of the eastern branch of the Potomac, and avenues climbing steep grades. In a letter to Thomas Johnson, March 8, Jefferson reports that: "We have questioned m͞r Ellicot very particularly whether the plan now in hand is exact. He says the conjectural parts are since ascertained by exact survey and that the plan is corrected from the survey, and may be relied on to the utmost minuteness."

On March 1, Jefferson advised the Commissioners to prepare to advertise for plans of the buildings. Thomas Johnson promptly wrote an advertisement for the Capitol competition based on the draft of September 8, 1791, and sent it to the President. It was amended and approved. Another draft was prepared at the same time for the President's House, using essentially the same format, with additions by Jefferson and Washington. The President noted, "I think particular situation of the ground wd require part[icula]r kind or shaped buildings." The final advertisement, as printed in the *Maryland Journal and Baltimore Advertiser* for April 3, 1792, is shown in Figure 21.

Jefferson notified the Commissioners that announcements had been placed in Freneau's, Fenno's, and Dunlap's papers in Philadelphia before March 21. The Commissioners themselves sent the advertisement to newspapers in Boston, Baltimore, Charleston, and Richmond.

By June 6, the Commissioners reported that they had received only two drafts, for the Capitol, from William Hart and Mr. Faw, not a heartening beginning for such a vital enterprise. It may well be that the paucity of decent designs at this late date impelled Jefferson to begin a new design for the President's House, which he submitted in the Competition under the pseudonym "AZ."

Fortunately, James Hoban of Charleston had become interested in the competition, and he began a meticulously planned campaign to gain the confidence and interest of the President and the Commissioners. He had been introduced to Washington in Charleston in 1791 by Dr. Thomas Tudor Tucker. Hoban no doubt saw the advertisement for the competition in the Charleston newspaper. His partner in the building and contracting business, Pierce Purcell, had gone to Washington earlier looking for opportunities in the new city, with a letter of introduction to Daniel Carroll.

James Hoban first went to Philadelphia, where he presented himself to Washington. He carried a letter of introduction from Colonel Henry Laurens, an old friend of the President. Laurens had been one of the delegates to France during the Revolution, and later, while negotiating in England, was the only American ever imprisoned in the Tower of London.

In Hoban's interview with Washington, the design of the President's House was discussed, as later letters from the President refer to his understanding of Hoban's intentions. Washington then gave Hoban a letter of introduction to the Commissioners, dated June 8:

> The Bearer of this, Mr. James Hoban, was strongly recommended to me by Colo. Laurens, and several other gentlemen of South Carolina when I was there last year, as a person who had made architecture his study, and was well qualified, not only for planning or designing buildings, but to superintend the execution of them.—He informs me that he intends to produce plans of the two buildings next month, agreeably to the advertisement of the Commissioners, and is now on his way to view the ground on which they are to stand.
>
> I have given him this letter of introduction, in order that he might have an opportunity of communicating his views and wishes to you, or of obtaining any information necessary for completing the plans. But, as I have no knowledge of the man or his talents, further than the information which I received from the Gentlemen in Carolina,—you must consider this letter merely as a line of introduction, for the purposes mentioned.—With esteem, and regard, I am &c.

Hoban also carried at least two other letters from prominent figures in South Carolina, addressed to Daniel Carroll.

Aedanus Burke, a former officer in the American Army and in 1792 a judge in the courts of South Carolina, wrote:

Charleston.May.12th.1792

> Dear Sir.
>
> The bearer of this is M^r. Hoban, an Architect who has followed his business in this place for a few years past with success. He is a man of Genius and considerable talents to his profession both for design and execution. He obtained from the Dublin Society two medals, the rewards of superior performance in a professional competition, and came well recommended to America. He wishes to be made known to one of the Commissioners as a

Fig. 21 Advertisement for the President's House competition.

Fig. 22 Capitol building designed by James Hoban, Columbia, South Carolina.

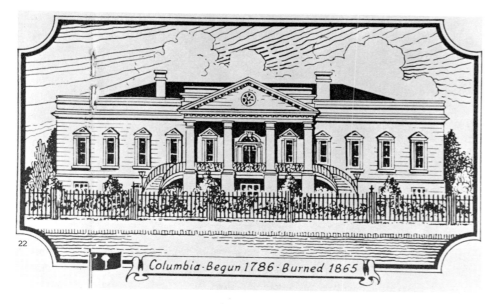

Columbia · Begun 1786 · Burned 1865

candidate in the business of the Federal Buildings, resting on his own abilities for the event, and I have taken the Liberty to introduce him to you

> With very great esteem & best wishes for you
>
> I remain Dear Sir
Your most obd^t hum. Ser^t
Æ. Burke

The "success" mentioned by Burke refers primarily to Hoban's design for the Columbia, South Carolina, capitol building constructed in 1787 and occupied in 1789.

Jacob Read, former member of the Continental Congress and from 1787 the speaker of the South Carolina House of Representatives, also spoke warmly of James Hoban to Daniel Carroll:

Charleston, May 24, 1792

Sir:

I formerly did myself the pleasure to address a Line to you by Mr. Pierce Purcell of this Place who visited the intended seat of the federal Government to offer for some of the work intended to be done there—and I thank you for the attention you were pleased to shew to my recommendation of Mr. Purcell & for the very obliging Letter you were pleased to write to me in answer to mine.

Mr. James Hoban who is Mr. Purcell's Partner and a very Ingenious Mechanic & draftsman will have the Honour of presenting to you this Letter He is a Man of Character & deserving of encouragement—He now comes to the federal seat to make his offer & an Essay towards a Plan for some of the buildings to be erected—I request your patronage of him & that you'l please to mention Mr. Hoban to the other Gentlemen Commissioners—From what I have seen of Mr. Hoban's Draughts I think he will stand a fair Chance to get some of the Premiums offered for Drafts

I am Sir
With very great esteem & regard
Your most obedient
Humb^e Ser^t
Jacob Read

Hoban is the only architect in the competition for either building to have made such an effort to establish himself professionally with the Commissioners. It served him well. The Commissioners reported to Jefferson on July 5 that "Mr. Hoban applies himself closely to a Draft of the President's House. He has made very favorable Impressions on us."

In the same letter, they mentioned that several plans had been received and more were expected to be presented: "Our Affairs in general are in rather a Pleasing Train and we hope that as soon as plans are approved we shall be able to proceed with Vigour."

The competition closed on July 15, 1792. Plans for the President's House were submitted by Andrew Mayfield Carshore of Claverack, New York; John Collins, probably of Richmond, Virginia; James Diamond of Somerset County, Maryland; Stephen Hallet of Philadelphia; James Hoban of Charleston; Thomas Jefferson (anonymously), then in Philadelphia; and Jacob Small of Baltimore. Of these, only two, Jefferson and Small, were native Americans; one, Stephen (Etienne Sulpice) Hallet, came from France in the 1780s; the other four were born in Ireland, but only James Hoban is known to have studied or practiced architecture there. One more entry was submitted by Collen Williamson of New York. It arrived on July 16, after the deadline, and was declined by the Commissioners.

Washington came to Georgetown on July 16 to view the entries with the Commissioners. On July 17, the premium for the best design was awarded to James Hoban. Unexpectedly, an award was also made to John Collins; the plan for the President's House prepared by him "appearing to be scientific and the second in merit which has been laid before them, they directed the payment of $150 . . . as a token of their sense of the merits of his essay." Jefferson's entry, not mentioned in the awards, would have come next in merit. The others could not have qualified under any circumstances.

Designs submitted in the competitions for both the President's House and the Capitol present a valuable view of the status of the art of building throughout the country. Architects or builders in or near every city in which the competitions were advertised sent entries, and the number of entrants is almost directly proportional to the population of the city:

Boston:	Samuel McIntyre, Samuel Blodget
New York:	Andrew Carshore, Collen Williamson, Charles Wintersmith
Philadelphia:	Stephen Hallet, Thomas Jefferson, William Thornton, George Turner
Baltimore:	James Diamond, Abraham Faw, Philip Hart, Jacob Small
Richmond:	John Collins, Samuel Dobie
Washington:	Robert Lanphier
Charleston:	James Hoban

Some of the best architects did not enter the competitions. L'Enfant was out of favor; John McComb of New York had designed a President's House there which Washington never lived in; and Charles Bulfinch was too busy in Boston.

Five

Competition Designs for the President's House

In 1792 no schools of architecture existed in America, and competence in the profession varied greatly. There were enterprising self-taught builders, like Diamond, McIntyre, and Small; amateurs like Jefferson, Thornton, Blodget and Carshore; and a small group educated in Europe, including L'Enfant, Hallet, and Hoban. The entrants in the President's House competition covered the entire spectrum of talent and training.

Andrew Mayfield Carshore

Having escaped or been released from the British Army upon Burgoyne's surrender at Saratoga in 1777, Irish-born Andrew Mayfield Carshore made his way down the Hudson River to Kinderhook, where he lived for some time. Possessing a good education, he ran an "English school" until moving to Claverack, where he taught at the Washington Seminary. It is not likely that Carshore ever received formal training in architecture, or designed any local buildings. He was known for his artistic penmanship, evident in the titles and notes on his drawings.

His design complied with a provision in the program for expansion: the eleven central bays could be built as a unit and four corner pavilions added later as needed. The twin cupolas are unusual, but not unique in America. They were to be found, for example, on the great mansion at Rosewell, Virginia.

The exterior is reminiscent of a late-seventeenth-century English building, with characteristics that Sir John Summerson has named "Artisan-Mannerism." This style grew from an amalgam of old Tudor and Dutch idioms among builders and contractors acting as their own architects, quite separate from the sophisticated architecture being developed simultaneously by Inigo Jones and his peers. Carshore's building is a bourgeois version of Clarendon House (1664), which was widely imitated in England. The smaller Beaulieu (1667) in Ireland is typical of the same style. Perhaps the Dutch influence, persisting longer in the Hudson River valley seminary buildings Carshore knew so well, gave his entry the appearance of the earlier English vernacular.

Buildings of this size and type in America in 1792 were those of the older colleges and state capitols, engravings of which were frequently published in the illustrated magazines. Carshore's building has the quaintness of the 1726 Burgis view of Harvard, printed in the *Columbian Magazine* as late as 1788. Most such architectural views for public enjoyment were drawn in perspective, the mode for over half a century. The realism of these engravings may have prompted Carshore to prepare his perspective view of the front of the President's House to show explicitly how the flanking pavilions would look when added to the central block. This drawing and a similar one by Carshore for the Capitol are possibly the first use of perspective for an architectural proposal in America.

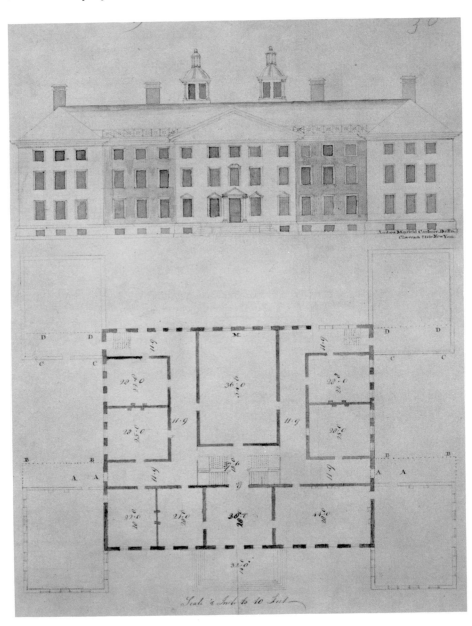

Fig. 23 Andrew Mayfield Carshore: front view and ground-floor plan for the President's House.

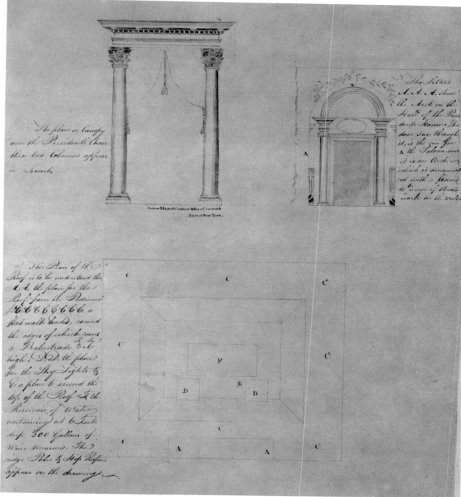

Fig. 24 Carshore's perspective view showing how the flanking wings would appear when built.

Fig. 25 Carshore: canopy over the President's chair; a view from the entrance hall toward the saloon; and the roof plan of the central block.

The principal floor plan is not a skillful use of space. Large windowed areas in the rear are wasted on stair halls, and there is a woeful lack of fireplaces for such large rooms; the largest has none at all. Moreover, the intersection of the main stairs and the corridor from the entrance hall is an impediment to convenient circulation.

In the front hall of Carshore's house, opposite the entrance, Ionic columns support an imposing arched opening crowned with a garland of leaves made of stucco. Across the stair hall an oval design fills the wall over a second wide doorway which leads to the grand saloon. Here the Presidential throne sits beneath an elaborate canopy. Corinthian columns support great draperies held back by tasseled ropes, rather like a four-post bed, and a large single tassel dangles over the President's head.

Although it is not immediately apparent from the elevation, a flat leaded walk about 10 feet wide follows the perimeter of the roof, protected by a balustrade 3½ feet high. The pitched roof then rises to a second flat area, which holds a 300-gallon cistern. The reason for the twin cupolas now becomes clear; they are skylights for the twin stairwells. While showing some ingenuity, the design is clumsy, and technically inadequate.

Carshore continued to teach at Washington Seminary in Claverack for more than 25 years. He then moved to Hudson, New York, where he became principal of the Hudson Academy. In 1810 he returned to Saratoga, where he spent the remaining years of his life.

John Collins

Nothing whatever is known definitely about John Collins or his second-prize-winning drawings. It is not certain that he is the John Collins who was employed on the construction of a new state capitol at Richmond, although for want of a better candidate it has been assumed by Fiske Kimball and Wells Bennett that the connection is sufficiently likely. John Collins of Richmond had worked on the Virginia capitol under the direction of Samuel Dobie, who entered the federal Capitol competition.

The wide gap between the professionalism of Hoban and the naïveté of the other entries, excepting Jefferson's entry, "AZ," makes the loss of Collins's drawings, and the uncertainty of his identity, extremely unfortunate. No second prize was contemplated. To impel the Commissioners to create one on the spot, the quality of Collins's work must have been extraordinary.

James Diamond

Of the known competition drawings those of James Diamond rank next to Hoban's in competence and finish. Only this set satisfies the full requirements of the competition program. Diamond shows both front and rear elevations, gives the principal floor plans, makes provision for wings connected to the central block by arcades, and shows a section of the building, the only one existing. See Plate 3.

His elevation has been traced by Kimball and Bennett to themes taken from *Vitruvius Britannicus;* bits and pieces of Vanbrugh's Grimsthorpe and Campbell's version of the Porto-Colleoni palace seem to furnish many of the elements found in the facade. The plan is similar to some in the same volumes. It may also be an

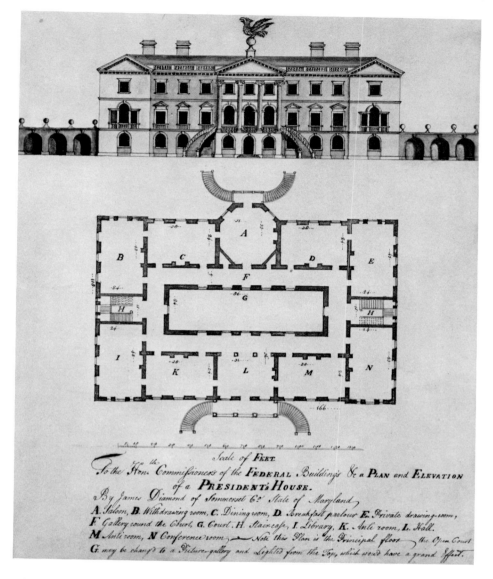

adaptation of a "plan of a mansion for a person of distinction" in Crunden's *Convenient and Ornamental Architecture* (1785).

Diamond is a shadowy character, like Collins; nothing much is known of his life in America. He died in 1797, leaving his property to a wife and three sons in Ireland.

Kimball and Bennett remarked that "the degree of organization and orthodoxy of Diamond's facade lead one at once to suspect the following of some published design." With the Irish connection as a clue, a review of well-known buildings in Ireland for one which may have been Diamond's model leads immediately to Carton, the country seat of the Duke of Leinster. Richard Castle had enlarged a nine-bay, two-story house in 1739 by adding protruding, monumental end pavilions and a third story. The new pavilions at Carton were much like those of Grimsthorpe, which was built some 15 years earlier, and had been published in volume III of *Vitruvius Britannicus.* More changes were made by Richard Morrison in 1817.

Fig. 26 James Diamond: principal floor plan and elevation.

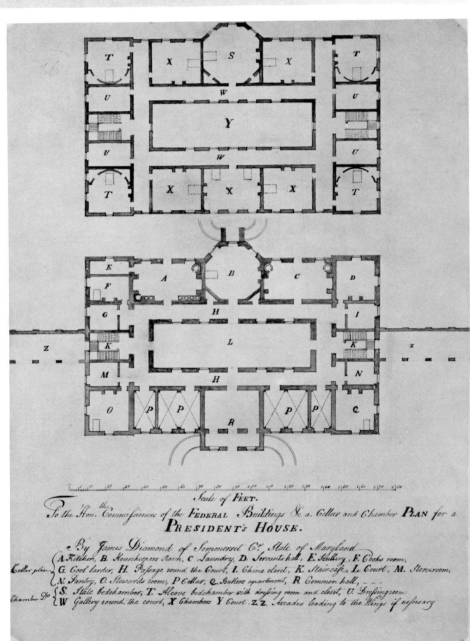

Fig. 27 Carton House as it appeared in the eighteenth century.

Fig. 28 Cellar and chamber floor plans, James Diamond.

The basic structure in Diamond's elevation bears a strong resemblance to eighteenth-century Carton. The ornament introduced by Diamond to embellish the coolness of Castle's work is in the main detrimental. The scale of the bird cannot be taken seriously, and the colonnades at each side are not as graceful as those at Carton.

Diamond's internal design is far better than that of any other entry, always excepting Hoban's. If Diamond's central court were a simple transverse corridor, the plan would be quite similar to the Hoban scheme. Hoban's ellipse becomes Diamond's octagon. On the upper floor, Diamond introduced four alcove bedrooms, a novelty in American architecture at this time. The use of a curved wall to create the alcove is not only arresting visually, but is an ingenious way to provide closets and dressing rooms. Stairways are provided only at the ends of the building, as at Carton.

His arcades, "leading to the Wings, if necessary," are the same solution later chosen by Jefferson to extend the offices and are exactly the arrangement used in the White House today.

Stephen Hallet

Until now the only reference to an entry by Hallet was in a letter from Jefferson to the Commissioners, of July 11, 1792, received by them July 16, the day after the competition closed. Jefferson reported:

> The President has left this place, this afternoon—being encumbered with lame and Sick horses he was uncertain when he should reach George-Town—perhaps on Monday morning—I forward to you by Post this morning two Plans you had formerly sent to the President, and a plan of a Capitol and another of a President's House by a Mr. Hallet . . .

Because of this solitary reference to Hallet's entry, it has been suggested that Jefferson, in glancing through the material, mistook some of Hallet's Capitol drawings as those for the President's House. If anyone else had written the letter, some credence could be given this theory, as similar errors have been found in other contexts. It is difficult to believe that Jefferson would make such a mistake.

In a volume of original documents in the National Archives entitled *Bonds, Powers of Attorney, Capitol and Other Buildings, Miscellaneous Accounts from June 4, 1792 to March 30, 1868,* a memorandum bearing Hallet's signature has been found, which begins:

> The following are the full contents in cubick feet of the brick work and masonry of the Federal Hall, and President's hotel as planned by the Subscriber and calculated to answer the directions of the Hon[ble] Commissioners:

Following this paragraph there is a two-page calculation for the volume of solid structure in the Capitol. The calculation for the President's House apparently has been detached, and if existing might not have Hallet's signature, which is on the first page in the left margin. The wording of this document seems to comply with the requirement in the advertised program for "an Estimate of the cubic Feet of Brick-Work composing the whole Mass of the Walls." If it is a specification accompanying the competition drawings by Hallet, it is the only such document known.

However, there is a possibility that it was prepared just prior to August 29, 1793, when the public building projects were being reviewed. A rather similar memorandum signed by Thomas Carstairs has been found in the same volume, with a preamble referring only to the Capitol. Conversely, since neither document is dated, this may be part of a long-suspected entry by Carstairs in the Capitol competition.

Regardless of the dating of these recent discoveries, the definite statement "the Federal Hall, and President's Hotel *as planned* by the Subscriber," establishes a strong basis for Hallet's participation in the President's House competition. No other documents or drawings regarding Hallet's design for this building are known.

The memorandum mentioned above is in English and the handwriting does not appear to be Hallet's. In these early years, Hallet did not write English very well, and may have had someone transcribe it for him. Also, this is not unusual for file copies of such records. The signature, however, is authentic, and the use of the word "hotel" for "house" is consistent with Hallet's style of writing.

Hallet did not have an extensive career in America. A professional architect in France, he came to America before the French Revolution, and appears to have resided in Philadelphia. In 1792, he presented a scheme for the Capitol building, well in advance of any plan to hold an open competition. From subsequent letters, it has been thought that this composition was a lavish one, later simplified to reduce cost. There was a recessed central section surmounted by a dome, and wings extending forward on either side. Hallet's concept may be the source of the Capitol plan on Ellicott's map of the city drawn in February 1792. After the competition closed, Hallet was occupied for some time at the Capitol, adapting Thornton's design. He was never entirely happy with the strange responsibility for constructing a building of which he could not heartily approve. He was "discontinued" in 1794, to be replaced by Hadfield in 1795. After a few years in Philadelphia, he spent most of the following decade in the Caribbean, returning to New York about 1812, where he remained until his death in 1825.

Thomas Jefferson

Only Carshore and Diamond signed their drawings; all other entries have been attributed to various architects by purely circumstantial evidence. Jefferson alone deliberately disguised his identity, using the pseudonym "AZ," and rightly so; it would have been highly unethical for one in his position to have competed publicly. Because his entry lost, the secret was kept until Fiske Kimball recognized identical preliminary drawings, unmistakably by the hand of Jefferson, in the Coolidge collection in 1915.

Jefferson's competition design is based on Palladio's residence for Monsignor Paolo Almerico at Vicenza. Palladio did not consider it a villa, and grouped it with the palazzi in his chapter on town-house design. "La Rotonda," as it became known, stood in an open setting on a small hill overlooking a navigable river, surrounded by vineyards and orchards. The site was "pleasant and delightful," yet "in the very city." Thus the location was much like that of the President's House, standing on a ridge in a large park leading to the waters of the Tiber and Potomac.

But here the analogy ends. La Rotonda was the home in retirement for an aged

and distinguished citizen. It was his Monticello. The President's House, as the advertised program emphasized, was to be the nucleus of a great executive establishment for the future. The basic dichotomy of viewpoints was not successfully resolved in Jefferson's adaptation.

In an undated personal memorandum Jefferson outlined the following requirements:

```
President's house
    Antichamber area ........................10 squares of full elevation

    Audience room  ..........................15
    Parlours. 1 of ...........................15
             1 of ...........................10
    Dining Room 1 of .......................10
                                            60 squares of full elevation

    Parlours. 1 of ...........................7½
             1 of ...........................5
    Dining Room 1 of .......................5
    Study ...................................5
    Library .................................10
    Clerks room 2 ..........................10
    Bedrooms with anti-chamb. &
    Dressing room to each. 4 of .............32
    Bedroom single 6 .......................24
    Making altogether ......................98½
    squares of half elevation to be
    counted as  ............................    49½
                                           109 squares or 105 f. sq.
```

Servants' apartments, the kitchen and its appurtances to be in an interval of 7 f. pitch between the floor of the house and cellars, consequently to be sunk a foot or two beneath the surface of the earth.

Cellar, woodrooms etc. to be below the servants' apartments.

Estimated in squares of 10 feet or 100 square feet.

Fig. 29 Elevation drawing, "AZ."

A careful comparison of this list to his competition drawings shows clearly that the estimate was not a general guide for *any* President's house, but was intended specifically for his own competition entry.

The first group of state rooms comprise 60 squares, or 6,000 square feet of "full elevation." As shown on the elevation drawing, the principal story is $23\frac{4}{10}$ feet high. Leaving space for floor and ceiling supports, the rooms of "full elevation" have a ceiling height of 20 feet. "Elevation" on the specification is translated into "pitch" on the floor plans.

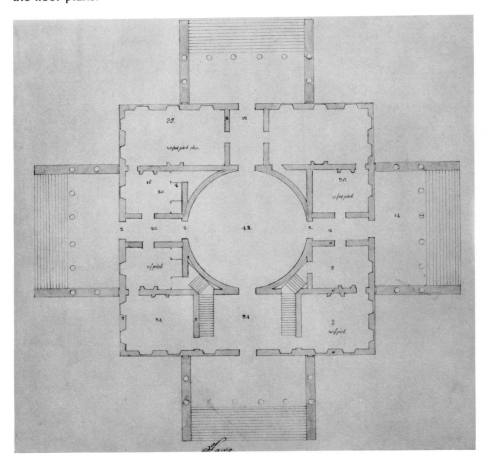

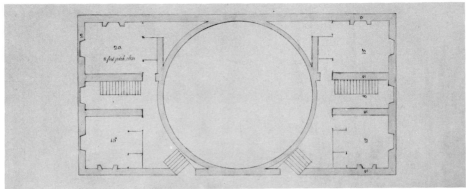

Fig. 30 First-floor plan, "AZ."

Fig. 31 Plan of mezzanine, "AZ."

There are three rooms of 20-foot pitch en suite along the entrance side, and a similar pair, plus a corridor, along the opposite facade. The central room rises as a great tube to the full height of the building. There are six rooms, therefore, to provide for state functions, although only five are required by the specification.

The other four rooms on the main floor, adjacent to the side porticos, are marked "11 ft. in pitch." They therefore fall in the second group of rooms on the list. Two are first-floor alcove bedrooms, which Jefferson always seemed to prefer. The other two are probably the small dining room and a parlor.

In the only published analysis of this set of drawings, the stairs are said to "terminate awkwardly" on the second floor level, "suffering from an apparent lack of the requisite circular balcony in the original model." This interpretation, and the identification of the drawing of four bedrooms as the "third floor plan," shows a misunderstanding of the ingenious internal structure proposed by AZ. There is no third floor, and the stairway problem was solved in a beautifully simple manner typical of the inventive Jefferson.

The drawing showing four bedrooms is the plan of a mezzanine, cleverly inserted between the upper portion of the first-floor rooms of 20-foot pitch, resting on the rooms of 11-foot pitch. The ceiling height on this mezzanine floor is marked "8-foot pitch." The ensemble therefore provided a clear, level platform for the second floor.

By so rearranging the plans in their proper order, it can be seen that the twin open flights of stairs from the entrance hall rise to curved corridors on the mezzanine, without awkwardness or obstruction. Access to paired bedrooms is provided by this corridor, which is lighted by the central room. The twin corridors also lead to pairs of stairs rising to the second floor.

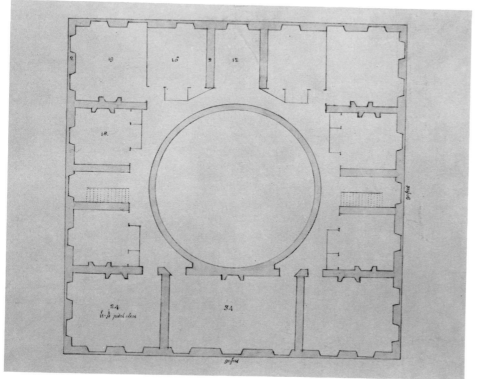

Fig. 32 Second-floor plan, "AZ."

33

Fig. 33 Halle au Blé, Paris. The dome shown is a steel-and-glass replacement of the wooden structure erected by Legrand and Molinos in 1782, accidentally destroyed by fire in 1802. Jean Bullant built the column at left in 1572 for astronomical observations by Ruggieri, astrologer and adviser to Catherine de Médicis.

Fig. 34 Philibert de l'Orme's method for constructing laminated wooden ribs of great length. From *Nouvelles Inventions pour bien Bastir, etc.*, 1561.

The roof rises at an angle of only 25 degrees. If there were rooms on a third level extending to the outer walls as previously thought, the ceiling height would be zero at the wall, increasing to about 6½ feet at the higher side of the room, hardly a suitable arrangement for the President's House.

The three rectangular skylights shown on the elevation are not intended for lighting the attics, but to illuminate the second floor rooms cut off from the outside by the portico roofs. The skylights are quite large, about 4 by 11 feet each. The size is not apparent at first glance as the skylight, unlike a dormer, lies flat against the roof and the low angle of projection in the elevation foreshortens the true length. Two small bull's-eye windows above each portico augment the skylight illumination.

Four large chimneys mar the perfection of Palladio's roof; Jefferson seems to have sketched them lightly to minimize their appearance. It is doubtful that sufficient draft could be generated under all wind conditions, as the great dome would buffer the air flow. Much taller chimneys would have been needed. At Mereworth Castle, an English version of La Rotonda, Colen Campbell hid flues between the inner and outer walls of the dome; the lantern served as a chimney rather than as a skylight, and the beauty of the design was preserved.

Jefferson proposed one more innovation: a dome composed of alternate segments of solid structure and glass, flooding the central room with light. The effect surely would have been spectacular. The scheme was inspired by the Halle au Blé (Grain Exchange), one of the buildings in Paris Jefferson most admired.

The Halle au Blé was a circular two-story building, with arcades below for wagons and traders, and granaries above; it stood on the present site of the Bourse. In January 1783, just prior to Jefferson's arrival in Paris, the large open center court had been covered by a dome, in a manner devised by Philibert de l'Orme for the Chateau de la Muette at Saint-Germain-en-Laye before 1561. The ribs of the dome were of wood, and the spaces between formed windows. This great expanse of glass gave a brilliant effect, and the Halle au Blé became one of the wonders of the city.

Jefferson's library contained a copy of *Invention pour batir les couvertures courbes. fol. (Nouvelles Inventions pour bien bastir a petits fraiz, trouvées naguères par Philibert de l'Orme*, Paris, 1576). This book described in detail de l'Orme's technique of assembling overlapping planks to form lightweight ribs. The book was bought while Jefferson lived in Paris, and was sold to the Library of the United States in 1815.

It is probably for the best that Jefferson's house was rejected, interesting though it was. Although L'Enfant was advised to look to "modern" models, Jefferson himself tried to adapt a design more than 200 years old. He violated the requirement that the building be easily extended; it is difficult to see how wings could be added without destroying its unique character. The curious mixture of private and public rooms on both floors would have made a President's life chaotic; it was complicated enough in Hoban's plan. This was really a house for the life of a country gentleman. The Rotonda design stands in silent testimony to the difference in political ideals between Washington and Jefferson, which led to their parting in January 1794.

Jacob Small

Jacob Small, Sr., was a successful builder in Baltimore. He had designed and constructed for "ten thousand dollars" a small church in 1785. His gravestone seems to be dated September 27, 1791, so far as anyone can decipher, yet there are legal documents recorded as signed by him in 1793. The more likely date of his death is 1794.

In 1792, Jacob Small, Jr., was also engaged in the trade of carpentry. Fifteen to twenty years later he began to be recognized as having some talent as an architect, and to advertise himself as such. He also developed a successful lumber business.

The competition drawings submitted by one of these men are the most numerous of all entries. A group of four designs is considered to be the work of "Jacob Small." Each consists of a plan and elevation on a single sheet. Three have ink inscriptions: "For the President's House, Jacob Small"; "Jacob Small, Plan of the President's house"; and "Presidents House Jacob Small." The fourth design is not inscribed. The handwriting appears to be by different persons, for identification purposes, rather than the signature of the architect.

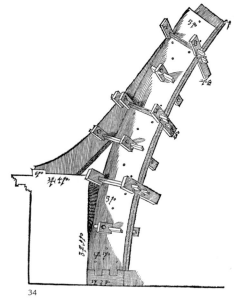

34

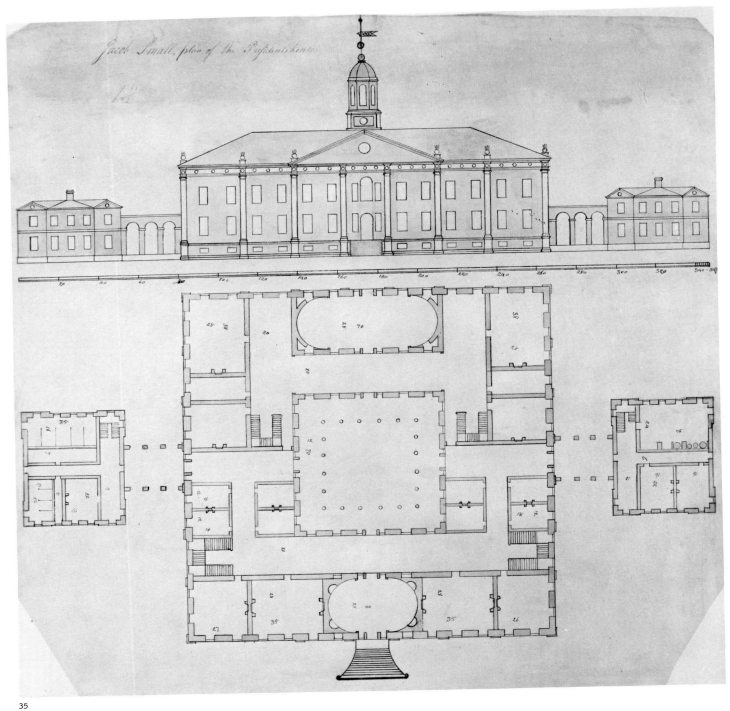

35

Fig. 35 Jacob Small submitted several plans
for the President's House; this is the largest.

Fig. 36 Plan and elevation, Jacob Small.

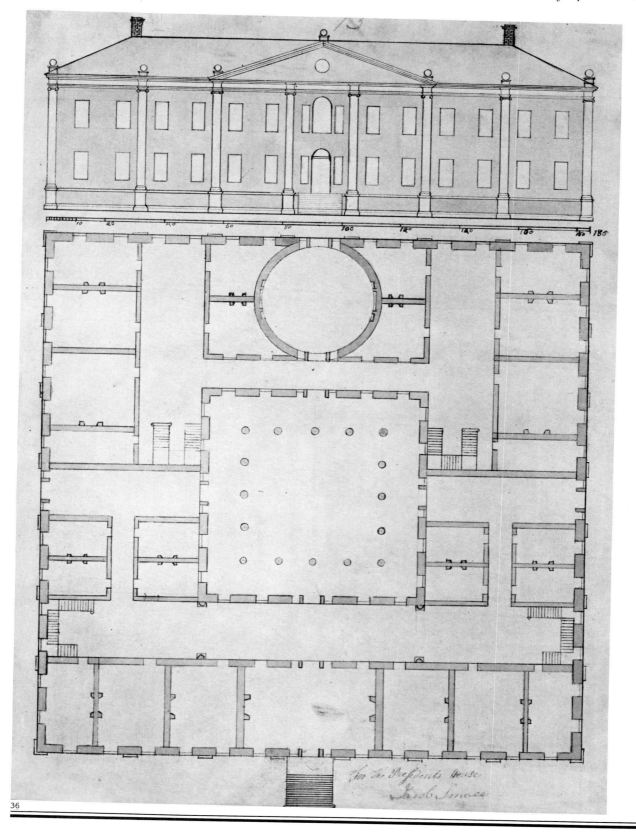

For The Presidents House
Jacob Small

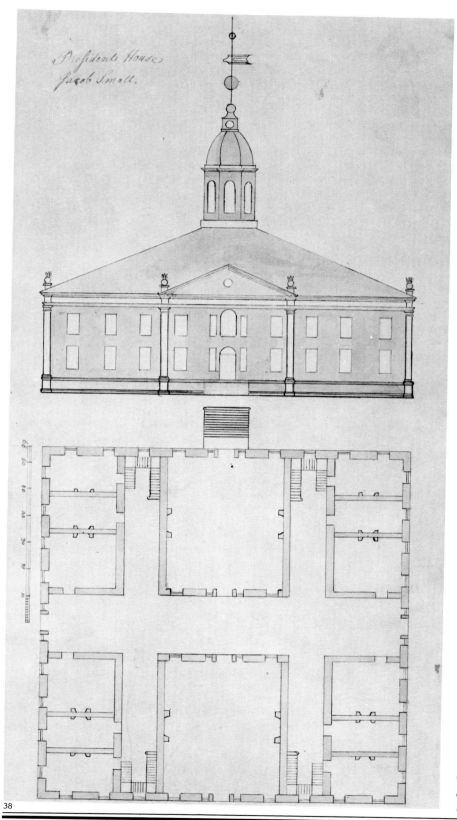

President's House
Jacob Small.

38

Fig. 37 Plan and elevation, Jacob Small.
Fig. 38 The roof is clearly copied from the Maryland State House, Jacob Small.

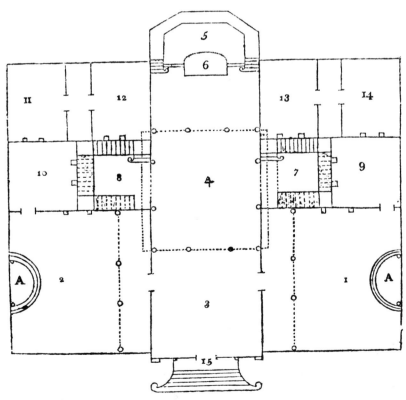

Fig. 39 View of the Maryland State House, Annapolis.

Fig. 40 Plan of the main floor, Maryland State House. Small used elements of this plan for both his President's House and Capitol designs.

Plate 1 The Washington family examining a map of the federal city.

Plate 2 Construction of the Hotel de Salm, Paris, 1786. Building activities around the President's House were much the same, 1792–1800.

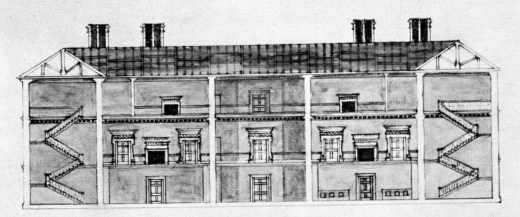

Section of the Back Front.

Back Front.

Scale of FEET

To the Honble Commissioners of the FEDERAL Buildings &c.

An ELEVATION and SECTION of the Back Front of a PRESIDENT's HOUSE

By James Diamond of Somerset County

4

WEST FRONT OF Leinster House.

5

Plate 3 Section and elevation of the back facade, James Diamond.

Plate 4 Elevation drawing of the President's House by James Hoban.

Plate 5 Leinster House, Dublin. Drawing by T. Cunningham, 1790.

6

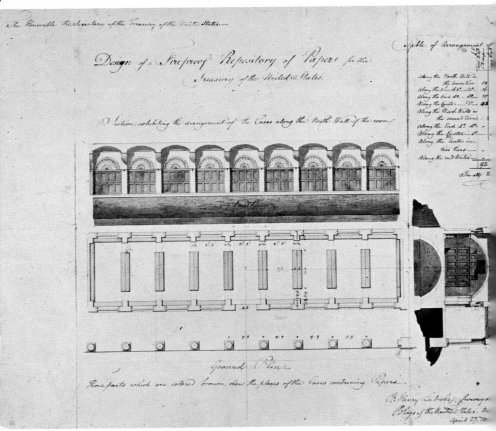

7

8

View of the East front of the President's House, with the addition of the North and South Porticos

9

10

11

12

13

14

Plate 12 Benjamin Henry Latrobe; a portrait by Charles Willson Peale.

Plate 13 St. John's Church and the burned President's House, 1816. Some of the damaged stone wall on the west side has been removed.

Plate 14 Corner of F and Fifteenth Streets, at the Treasury, 1817. The 1797 structure of the "Bank Metropos" is still standing. Hoban's "Little Hotel" immediately behind it is at the extreme right.

Plate 15 Anthony St. John Baker's watercolor of 1826 vividly shows the unfinished appearance of the city.

Plate 16 A watercolor by the Baroness Hyde de Neuville of the President's "campus" in 1820. Jefferson's wings were apparently being reconstructed.

Plate 17 The portrait of George Washington acquired in 1800 for the President's House.

Plate 18 Admiral Cockburn directed the burning of the Capitol and the President's House, but spared private property.

Plate 19 President Madison's medicine chest, carried off by a British soldier, was returned by his descendants.

15

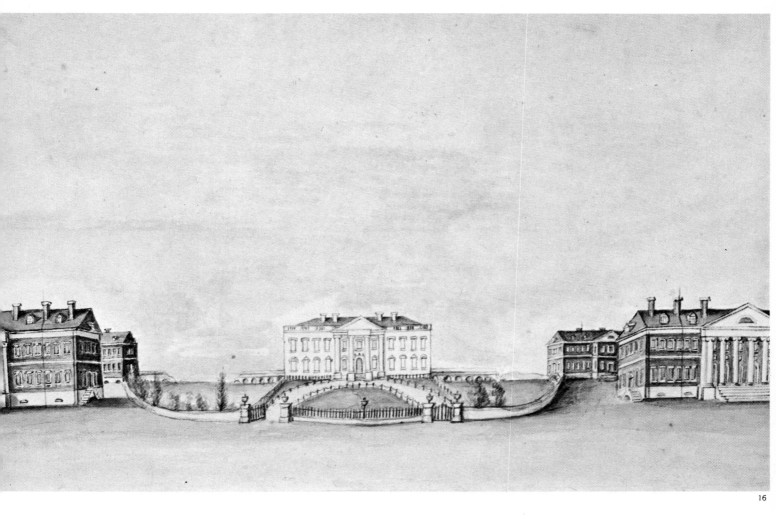

16

19

17

18

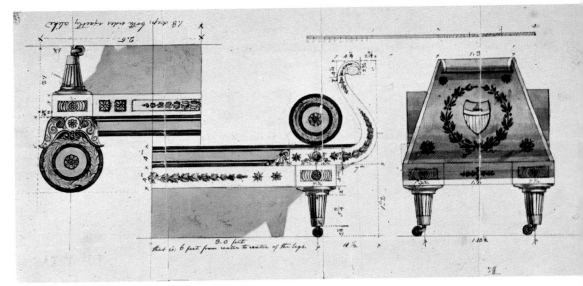

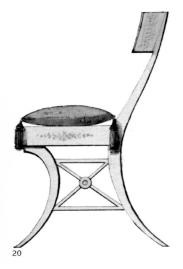

20

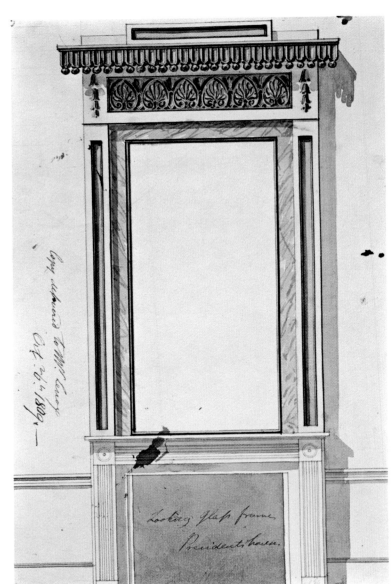

21

22

Plate 20 Latrobe designed chairs and sofas in the "Greek" style for the oval drawing room.

Plate 21 Latrobe's looking-glass frame for the oval room.

Plate 22 One of twenty-four chairs built by William King of Georgetown for for the East Room.

Jacob Small was equally prolific in the Capitol competition, entering three elevations and four floor plans, a section and two detail drawings of conference rooms. The two conference room sketches have notations and the name of Jacob Small in the same penmanship. These signatures are identical, and match that on the design for the President's House marked "13." The old-fashioned script and poor spelling of the captions make the elder Small the better candidate. A badly spelled letter from Jacob Small dated March 9, 1793, to the Commissioners asked for return of his plans. The signature on this letter is slightly different from those on the drawings; a clerk may have identified all the drawings.

The Small entries are essentially derived from the State House at Annapolis, erected in 1772 and twenty years later still the best-designed building in Maryland. The schemes vary from nine to thirteen bays, of which three or five are grouped under a central pediment. The main entrance and the window above it are always flanked by small windows in a simplified Palladian motif. The principal ornament consists of giant-order pilasters. Two of the four designs show flanking colonnades connecting to small wings, reminiscent of the Pennsylvania State House (Fig. 1). All but one are topped by a cupola broadly copied from the Maryland State House, but with details either from the belfry of the church built by Small in 1785, or from a cupola like that of the Pennsylvania State House.

None of the floor plans are well-organized or suited for a President's House. Almost every conceivable architectural stereotype is used somewhere, including inner courtyards; oval, lozenge-shaped, and round rooms; niches; and circular stairs.

While the plans of Small's designs leave much to be desired, the elevations, except for the smallest, have some merit. His eleven-bay facade is similar in its proportions to Hoban's later two-story design. The inept, almost rude, drawing presents the concept poorly. Bulfinch's University Hall at Harvard College, also dependent on giant-order pilasters for dignity and ornament, seems almost ugly in contemporary drawings and engravings, yet today it is considered attractive and well-designed.

Six

James Hoban's Design for the President's House

Only two eighteenth-century architectural drawings for the President's House as built have survived.

One is an elevation presented to the Maryland Historical Society in 1865 by John H. B. Latrobe, one of its founders, in a collection of drawings accumulated by his father. The right of B. Henry Latrobe to have retained the drawing, along with several others in the same category, is perhaps debatable. They were undoubtedly in the collection of government documents turned over to him in 1803, upon his appointment as Surveyor of the Public Buildings. Latrobe resigned in 1817, and on November 24 of that year Colonel Samuel Lane, then Commissioner of the Public Buildings, required that he surrender all "books, plans, instruments, etc. belonging to the Public in your possession" to Captain Lenox, Latrobe's successor pro tem. In any case the Maryland Historical Society has given the drawings the kind of protection and preservation not often provided such valuable historical materials.

This elevation was first published in 1903, in a report on the restoration of the White House completed in the previous year. It shows the north front essentially as it appears today, except for the absence of the porte-cochère. See Plate 4.

The other surviving drawing has two figures: a floor plan, and a section of the north wall incorporating orthographic projections of major architectural elements applied to the inner and outer surfaces. The floor plan closely resembles Latrobe's version of the President's House as it was in 1803. The drawing, identified as Hoban's creation by Fiske Kimball in 1915, was among the Jefferson papers and drawings in the collection deposited in the Massachusetts Historical Society in 1912 by Thomas Jefferson Coolidge, Jr., a descendant of Jefferson.

Although no documents have ever been discovered to establish conclusively that Hoban was the architect who prepared the undated and unsigned drawings, the circumstantial evidence is very persuasive. The strength of the evidence is demonstrated by a simple syllogism: Hoban won the competition and constructed the President's House; the drawings show the building as it was built; therefore Hoban drew the plans. Equally important is the negative evidence. No other person active

Section of the Wall

Basement Level

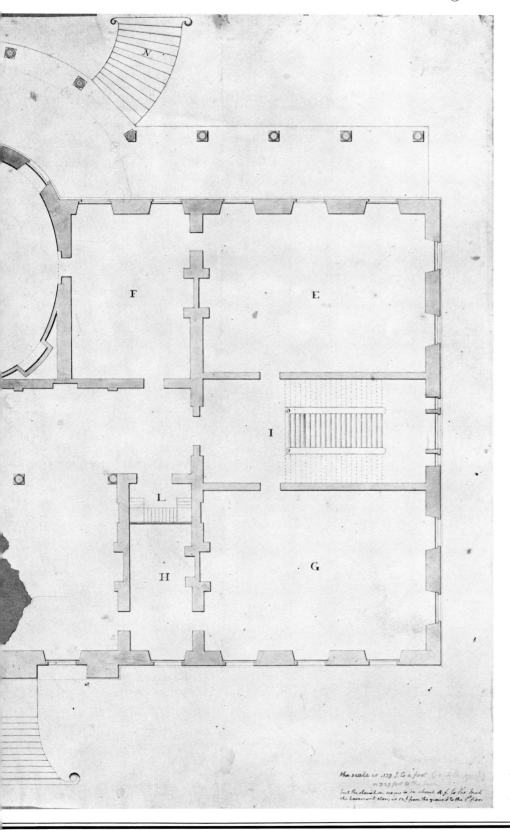

the scale is .137.5. to a foot

or 229 feet to the inch

but the elevation seems to be about ⅘ to the inch

the basement story is 13½ from the ground to the 1ˢᵗ floor

Fig. 41 Principal floor plan and wall section, President's House competition drawing, James Hoban.

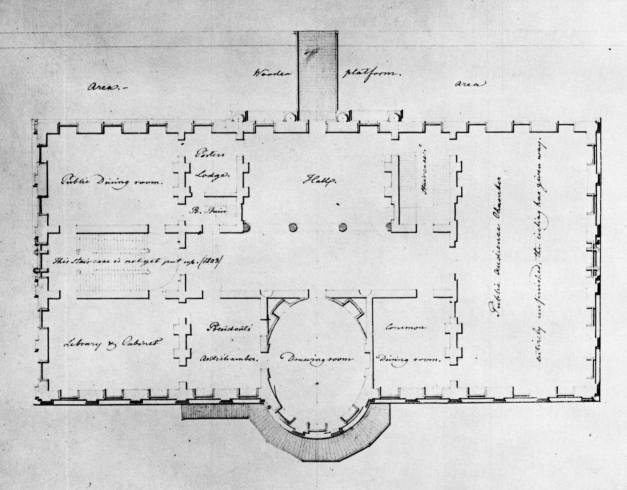

The surrounding Ground was chiefly used for Brick yards,
it was enclosed in a rough post and rail fence. (1803)

Area.—   Wooden   platform.   area

Public Dining room.   Porters Lodge.   Halls.   Staircase.

                       B. Stair

This Staircase is not yet put up. (1803)

Library & Cabinet   Presidents' Antichamber.   Drawing room.   Common Dining room.   Public Audience Chamber   entirely unfinished. the ceiling has given way.

During the short residence of President Adams at Washington, the wooden Stairs & platform were the usual entrance to the house, and the present drawing room, was a mere Vestibule.

Plan of the Principal Story in 1803.

in the area at the time could have drawn plans in the same professional style and with the same competence.

A third drawing by Hoban was recently located; it was attached to a letter he wrote to the Commissioners of the District of Columbia. It is a small, neat, utilitarian sketch of a brick storm drain for the War Department building. Unfortunately its character neither confirms nor disputes the authorship of the President's House drawings.

Conceding that the plan, section, and elevation are by Hoban, are they necessarily the original drawings submitted by him in the competition of 1792? If they constitute a set or part of a set, all three should show corresponding views of the same building. The plan does agree with both the section and the elevation, but the section shows a three-story building on a basement partly below grade, with window treatment and other details quite different from both the elevation drawing and the building itself. The disparities between the two drawings are explained by a series of letters written in 1793.

On January 5 the Commissioners told the President:

> You have in your memory no Doubt, the general Idea of the Expence *at the time of your Adoption of the Plan for a President's House with the Increase then directed and highly Ornamented* [our italics] as Mr. Hoben has since collected, though from what grounds we do not know in proportion to the Cost of the Royal Exchange in Dublin this cost near 77900 Sterling on a view of our means, and we enclose a State[ment] for next year, we submit whether it will not be best to take the Plan on its original Scale, adding something to the Elevation, as was agreed to be proper—There will be also the greater probability or rather Certainty of effecting the necessary work in Time—. . .

The President responded on March 3:

> . . . When it was suggested to increase the dimensions of the President's House one fifth, I had no idea that it would carry the expence of that building to anything like the sum of £77,900—Sterling, which is estimated by Mr. Hoben.—And if that should be the case, I am decidedly of opinion that it would be best to take the plan on its original scale as you mention.—. . . But I confess that I cannot see how so great an increase of expence would arise, from the small increase in dimensions proposed; & am much mistaken indeed if it does not far exceed any ideas he let out at the time his plan was adopted. However, as I do not profess to be an accurate Judge in these matters, I cannot undertake to say that the additional expence is inconsistent.—. . .

George Washington himself, therefore, on July 17, 1792, instructed James Hoban to increase the size of the original three-story plan by one-fifth, and to add ornamentation to the rather plain exterior. This would account for the presence of window pediments and pilasters on the elevation, and their absence on the plan-and-profile.

The unexpected increase in cost is not really inconsistent. The President apparently overlooked the geometric factor. A linear increase of one-fifth is a cubic increase of almost 73 percent. Hoban's first estimate might have been as low as £45,000; but it is also easy to imagine an eager architect minimizing the costs and difficulties during negotiations for the commission.

Fig. 42 Plan of the principal story, the President's House, 1803. Drawing by B. Henry Latrobe, 1807.

Several days later the Commissioners surprisingly made a decision contrary to the President's inclination. With Hoban's assistance, they devised a plan to allow flexibility and defer irrevocable commitment on the total cost of the building. On March 14 they wrote to Hoban:

> On reflecting on our circumstances we believe it will be best to begin the President's House on the large plan with a present Intent of Dropping a Story in the execution. It will according to your idea described bring it on the whole, to much about the same Expense as in the smaller Length and Bridth, with the addition of the story—& will certainly not sink the neighboring buildings so much and perhaps the Beauty of the whole may be increased.—Besides if the funds run out and Opinion should lend to it in the progress of the work the large scale may be carried through.

The final form of Hoban's design was not determined until the following October. On the fifteenth of that month, Hoban wrote to the Commissioners:

> Gentlemen
>
> The present state of the President's House, and the situation of the business in the Stone cuting department carrying on at the President's Square; makes it necessary that you would come to a final determination respecting that building. The whole of the Stone cuters now in employ^t are preparing Aslar, and Architraves, calculated to suit the President's House; either to finish with two storys on the present basement agreiable to your idea given me some time ago; or to finish with three storys, so as to accord with the plan.
>
> Under the idea that the President's House should be proceeded on with spirit the ensuing year, it is now the time to make the necessary arrangements for that purpose; as to the various dimentions of Stone that may be wanted, which cannot be concluded on, untill your mind is made up as to the elevation—
>
> It may not be improper for me to observe, that the Aslar now cuting may be applyed to building the Capitol, if it is found on investigation, that it can be conveyed there by way of the Commrs. Wharfs and out of the President's Sq.^{r} in the same terms as by any other rout—and that the forwarding of the Capitol required it—
>
> [The next four paragraphs discuss lumber and other details]
>
> Herewith is an estimate from Mr. Blagdin, specifying the mode of measurement and the price of cuting and seting such work as the President's House and Capitol, to be done in a compleat manner this point requires serious consideration—
>
> I am gentlemen with great respect
Your Ob^t Servt
James Hoban
>
> N.B. Should the President's House be found sufficient for the purposes intended, with two Storys on the present basement, still retaining the same proportions as the original design, I am of the opinion in point of Elligance it will have a better effect—
>
> James Hoban

In the margin of the letter, opposite the number of stories, is written "two" in a different hand. The elimination of the third story is more fully confirmed by an entry in the proceedings of the Commissioners for their meeting of October 22, 1793:

"The Elevation of the President's House to be two stories only, besides the Basement."

This series of documents proves the validity of the plan and profile of a three-story building as an original competition drawing. It also strongly suggests that there was no two-story elevation drawing prior to October 1793. The footnote to Hoban's letter implies that neither he nor the Commissioners knew what the two-story version would look like.

A scale between the inner border and the green band on the drawing of the elevation shows that the facade is 168 feet wide, the size of the present building, and therefore one-fifth larger than Hoban's original. This elevation obviously cannot be an original competition drawing, and may have been prepared in late 1793 or early 1794.

It shows the President's House after at least two successive modifications. The original elevation proposed by Hoban has not survived, although it is certain that such a drawing was submitted; the program required one, and the letters quoted refer to the elevation several times.

On July 18, 1792, just after the competition closed, the Commissioners happily wrote to Samuel Blodget,

> That the President has approved the plan for a Palace, which we think convenient, elegant, and within a moderate expence—this plan was produced by a practised Architect from Charlestoun, who we expect will superintend the Building.

When Hoban was finally paid the premium he had won, the journal entry indicates that at least two drawings were submitted:

> Sundrys D^r to James Hoban
>   Presidents House for the Drawings of ditto
>   p Advertisement 500 dollars
>   @ 7/6 p dollar is £187..10..

This notation shows also that despite references to "a building lot in the city, a medal worth 10 guineas, and the balance in cash," Hoban received the entire premium in cash. A building lot was offered as an additional premium in the Capitol competition only.

Principles of descriptive geometry fortunately enable us to derive from the competition plan-and-profile drawing a reproduction of nearly all the missing original north elevation. Hoban provided hundreds of details which, when plotted in correct planar relation horizontally and vertically by an appropriate method of projection, result in the reappearance of the facade as originally proposed.

The front wall of the floor plan shows the width of wall and window, the projection for the piers supporting the columns, and the grand flight of stairs at the entrance.

The wall section at the left; the orthographic projections of the basement, moldings, window framing, ornamental brackets, ashlar piers with incised mortar joints; the three-quarter engaged columns; and the complete details of the entablature and balustrade speak volumes. For some time, it seemed that there was no way to verify the familiar central pediment above the colonnade from evidence on the drawing. The balustrade could have continued uninterrupted, as the profile persuades us to believe. At last, under magnification, six small dots, in a straight vertical line from the top of the cornice, were detected among the grime, the specks of mold, and foxing at the worn upper left corner of the paper, confirming that a pediment was indeed intended.

To reconstruct the facade graphically, the scales of the section-profile and of the floor plan must be determined, as none are marked on the drawings. In the lower right corner, a note obviously not part of the original drawing says:

> the scale is .137. l. to a foot (i.e. 2 Fr. *lignes*?)
>   or 7.29 feet to the Inch
> but the elevation seems to be about 4. f. to the Inch
> the basement story is 13. f. from the ground to the 1st floor

Kimball has identified the handwriting as Jefferson's and a comparison of the style of other known writing of his shows close similarity. However, the part in parentheses—(i.e. 2 Fr. *lignes*?)—is much lighter than the rest of the note, and the figure 2 is written in a rather elaborate manner very unlike Jefferson's usual stubby 2, which is more typically shown on the second line. Further, having lived in France and studied architecture there for several years, Jefferson would have known that two French *lignes* (units of linear measure of the *Ancien Regime*) would be greater than .137 inches. The French *pied* was slightly longer than the English foot, and the conversion of the smaller units, the *pouce* and the *ligne*, was as follows:

> 1 *ligne* = .08883 inches
> 12 *lignes* = 1 *pouce* = 1.0658 inches
> 12 *pouces* = 1 *pied* = 12.7892 inches

A scale of 2 French *lignes* to the foot would have resulted in a building width of about 220 feet, far beyond the known dimensions. Did another hand, perhaps Latrobe's or Mills's, add the query at the end of the first line?

The scale given by Jefferson's note for the section—4 feet to the inch—seems to be correct. It agrees with his measurement of the basement height, which is quite important since Hoban built the basement according to his original elevation, before the change to two stories. It also gives a pleasing proportion to the building, and the dimensions of elements in the sketch are exact multiples, or simple fractions, of a foot. The odd scale for the floor plan, however, is unrealistic. The dimensions of doors, windows, stairs, walls, and other details become irrational numbers, a scheme no architect would consider. Kimball suggested a reasonable explanation, which can be corroborated mathematically. Washington's letter of March 3, 1793, to the Commissioners notes an increase in dimensions by one-fifth. Kimball found that by reversing this enlargement Jefferson's approximation, based on the actual building, became a logical scale of 6 feet to the inch for the original drawing. Dimensions of the various parts then are simple numbers.

Hoban's original scheme, therefore, envisioned a building 140 feet wide, 72 feet deep, and 66.5 feet from ground level to the top of the parapet. For some mysterious reason, Kimball described the scale as: "for the plan, originally six feet to the inch, later taken as 7.25 to the inch, for the section, twice these figures." In the first place, using his own hypothesis, the "later scale" of the plan would be 7.2 feet to the inch, not 7.25. But it is naïve to imagine that an architect would simply

change the scale of a plan in order to enlarge it. The thickness of walls and plaster, windows, fireplaces, and countless other parts of the building do not change in direct ratio to the increase in size of the rooms. A practical architect would therefore put the smaller drawing aside and prepare a properly scaled new one. The remark that the section is "twice these figures" is also unsupportable. No matter how he meant it, the proportions would be grotesque. The only logical scale, giving rational numbers for the dimensions of the facade, is the one specified by Jefferson's note, namely 4 feet to the inch.

Despite these errors, Kimball's figures have persisted, copied and recopied, to the present day. Careful measurement of a photographic print of the Hoban drawing shows a slight distortion, some of which may be in the print itself. The scale parallel to the north facade is about 1.6 percent greater than that along the east side. This differential shrinking of the paper is of negligible significance historically, but may account for Jefferson's close, but not exact, scale for the plan.

Having ascertained the correct scales, a point-by-point plot of the windows, doors, columns, pediment, and other elements along Cartesian coordinates will result in an exact reproduction of the original facade. This geometric synthesis of the missing competition elevation is shown in Figure 43.

One feature of the reconstruction is conjectural. The treatment of the spaces over the windows and door on the first floor of the central pavilion cannot be determined from the plan and the profile. Of three or four possible choices for tying the piers

Fig. 43 Reconstruction of James Hoban's competition drawing; elevation of the President's House.

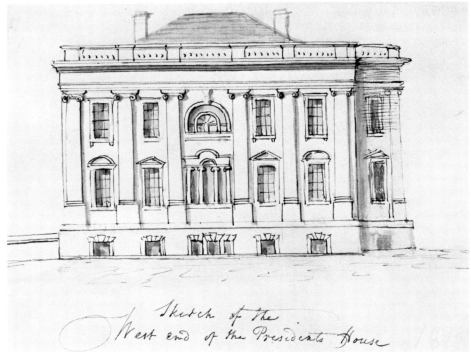

Fig. 44   North elevation of the President's House, before 1805, Samuel Blodget, Jr.

Fig. 45   West elevation of the President's House before Jefferson's household offices were added. Drawing by Samuel Blodget, Jr.

together structurally and visually, the round arch was the overwhelming favorite of the period. Hoban himself employed it in the design for Blodget's Hotel, where he created a similar arrangement of windows and a door flush with the wall, recessed between piers of supporting columns. All other elements of the composition are shown in enough detail in the original drawing to be recognizable. A surprising deviation from the final design of the President's House is the lack of alternate rounded and triangular pediments over the windows.

Hoban developed his presentation drawings in twenty days after arriving in Washington. In that short span of time, only minimum drawings required by the competition program could have been prepared. After Hoban's plan was accepted, July 17, 1792, a more detailed set of drawings for the actual construction would have been needed. The decision to increase the dimensions by one-fifth would also have involved revised drawings. There is a strong likelihood that only one set of working drawings, showing the three-story building, one-fifth larger than the original, with additional detail and ornament, was prepared and used to construct the foundations. After October 22, 1793, when the building was limited to two stories, no new major drawings would have been necessary. The elevation showing the appearance of the two-story version may logically have been drawn at this time, completing James Hoban's initial architectural contribution.

An unexplained departure from the elevation was introduced in the actual construction of the building, perhaps years after the drawing was made. A large blank panel sits over the two center columns in all early engravings of the north front, and at the center of the architraves on the east and west fronts as well. In classical buildings such panels contained an inscription, or carved decoration. No reference to the panels has yet been found in the records of construction. The original drawing contemplated an enormous carved eagle in the pediment, which was never executed. A drawing by Samuel Blodget made shortly after the President's House was completed shows a different ornament, probably of Blodget's invention.

Seven

The Ancestry of Hoban's Design

Since 1916, when Fiske Kimball first published Hoban's plan for the President's House, there has been much speculation regarding the possible source of his concept. Ordinary house-builders of the eighteenth century, not particularly skilled at architectural design, frequently chose a plan and elevation from one of the many illustrated books available, modifying the pattern to suit the needs of the client.

A common view, based on Kimball's intense conviction and widely accepted because of his stature as a scholar and critic, is that Hoban used plates 52 and 53 of James Gibbs's *A Book of Architecture* as a model for the President's House. Gibbs's book, first published in 1728 and reprinted in 1739 was a basic reference throughout the middle and late eighteenth century. It is known to have been a text-book in the architectural school of the Dublin Society, where Hoban was a student. No one really questions that Hoban was familiar with the book, and perhaps owned a copy, but documentary proof does not exist to support any connection between designs in Gibbs and the drawings that Hoban produced.

The fundamental flaw in the "Gibbs plates 52 and 53" theory is the premise that the extant plan and elevation were prepared more or less simultaneously, that they were both Competition drawings, and that they were closely related conceptually. The historical facts show that the elevation was drawn much later than the plan, and represents an alteration of Hoban's original idea. Hoban designed a three-story house, and there are none in Gibbs which resemble this composition.

Three contemporary sources have stated that Hoban was inspired by the house of the Duke of Leinster in Dublin. (See Plate 5.) The earliest reference was made by Hoban's successor as architect for the President's House, B. Henry Latrobe. In 1806, he wrote:

> General Washington knew how to give liberty to his country but was wholly ignorant of art. It is therefore not to be wondered, that the design of a physician, who was very ignorant of architecture was adopted for the Capitol and of a carpenter for the President's House. The latter is not even original, but a mutilated copy of a badly designed building near Dublin. If these buildings are badly designed, they are still more indifferently executed.

The second reference is in David Bailie Warden's *A Chorographical and Statistical Description of the District of Columbia,* published in Paris in 1816, where

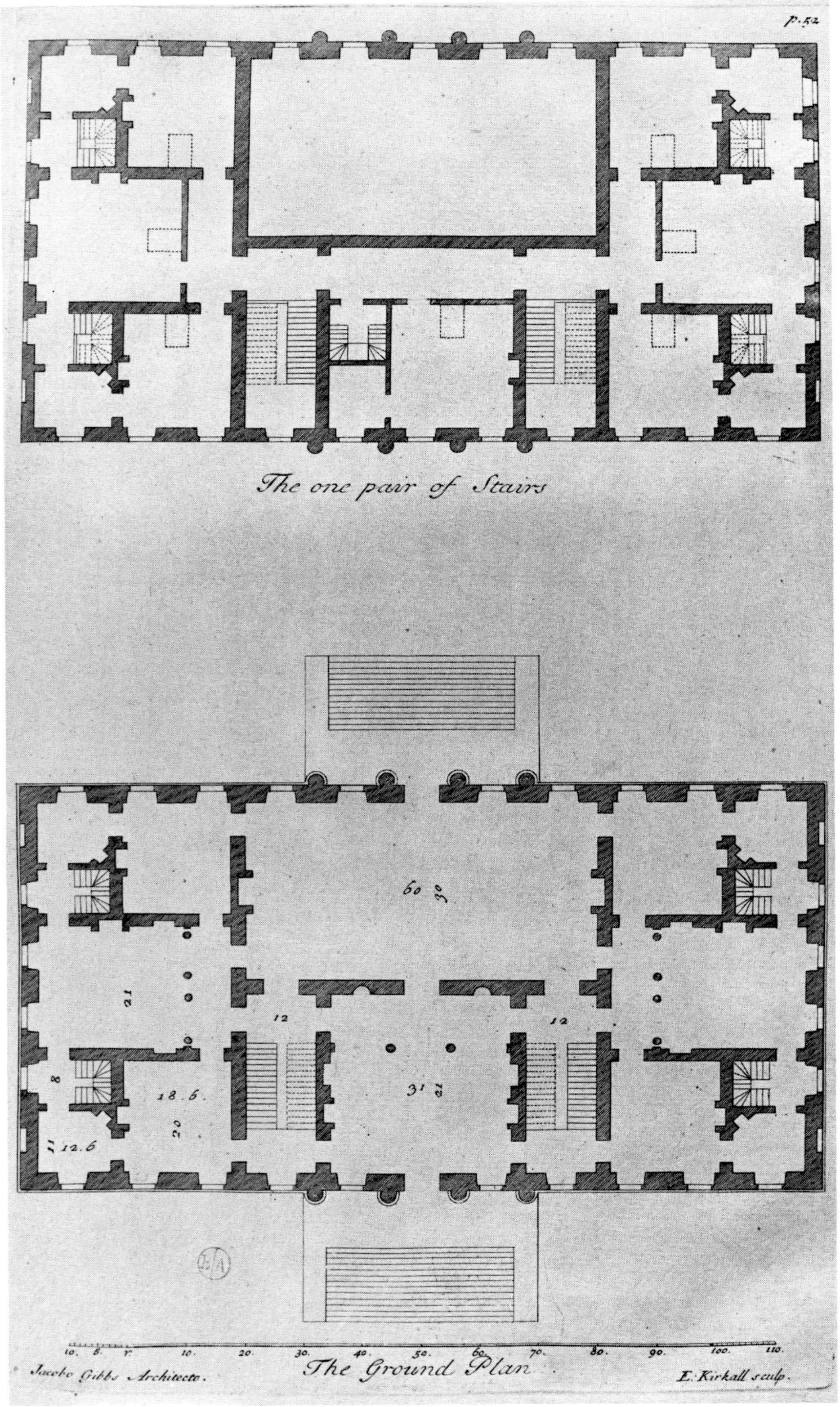

P. 52

The one pair of Stairs

The Ground Plan

Jacobo Gibbs Architecto.

E. Kirkall sculp.

Fig. 46 Plan for a gentleman's House. James
Gibbs, *A Book of Architecture,* 1728, Plate 52.

Fig. 47 Elevation for a gentleman's house.
Gibbs, plate 53.

46

Warden had been employed in the United States consular office. The book states on page 36:

> The President's House consists of two stories, and is a hundred and seventy feet in length and eighty-five in breadth. It resembles Leinster-House in Dublin, and is much admired. Even the Poet Moor [Thomas Moore] styles it a "grand edifice," a "noble Structure."

Warden lived in Washington during part of 1810 and 1811, and was well-acquainted in local society. His book is dedicated to Mrs. Custis. He had the opportunity to obtain firsthand information on the building, and a natural curiosity about anything pertaining to the new federal district. Latrobe was still architect at the President's House during Warden's residence in the capital.

On March 22, 1817, Latrobe wrote to William Lee, an aide to President Madison, recommending a revision of the basement plan of the President's House then being reconstructed by James Hoban:

> I will first, however, observe that I feel no delicacy whatever on this subject toward Mr. Hoban. If the plan was his design, I should be guilty of great professional impropriety in interfering with his operations. But as it is acknowledged to be that of the palace of the Duke of Leinster, which I have now before me, in a book containing the principal edifices of Dublin, he cannot be offended even if he should see these remarks.

In the same letter Latrobe again refers to Hoban as the "copyist of a bad plan."

The last known contemporary attribution was made by the Duke Bernhardt of Saxe-Weimar-Eisenach, who traveled to America in 1825 and published his journals in 1828. On November 15, 1825, the Duke visited the city of Washington, where he was received by the President. He describes the house of the President, and states that the palace of the Duke of Leinster was the model for the building.

None of these references to Leinster House appear to have been copied from one

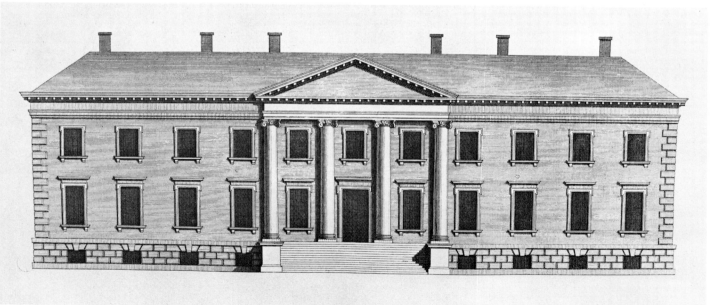

47

another. Latrobe's first remarks were expressed privately in a letter to Philip Mazzei. In each case the writer was personally familiar with Hoban's building; some possibly knew Leinster House as well. These independent, consistent references by competent people indicate that the origin of the design of the President's House was no secret.

Hoban's composition was utterly new to America; no other building like it existed in the colonies or the early republic. It was the first great house faced entirely with dressed stone, antedating the Parkman houses in Boston by more than a decade.

Homes of the wealthy and powerful in America were comfortably large, in good taste and style, but not intended as ostentatious symbols of the owner's financial status, as in the British Isles and Europe at that time. The President's House was the largest dwelling yet proposed, befitting the dignity of the office. Hoban's building was a few feet wider than Leinster House, then the largest townhouse in Ireland and the residence of its highest-ranking nobleman.

Hoban had been trained at the Dublin Society architectural school, where he won a medal for excellence in drawing. He subsequently worked on some of the most distinguished buildings being erected in Dublin during his residence there. These included the building for the Newcomen Bank, designed by his teacher, Thomas Ivory; the Royal Exchange, designed and built by Thomas Cooley; and the Customs House, designed by James Gandon. His name does not appear on any known roster of mechanics or craftsmen in Dublin. Since his special talent was in drawing, it is possible that he was employed by Cooley as a draftsman, along with Richard and Francis Johnston.

Although under considerable pressure of time, Hoban produced a remarkably satisfactory and elegant plan for the Competition. That it should resemble existing buildings in many respects is not surprising. The creation of an entirely new design would have taken longer than the competition deadline permitted. As it was, Hoban did not use Leinster House as his only model. Elements of at least two other buildings near Dublin can be identified in his drawings.

The framework for Hoban's competition plan and elevation can first be found in Castletown, a large country house a few miles west of Dublin. It was designed by the Italian architect Alessandro Galilei, and erected in the 1720s. Both the exterior and interior decoration was "improved" in later years, but the general design was never altered. It is the oldest of the models on which Hoban based his competition design. From it, Hoban abstracted several important features for the President's House.

Castletown is a free-standing building which consists of a sunken basement story surmounted by three full stories, topped by a balustraded roof, just as Hoban proposed in his profile and section. The height is about 66 feet to the top of the parapet; Hoban's section is 66½. The proportion of width, depth and height above ground of the main block at Castletown is 132 feet: 66 feet: 66 feet, or 2:1:1, a double cube. Hoban's first plan of the President's House was 140 feet: 72 feet: 66.5 feet, or 2:1.02:.95, almost the same shape.

In the words of Sir John Summerson, Castletown has "a front of stupendous monotony." In 1734, Lady Anne Conolly, just married to the nephew of the builder, writes:

> ... I don't think the place very pleasant, though the house is really a charming one to live in. The front is quite without ornaments of any sort, not even so much as pediments over the windows. . .

Fig. 48   Medal awarded James Hoban by the architectural school of the Dublin Society, 1780.

Fig. 49   Castletown, Celbridge, County Kildare. Designed by Alessandro Galilei; built 1722.

Fig. 50   Ground-floor plan of Castletown.

This early statement has special significance in the light of Hoban's section-profile, which also does not show pediments over the windows. It has been assumed that pediments were added to the windows on the second story of Castletown in the 1760s, when the sills of ten of the twelve windows on the first floor were lowered. But Lady Louisa Conolly continued to embellish the architecture of Castletown for several years more, and Hoban may have known it in its original state.

Castletown has a balustrade around the roof, and so does Hoban's design for the President's House. Leinster House has a plain roof. Hoban's inclusion of this feature may have been motivated by the preferences of President Washington, who had strongly criticized both Turner's and Hallet's roof plans for the Capitol. Later, in a letter to William Thornton, he said that when a roof is to be seen, something to relieve the view of a plain and dead surface was indispensable. Dormers, for instance, would suffice; otherwise, an unadorned roof should be hidden by a parapet. It may be significant that most of the designs in both of the 1792 competitions had balustraded roofs.

49

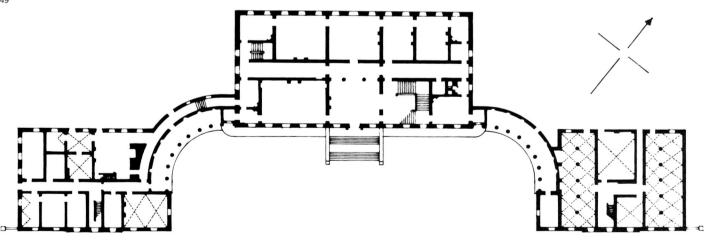

0 10 20 30 40 50   100 FT

50

The remaining structural element of Hoban's profile view also found at Castletown is the basement story that is partially sunken into the ground, but high enough to provide good light for the windows of the service rooms. Leinster House sits flush upon the earth, and the basement is lighted on the entrance side only through gratings let into the pavement. The sloping terrain at the site of the President's House may have determined Hoban's choice; on the south side, the floors of the basement rooms are at grade, permitting easy access.

A wide central transverse corridor extends the full width of the basement floor of Castletown. Its ceiling is supported by handsome groined vaulting. A nearly identical passage was designed for the basement of the President's House by Hoban.

In spite of the seemingly extensive borrowing from Castletown, Hoban's competition drawing was primarily derived from the plan and elevation of Leinster House, built in 1745 from a design by Richard Castle. Coming from Germany to England about 1725, a civil engineer by training, Castle became acquainted with the new English Palladian style being popularized by Campbell, Burlington, and Kent. He was a subscriber to volume III of *Vitruvius Britannicus.* Though he stayed in London 4 years and seems to have absorbed the essence of Palladianism very well, no buildings by Castle are known in England. His first commission was a house in the north of Ireland for Gustavus Hume. After completing Castle Hume, Richard Castle went to Dublin in time to associate himself with Sir Edward Lovett Pearce, the leading Irish architect, who died unexpectedly in 1733. Castle took over his practice, and built a greater number of important public and private buildings than any other architect in Ireland in the eighteenth century.

Leinster House is a reserved but correct Palladian building. The floor plan closely resembles Castletown; the entrance hall and axial corridor are almost identical, although the arrangement of the rooms and staircase have been changed somewhat. Certain details are similar to those in the architectural pattern books of the time, which may well account for Kimball's idea that Hoban drew his plans from Gibbs in 1792.

For the competition design, Hoban adopted only the general floor plan and the entrance elevation of Leinster House. The rest of the exterior of the President's House, including the unusual south front, was an original composition. While no record of the interior has survived, it was simpler than the elaborate and lavish decoration of Leinster House. The talented woodcarvers and joiners needed to execute this kind of work were not available.

There is some curious evidence that Hoban worked from the engraving of Leinster House in *Views of the most Remarkable Public Buildings Monuments and other Edifices in the City of Dublin,* by Robert Pool and John Cash, published in 1780 under the auspices of the Dublin Society. In their engraving the windows are mistakenly grouped in a 4-3-4 arrangement; the wall space between groups is nearly twice the space between windows within a group. Leinster House itself was built with equal window spacing across the entire front, and so was Castletown. The Gibbs plate also shows uniform spacing. Pool and Cash made the same mistake in their engraving of the Lying-In Hospital in Dublin, also designed by Castle and almost a twin of Leinster House.

Hoban was a student at the Dublin Society in the year the book was published, and no doubt owned a copy, since he duplicated the Leinster House window

51

52

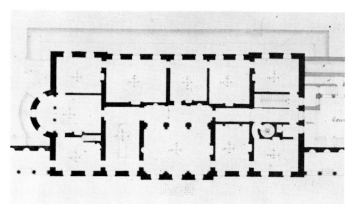

53

Fig. 51 View of Castletown as it is today.

Fig. 52 Drawing of Leinster House, Dublin, by Richard Castle.

Fig. 53 Ground-floor plan of Leinster House before the modifications made about 1780.

spacing so accurately. The grouped windows introduced a distinctive enhancement of the central pavilion not found in any of the prototypes themselves.

The original plan of Leinster House included three rooms arranged along the north side, the entire outside wall of the center room forming a semicircular bay, which permitted a better view of the lawn and garden and provided an eye-catching terminus for the long central passage. About 1780, this part of the house was being drastically remodelled, as the description accompanying the Pool and Cash engraving mentions that "the present possessor, William Robert Duke of Leinster, has displayed an elegant taste in some considerable alterations lately being made at the north end of the house." Three years later, Thomas Milton published a view of the garden front of Leinster House. This time the text states that "on the North Side [is] a long Room running the whole depth of the House, under the Picture Gallery, and of the same shape and dimensions, this is called the Supper Room; it is adorned with sixteen fluted Columns Ionic, supporting the enriched ceiling."

Overhead, "the Gallery on this Floor is upwards of Eighty Feet long and twenty-four feet wide, with a Bow of three windows on the side; the Ceiling is arched the Portion of a Circle, highly enriched and painted in different colours, from the designs of Mr. Wyat." These great rooms running from front to back inspired Hoban's design for the East Room.

The plan of Leinster House and Hoban's first plan are almost identical in size: 140 feet by 70 feet and 140 feet by 72 feet, respectively. The extra width of Hoban's building is added to the central corridor. Some additional space is stolen from the rooms at the west end to expand the grand staircase. By substituting a less extravagant stairway in the original Leinster House location, Hoban was able to widen the East Room not only to correct Palladian proportions, a double-square, but to use the whole first floor more efficiently. Wyatt had achieved the right proportions at Leinster House in the Supper Room by introducing vestibules at the ends, reducing the extraordinary length to balance the maximum width available. The area between the sets of columns is also a double square, but the solution is a costly waste of space.

At the rear of Leinster House a sunken terrace about 11 feet wide surrounded by a balustrade runs the full length of the building at the basement level. On Hoban's

Fig. 54 Robert Pool and John Cash, engraving of Leinster House, 1779. The erroneous window spacing is the same as in Hoban's elevation of the President's House.

Fig. 55 Elevation, Leinster House, 1913.

Fig. 56 Ground-floor plan, Leinster House; measured drawing, 1913.

Fig. 57 Principal floor plan, Leinster House, 1913.

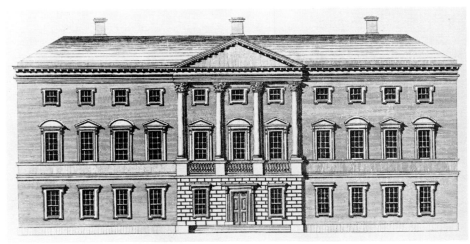

54

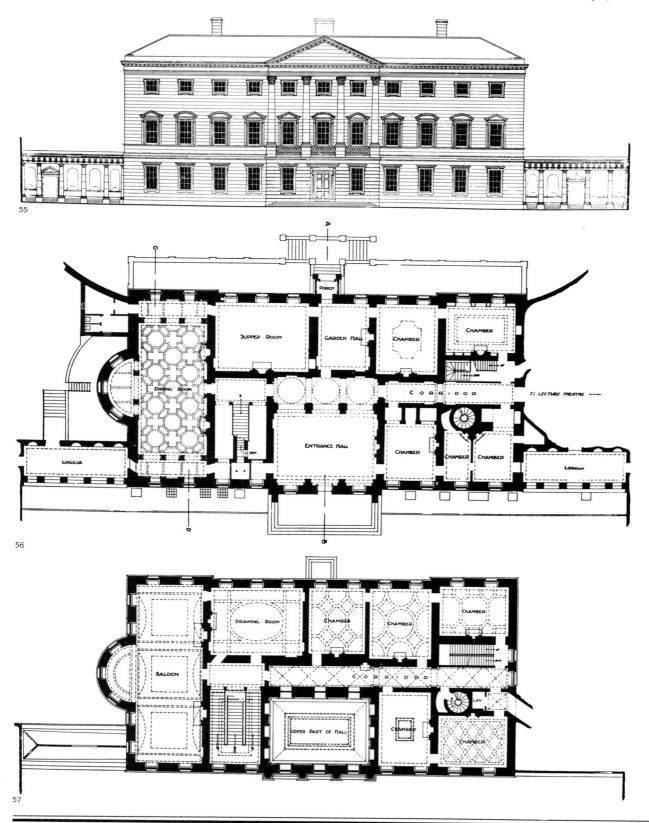

55

56

57

plan, a piazza of the same width, never built, also extends the length of the building. It was June and July in Washington when Hoban worked so diligently to meet the competition deadline. The oppressive summer heat would remind him of the desirability of a cool, shaded verandah on the south side of the house. Whether Hoban was inspired by Leinster House, by the great verandah at Mount Vernon, or by a similar feature in a South Carolina house is not known. However, Mount Vernon, close by, overlooked the Potomac, just as the President's House was destined to do. Its verandah was designed by the man who would be the final judge of the Competition, and Hoban was not only a clever architect but an astute politician.

The program for the President's House competition mentioned that "It will be a Recommendation of any Place, if the central Part of it may be detached and erected for the present, with the Appearance of a complete whole, and be capable of admitting the additional Parts in future, if they shall be wanting." This idea had been suggested by President Washington.

In Hoban's design, a few historians have considered the possibility that he meant to lop off three bays on each side, building only what was left, if a small house were required. However, the documents show that from the beginning Washington thought Hoban's plan too small, and ordered it enlarged by one-fifth. The alternative, then, would have been to add wings to the original block as the needs of the President increased.

The Palladian villa scheme, with loggias at each side leading to outbuildings, was suited for exactly this kind of extension. The traffic between the wings and the central house would be largely that of civil and domestic personnel. The logical connection, to avoid bothering the President in his private and state quarters, would be the spacious and handsome corridor at the basement level. Both Castletown and Leinster House had monumental colonnades linking the main block to outbuildings. James Diamond's entry in the Competition suggested "Arcades leading to the Wings if necessary," and Jacob Small's drawings had plans and elevations of both the arcades and the terminal buildings as well. Twelve years later President Jefferson began construction of similar passages which he intended to run from the President's House to the Executive office buildings then erected on either side, with a pavilion at the halfway point to break the monotony of the long straight line. Jefferson's experience at the President's House could have been the source for the same feature in his design for the University of Virginia.

As late as 1976, the source for Hoban's central oval room "on end" remained a mystery. The possibility existed that it was somehow derived from the oval salons Jefferson admired in Paris. Indeed, sketches by him incorporating oval rooms may antedate Hoban's drawing. The Jefferson sketches appear to be early studies for his first scheme for a President's House, which was never made public.

It is not likely that Hoban was familiar with Parisian architecture, and no evidence has come to light that Jefferson and Hoban ever communicated before the competition. Moreover, there are three Irish houses—Mount Kennedy, Lucan, and Castlecoole—that have oval rooms arranged in a manner exactly like Hoban's design for the President's House. It can be proved that the three were interrelated, and that Hoban was acquainted with either the architect or the builder of each of them.

The oval room on axis with the entrance hall evolved from the conjunction of a rectangular room with columns, representing a basilica, leading to a circular room, representing a classical temple, thereby uniting the two most exalted interior forms in Renaissance architecture. The oval is a baroque innovation, probably appearing first in the Palazzo Barberini in Rome.

Palladio never used an oval except for stairs. From Italy, the oval spread with the baroque style to most of Europe, and was much used in the seventeenth and eighteenth centuries. The most famous French example of an oval room on axis is in the Chateau Vaux le-Vicomte, built by Le Vau in 1661.

In England, Inigo Jones used oval rooms in a minor position in his grand design for a new Whitehall, the palace that was never built. The first house in the British Isles with an oval room on axis was Ballyhaise, County Cavan, Ireland, designed about 1733 by the same Richard Castle who created Leinster House. Transplanted from baroque Germany to Palladian England, Castle was the ideal man to combine elements of the two schools. At Ballyhaise, as in all previous plans, the long axis of the ellipse was parallel to the facade. Other English architects later used the oval room, particularly Sir Robert Taylor, a prolific and popular designer who was also a keen mathematician. Taylor even designed four oval rooms within a circle at Sharpham House, Devon, a scheme that Thomas Jefferson proposed later for the Capitol and adapted in the rotunda of the University of Virginia.

Other Irish houses with Castle's central oval room followed. Two were by Thomas Cooley, at Caledon House and Rokeby Hall. In all these early examples the long axis of the oval room was parallel to the rear wall.

Fig. 58 Luton Hoo, Bedfordshire. The original portico shown here was destroyed by fire early in the nineteenth century. Hoban's proposed verandah for the President's House was similar in style, but extended the full width of the building.

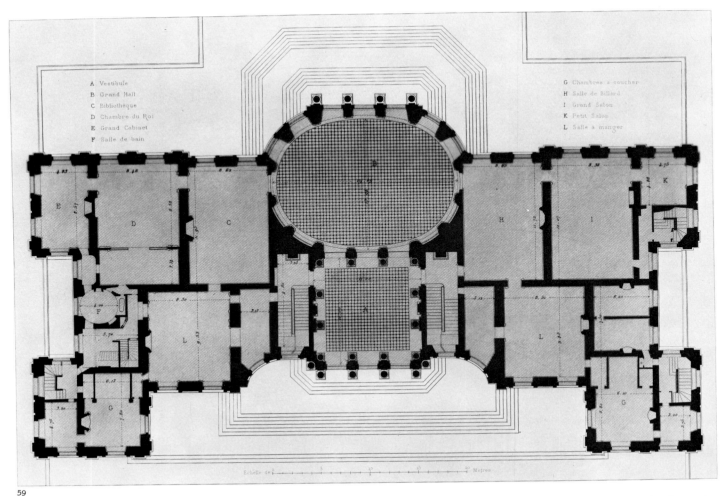

A Vestibule
B Grand Hall
C Bibliothèque
D Chambre du Roi
E Grand Cabinet
F Salle de bain

G Chambres a coucher
H Salle de Billard
I Grand Salon
K Petit Salon
L Salle a manger

59

Fig. 59 Chateau Vaux-le-Vicomte. Principal floor plan.

James Wyatt invented the central oval room with its long axis perpendicular to the facade in his plan for Mount Kennedy, County Wicklow, in 1772. This idea is far more ingenious than appears at first glance. By adding only a slight bulge at the back of the house, costing little in extra material, a commodious and graceful room can be fitted into a relatively narrow space, leaving enough width in a modest house for a chamber of normal size at each side. The open appearance which greets the eye upon entering this oval room from the entrance hall is more pleasing than the short view seen when the oval is oriented the other way around.

Irish houses of the period were rather plain on the outside, in contrast to the richly decorated interiors. At Mount Kennedy, no special ornament set apart the exterior of the curved bay. Hoban followed this tradition in his first plan for the President's House.

Although Mount Kennedy was planned in 1772, Thomas Cooley did not begin to build until 1781. It was completed in 1784. In that year Cooley died, leaving his practice in the hands of the Johnston brothers.

Lucan was built from 1776 to 1779. Agmondisham Vesey, the owner and an amateur architect, has been credited with the overall design. Plans for Lucan were drawn by William Chambers in 1773, but John Harris has noted that neither the

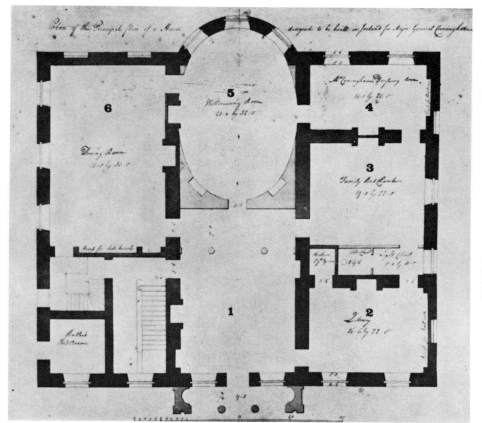

60

62

61

𝓕𝓲𝓰. 60   James Wyatt's plan for Mount Kennedy, 1772.

𝓕𝓲𝓰. 61   Rear facade, Mount Kennedy.

𝓕𝓲𝓰. 62   Plain walls offer a striking contrast to the ornamented ceiling in the oval room at Mount Kennedy.

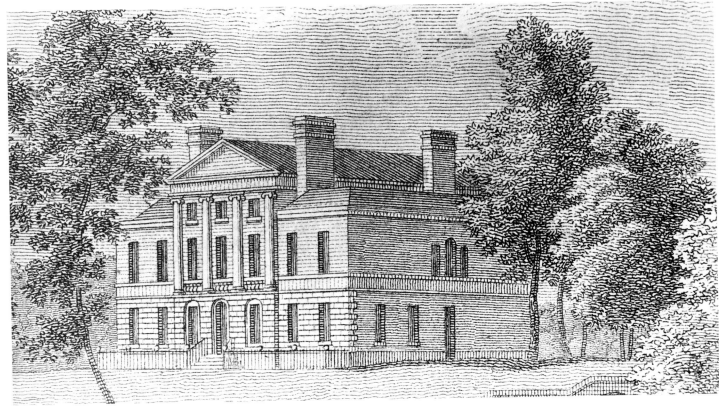

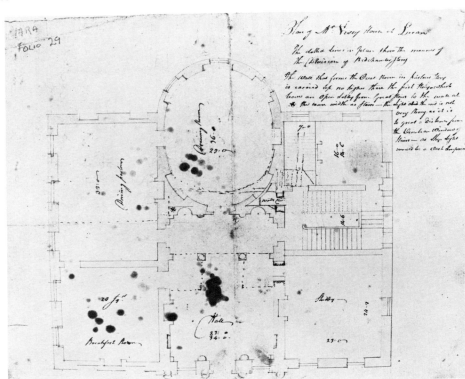

Fig. 63 Lucan House, County Dublin. Detail of an engraving by Thomas Milton, 1783.

Fig. 64 Principal floor plan of Lucan. The design of the oval room resembles Hoban's "Eliptic."

floor plan nor the elevations of the executed building are characteristic of Chambers's style. New plans were made three years later. Elizabeth Carter, the famous bluestocking, wrote to Mrs. Montagu on May 15, 1776:

> [Mrs. Vesey] has this afternoon been looking over the plan of the new-house at Lucan, and seems greatly disturbed to find she is to inhabit a round room, where she conceives she shall be like an old parrot in a cage; upon which Mrs. Hancock and I have promised to add scarlet trimmings to her green gown.

The 1776 floor plan and design for the oval saloon, which still exist, have been attributed to James Wyatt.

Both Mount Kennedy and Lucan were built before Hoban emigrated to America. Either building could have been the immediate inspiration for the "Eliptic" at the President's House. Hoban seems to have had somewhat closer connections to Thomas Cooley, the builder of Mount Kennedy, than to Thomas Penrose, who is believed to have supervised the building of Lucan. However, both men had held the office of Clerk and Inspector of Civil Buildings, and Hoban, "being universally acquainted" in the building line in Ireland, would have known Penrose. James Wyatt, the London architect who designed both Mount Kennedy and Lucan, apparently never visited either place.

A third oval room, exactly the size and shape of the Blue Room in the White House, was incorporated in the design for Castlecoole by Richard Johnston. His drawings are dated 1789, five years after Hoban's departure. But Johnston had redrawn Wyatt's 1772 plan for Mount Kennedy prior to 1784, and just when Lord Belmore first consulted Johnston about his new house at Castlecoole is not known. In an odd reversal of roles, Wyatt was called upon to revise Johnston's plans for Castlecoole, and it is Wyatt's neoclassical building that stands today. See Plates 6 and 7.

Fig. 65 James Wyatt's oval saloon, now the dining room, at Lucan.

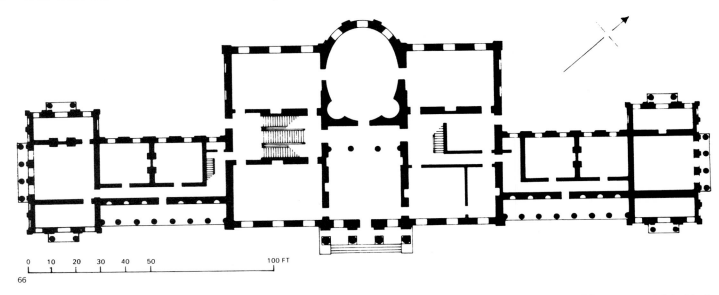

66

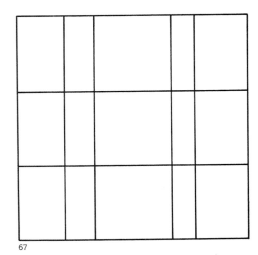

67

In the two earlier Irish oval rooms at Mount Kennedy and Lucan, straight-sided, set-in niches adjoin the entrance from the corridor. Those at Mount Kennedy have been covered over to accommodate the de Gree *grisailles* which graced the walls until recently. At Lucan, the niches contain imitation window sash.

Hoban's intended treatment of these niches at the President's House is not recorded, but Dolley Madison had five sets of red velvet curtains made for the oval room, and there are only three windows. The logical disposition of the remaining pairs would be over the niches, making them appear to be windows as at Lucan.

Three Irish houses—Castletown, Leinster House, and Lucan (or Mount Kennedy)—thus account for all the elements that Hoban needed to put together his plan. The Competition drawing is a cleaner, more academic composition than any of the prototype buildings. It shows that the architect had been well-schooled in the geometric principles of Palladian design, and adhered closely to the rules laid down in *The Four Books of Architecture.* Perhaps a more confident and experienced architect would have allowed himself more freedom from the textbooks, but Hoban had never undertaken a project of this magnitude before.

As Rudolf Wittkower has pointed out, Palladio's villa plans were variants of a fundamental scheme. By altering the dimensions and position of partitions, and by adding or subtracting according to the circumstances, Palladio obtained his vocabulary. He also recommended:

> The most beautiful and proportionable manners of rooms, and which succeed best, are seven, because they are either made round (tho' but seldom) or square, or their length will be the diagonal line of the square, or of a square and a third, or of one square and a half, or of one square and two thirds, or of two squares.

In addition to these ratios—$1:1$, $1:\sqrt{2}$, $3:4$, $2:3$, $3:5$, and $1:2$—Palladio often used other simple ratios, particularly $4:5$ and $5:6$. All the rooms of the President's House, both in Hoban's original drawing and after the building had been expanded one-fifth and slightly altered, follow these recommended proportions.

| | | Ratios of Width to Length | |
		Original Drawing	As Built
Entrance Hall	(A)	3:5	2:3
Oval Room	B	3:4	3:4
East Room	C	1:2	1:2
Red and Green Rooms	D & F	2:3	4:5
Dining Room and Study	E & G	3:4	3:4
Porter's Hall	H	1:2	4:5
President's Staircase	I	1:2	1:2
East Staircase	K	1:3	1:2
Porter's Staircase	L	2:3	2:3
Corridor	—	1:5	1:4

Hoban's adherence to these values showed an awareness of architectural theory above and beyond that of the ordinary builder. An incident in Charleston a few years earlier had demonstrated that he had considerable mathematical ability and was familiar with the geometric principles of the ellipse. The Charleston *Morning Post and Daily Advertiser* of April 21, 1787, had published:

A QUESTION.

In an eliptical acre of grass there is given,
Whose length to its breadth is as 9 to 7;
How long is the cord, and how brought to pass,
That a horse fed no more than his acre of grass.
J.C.

The paper of May 7 contained:

Answer to the Question inserted 21st April.

An English acre, in proportion as 9 to 7, its transverse diameter

is	207,694
Its conjugate ditto	267,036
Difference of diameter, is	59,342
Which, subtracted from semi-conjugate diameter, is	74,176

The length of cord necessary, which length being kept equidistant from the outlines of an elipsis, as above proportioned on both its diameters, gives the points to place 4 pins round, which pins said length of line is to traverse, which being equidistant from the outline, confines the horse to the oval described.

April 24th, 1787.   James Hoban.

Hoban's treatment of the Ionic order is also in accord with classical rules. The proportions of the architrave, frieze, and cornice and the relation of the entablature to the height of the column (1:5) are all correct. The spacing of the columns on the facade, so far as can be determined from the drawing, is consistent with the ratio of 1 module (diameter of the column) to an intercolumnar spacing of $2\frac{1}{4}$ modules, according to the dictum of Vitruvius.

In short, Hoban was a trained professional, an architect with a good academic background, but not broadly experienced. In those days, however, architecture alone did not offer a lucrative future. A set of plans by a London architect of the highest repute (such as those provided by Chambers for Lucan) cost about £25. An unidentified commentator remarked that "it's scarce worth the attention of an

Fig. 66 Richard Johnston's 1789 plan of Castlecoole contained many of the features of Hoban's later plan for the President's House.

Fig. 67 The geometric pattern underlying Palladio's villa plans. The President's House is derived from this scheme.

ingenious person to pursue and study the profession of an architect, unless he becomes mercenary and unites that disgraceful and illiberal one of a contractor and builder." Hoban's whole career in Washington shows that he was capable, intelligent, and politically adept. He used his architectural talent to provide an opportunity to profit by building, and earned himself a comfortable fortune in construction and land speculation. Latrobe, who stayed with architecture, died in debt, while Hoban, a builder as well, left $60,000, the equivalent of a million dollars today.

Eight

Building the President's House: 1792–1802

Preliminary surveys and site preparation had been the major accomplishments of 1791 in the new federal district. L'Enfant, Ellicott, and the Commissioners began work in the spring of that year. Trees were felled to obtain sight lines, and areas for the two principal buildings cleared as the form of the city appeared in L'Enfant's mind. Slaves rented from neighboring plantations built wharves at Hamburgh, dug clay for brickmaking, and began excavations for cellars at the President's House and the Capitol. An abortive sale of thirty-five lots held in October raised only $2,000 in cash, far less than was expected.

The Commissioners bought a copy of William Salmon's *Palladio Londinensis: or the London Art of Building,* a practical book of architectural geometry and methods of construction, presumably for L'Enfant. Shortly afterward he staked the outlines for the President's House, and in December 2,443 perches of foundation stone were delivered there. This was a significant beginning, as L'Enfant had estimated about 30,000 perches for the entire building.

In January 1792 Elisha Owen Williams of Georgetown and William Ray contracted to build eight huts at the President's Square by the fifteenth of March. The government not only provided shelter for workmen without homes, but fed them. The average daily ration per man was one pound of beef or pork, one pound of flour, a half-pound of cornmeal, one half-pint of spirits, whatever produce was available, and a weekly allowance of two ounces each of chocolate, sugar, and butter, and a pound of rice. For the times, this diet was surprisingly generous and well-balanced for men engaged in hard labor. Unfortunately, there is frequent evidence that food supplies were inedible or spoiled, and that shipments were uneven.

Initial funding for the public works was provided by Maryland and Virginia. The major financing for the construction was expected from the sale of lots, which Washington urged the Commissioners to pursue vigorously to compensate for the debacle of the previous October.

The large official map of the city was still not available, however, and this slowed the sale of lots. There were lame excuses from the engravers in Philadelphia for the delays, which Washington suspected were deliberate, inspired by those opposed to the relocation of the government. To circumvent any Philadelphia intrigue, he and Jefferson decided to have a plate also engraved in Boston, and asked Samuel Blodget, Jr., to make the arrangements. Blodget contracted with Samuel Hill, publisher of the *Massachusetts Magazine,* to produce a master plate at top speed. In spite of his promise to drop everything else and concentrate on the official plate, Hill found time to engrave a smaller version for insertion in the May 1792 issue of the *Massachusetts Magazine.* The plan was also published in the *New York Magazine* the following month. Thus, with the previously published map in the *Universal Asylum,* three excellent but unofficial printings of Ellicott's plan, all virtually identical, were circulating long before the so-called Boston plate was sent to Philadelphia and printed by Mr. Scott. The first copies went to the Commissioners at the end of August. In the confusion and rush, the soundings of the waters were omitted from this plan. In the meantime a small (20 by 27 inches) version of the Ellicott drawing had been engraved in Philadelphia by Thackara and Vallance, and printed by Scott. Copies were sent to the Commissioners in Washington by Jefferson's secretary, George Taylor, on September 14. Large numbers of both plans were sold in the next two months. The large "Philadelphia" engraving was completed by October 28, not in time for the second sale of lots. The first prints of the final plan were ready on November 13. Jefferson set the price at 75 cents a copy. The Boston plan, without soundings, sold for 37.5 cents.

In the meantime preparation for construction continued at the rapid pace dictated by the President. John Mountz contracted to make sledgehammers, wedges, and other tools. William Knowles erected a large shop, 50 feet long and 21 feet wide, at the site in April. Captain Williams seems to have made a good impression with his contract, as he was appointed general overseer of the work at the President's House for one year on April 13. In early May two kilns were built there, each to make 300,000 bricks.

Freestone began to arrive regularly from Virginia quarries. Collen Williamson, the late entrant in the competition, was hired as master mason to superintend the cutting and laying of stone at the public buildings.

With all the construction now in progress, the unpaid Commissioners found that their sporadic conferences did not enable them to direct the work adequately. In May, they instituted regular monthly meetings. The competitions advertised in March were beginning to bring responses, and by late June had grown to a substantial number. Most were proposals for the Capitol.

On July 15 the competitions officially closed. During the next two days the President and the Commissioners examined the entries. On the eighteenth, the records of the proceedings show that

> James Hobens plan pf the Palace being approved by the President, he is
> entitled to the reward published, and chuses a Gold medal of . . . 10 Guineas
> value—the Balance in money.

A second entry the same day states:

> James Hoben is retained in the service of the public by the
> Commissioners—he is to make the drawings and superintend the execution
> of his plan of the Palace and such other work of that kind as may be in
> execution—he is to find himself and receive three hundred guineas pr year.

The Commissioners informed Washington of these arrangements on July 19, 1792:

> Yesterday the Commissioners contracted with Mr. Hoban for his services by
> the year at 300 guineas. His draft and attention may be confined to the
> Palace or extended to other objects as they may choose. This morning we
> went with Mr. Hoban to the site of the Palace, that he might lay out the
> foundations. The plan being much less than Major L'Enfant's design will not
> fill up the diverging points marked by the stakes. This will necessarily
> occasion a division of the excess on the two sides, or to recede the whole
> distance on one side. This does not seem to create so much embarrassment
> as might be expected, but as the work may go on without any waste of labor,
> till you shall be here again, we have left the choice open, to be made by you
> on the spot. Hoban's affairs require his absence about a month. His return is
> expected to be as soon, as he will be much wanted.

The President responded:

> I think you have engaged Mr. Hoban upon advantageous terms, and hope, if
> his industry and honesty are of a piece with the specimens he has given of
> his abilities, he will prove a useful man and a considerable acquisition.

No entry was judged entirely suitable for the Capitol, and further revisions were
requested of Hallet, then the leading contender.

Partly because of the excavation already made by L'Enfant, and partly because of
the delay at the Capitol, it was possible for Hoban to lay the cornerstone of the
President's House October 13, 1792, with Masonic ceremonies. It was three
hundred years and one day after the discovery of America, a coincidence to have
great significance a century later.

The October 19 issue of Dunlap's *American Daily Advertiser,* Philadelphia, published a letter from Georgetown dated October 13, 1792, noting that "the cornerstone of the President's House was to be laid this day, at 12 o'clock, and the greater
part of the material being already on the spot, the edifice will be finished expedi-
tiously as the requisite attention to the security of the walls, in a building of such
magnitude, will permit." The only known description of this occasion was printed in
the Charleston *City Gazette* issue of November 15, 1792.

A brass plate engraved by Caleb Bentley was laid on the cornerstone. During the
reconstruction of the White House during the period 1948–1952, this plate was
located by an electronic mine-detector, but because the walls about it were in good
condition it was not disturbed.

Having begun the foundations, it was now important to get more highly skilled
craftsmen for stonecutting and carving, and carpenters for the interior frame and
finish. At Jefferson's suggestion the Commissioners wrote to an agent in Amsterdam to procure about 100 stonemasons, stonecutters, and bricklayers from
Germany. In a letter to the Commissioners dated November 3, 1792, Hoban offered
to import help from Ireland:

> Being universally acquainted with men in the Building line in Ireland,
> particularly with many able Stone Cutters in Dublin with whom I have been
> concerned in building, as the Royal Exchange, New Bank, and Custom
> House, all of which buildings were done in the same Stile as the business to
> be done here, and of nearly the same kind of Stone, to those men I would

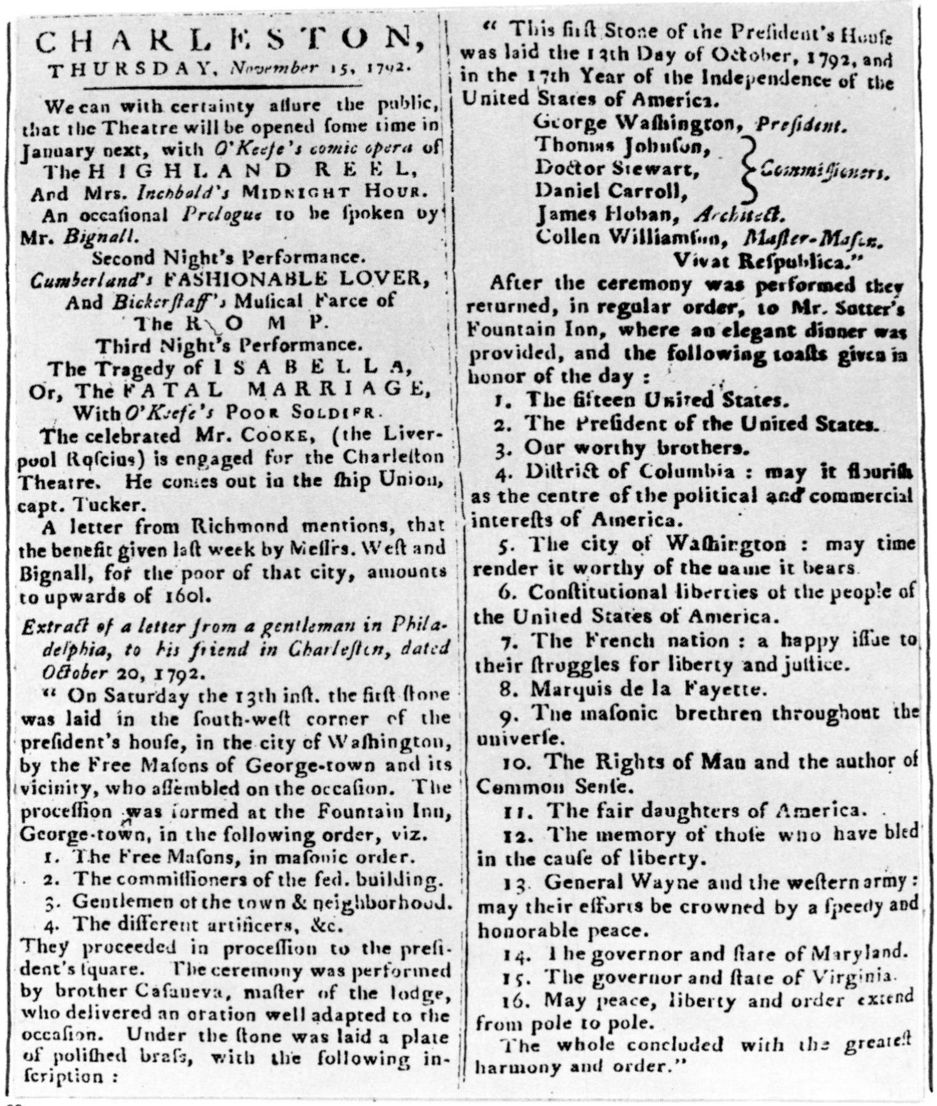

CHARLESTON,
THURSDAY, *November* 15, 1792.

We can with certainty affure the public, that the Theatre will be opened fome time in January next, with *O'Keefe's comic opera* of The HIGHLAND REEL, And Mrs. *Inchbald's* MIDNIGHT HOUR. An occafional *Prologue* to be fpoken by Mr. *Bignall.*
　　　Second Night's Performance.
Cumberland's FASHIONABLE LOVER, And *Bickerftaff's* Mufical Farce of The ROMP.
　　　Third Night's Performance.
The Tragedy of ISABELLA, Or, The FATAL MARRIAGE, With *O'Keefe's* POOR SOLDIER.
The celebrated Mr. COOKE, (the Liverpool Rofcius) is engaged for the Charlefton Theatre. He comes out in the fhip Union, capt. Tucker.

A letter from Richmond mentions, that the benefit given laft week by Meffrs. Weft and Bignall, for the poor of that city, amounts to upwards of 160l.

Extract of a letter from a gentleman in Philadelphia, to his friend in Charlefton, dated October 20, 1792.

" On Saturday the 13th inft. the firft ftone was laid in the fouth-weft corner of the prefident's houfe, in the city of Wafhington, by the Free Mafons of George-town and its vicinity, who affembled on the occafion. The proceffion was formed at the Fountain Inn, George-town, in the following order, viz.
　1. The Free Mafons, in mafonic order.
　2. The commiffioners of the fed. building.
　3. Gentlemen of the town & neighborhood.
　4. The different artificers, &c.
They proceeded in proceffion to the prefident's fquare. The ceremony was performed by brother Cafaneva, mafter of the lodge, who delivered an oration well adapted to the occafion. Under the ftone was laid a plate of polifhed brafs, with the following infcription :

" This firft Stone of the Prefident's Houfe was laid the 13th Day of October, 1792, and in the 17th Year of the Independence of the United States of America.
　George Wafhington, *Prefident.*
　Thomas Johnfon,　⎫
　Doctor Stewart,　⎬ *Commiffioners.*
　Daniel Carroll,　⎭
　James Hoban, *Architect.*
　Collen Williamfon, *Mafter-Mafon.*
　　　Vivat Refpublica."
After the ceremony was performed they returned, in regular order, to Mr. Sotter's Fountain Inn, where an elegant dinner was provided, and the following toafts given in honor of the day :
　1. The fifteen United States.
　2. The Prefident of the United States.
　3. Our worthy brothers.
　4. Diftrict of Columbia : may it flourifh as the centre of the political and commercial interefts of America.
　5. The city of Wafhington : may time render it worthy of the name it bears.
　6. Conftitutional liberties of the people of the United States of America.
　7. The French nation : a happy iffue to their ftruggles for liberty and juftice.
　8. Marquis de la Fayette.
　9. The mafonic brethren throughout the univerfe.
　10. The Rights of Man and the author of Common Senfe.
　11. The fair daughters of America.
　12. The memory of thofe who have bled in the caufe of liberty.
　13. General Wayne and the weftern army : may their efforts be crowned by a fpeedy and honorable peace.
　14. The governor and ftate of Maryland.
　15. The governor and ftate of Virginia.
　16. May peace, liberty and order extend from pole to pole.
The whole concluded with the greateft harmony and order."

68

Fig. 68　A contemporary account of the laying of the cornerstone of the President's House.

write if it meets the approbation of the Commissioners, to embark for this City, early in the Spring, and hold out such terms to them as the Commissioners may think proper . . .

In January 1793, the Commissioners hired Samuel Blodget, Jr., as their resident representative for one year. In their letter of January 5 to Blodget about his appointment, the Commissioners informed him:

We have taken the Measures most likely as we judge to succeed for the Introduction of foreign Mechanics—the number we have attempted is greater than we want, we shall probably fail of some of them, and if all should come the only possible bad consequence will be distressing our friends in no great degree. Plain Stonecutters we most want and they have been our principal Object, without a good many we shall be at a stand. Wherefore if it should be in your way we wish you to forward an immediate increase. We are strong

69

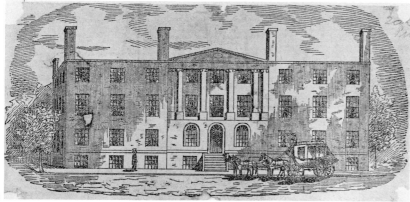

70

enough we are told in Carpenters, Mr. Hoban is to Endeavor to get a good Brick-maker from Philadelphia. We may have a good many Negro Laborours.

Blodget was so deeply involved in lot speculation and his lottery that the appointment did not work out well. It was not renewed in 1794.

Blodget's lottery was ostensibly to raise funds for a national university. The grand prize offered was a hotel costing $50,000, "in a desirable location in the city." The plans of the building were drawn by James Hoban, who appears to have leaned heavily on his original design for the President's House. The hotel was erected on a rise overlooking Pennsylvania Avenue, on the corner of 8th and F Streets where the United States Tariff Commission building, formerly the General Post Office, now stands. The cornerstone was laid on July 4, 1794. A brick structure trimmed with stone, it was the handsomest building in the city with the exception of the President's House and the Capitol. Never opened as a hotel, it stood empty and unfinished for several years; occasionally a theatrical performance or a meeting was held there. First rented and then bought by the government, it was eventually remodeled and became the Patent Office.

Fig. 69 The large building on the right is Blodget's Hotel, designed by James Hoban. In the distance the President's House and the Treasury Building can be seen.

Fig. 70 Blodget's Hotel was later remodeled for the Patent Office and General Post Office.

In February 1793 Jeremiah Kale was hired as foreman of bricklaying at the President's House, indicating that the building had begun to rise above its foundations. Before the end of the year, the basement story was finished to the point where the walls were painted, presumably to guard against damp and mold.

Political developments in Philadelphia were about to slow the construction of the President's House for some time. Jefferson had been uneasy about his position in the Federalist-controlled government from the beginning. He strongly opposed many of Hamilton's fiscal policies, especially the establishment of the United States Bank. Gradually, as their most prestigious spokesman, he became the leader of the Anti-Federalists. Party members were divided along traditional lines. Federalist financiers, traders, and manufacturers were centered in the cities of the North. Anti-Federalist farmers and planters ranged from the old South to rural Pennsylvania and New York and new agricultural areas developing to the west. Recognizing that Washington shared and supported Hamilton's views, Jefferson resigned from the Cabinet on December 31, 1793, and returned to Monticello. During the next three years as a private citizen, he continued to organize and foster an Anti-Federalist movement, which became known as the Republican Party upon Washington's retirement.

Edmund Randolph replaced Jefferson as Secretary of State, but resigned in August 1795 upon publication of a totally false charge of attempted bribery of the French minister. He was in turn replaced by Timothy Pickering, who completed the second term of Washington's administration.

While the government was preoccupied with these and other problems—the Whiskey Rebellion, the Jay Treaty, and "Citizen" Genet—activity had slackened in the capital city. Funds were scarce, lot sales desultory. The loans from Maryland and Virginia were nearly gone, and no organized lot auctions took place between September 13, 1793, and October 18, 1797, although private sales were made in the interim. The Commissioners, being without a local agent in 1794, had resumed direct responsibility for the work. Tiring of such unpaid, thankless duties, Stuart and Johnson wanted to resign. Washington persuaded them to stay a while longer, but finally replaced them with Gustavus Scott and William Thornton.

In a memorandum entitled "Expenses on the President's House to 1st January 1795—Remarks" the unknown writer (probably Thomas Munroe) stated in part:

> The first or principal story of this building is not finished—according to Mr. Hoban's information, it will take two of the Spring months to put it into a State to receive the Joice—All the Ashler Stone to carry it so far is prepared & particular ps. under the workmens hands in the Stone Carvers Shop—there are 20 Stone Cutters at work Besides Edwards & Blagden the principal men in the carver shop—We do not conceive it to be your intention that this building should remain in its present state, nor that no progress should be made in the next story during the present year—but that much the greater part of our funds should be appropriated towards procuring materials and carrying on the Capitol.

With the President's House in the doldrums, Hoban was soon diverted by his involvement with Blodget's Hotel (also known as the Great Hotel) and some private projects with his partner, Pierce Purcell. Together they had acquired six lots in 1792 and two more in 1793. While Hoban was busy at the President's House, Purcell erected buildings. In 1794 they built the Little Hotel, so-called, no doubt, because of the Great Hotel not far away. The Little Hotel was on Lot 5, F Street, just one lot from 15th Street. It opened in 1795 and closed in the fall of 1797. In 1799 William Rhodes rented and reopened it, only to move to the corner building in 1801, when the name was changed to Rhodes' Hotel. The Little Hotel building was sold in 1804 to Francis Clarke, a merchant, who converted it to a private dwelling.

There is no indication that Hoban neglected his duties as architect of the President's House, but when the work was slack, he occupied himself with other matters in addition to speculative construction. He founded the first Masonic Lodge in Washington on September 6, 1793, and was its first master; he became Captain of the Washington Artillery; and when Washington became a city, he was elected a councilman and remained one the rest of his life.

Hoban, with two associates, took the first census of the city of Washington. Their statement reads:

> By a census of the inhabitants of the City of Washington taken August 12, 1793, it appears that the number exceeds 820 and that for the last six months there has been no death of either man or woman taken place in the City. It is to be observed that of the above number a great proportion are artists in the different branches of building and from different parts of America and Europe. The climate agrees with their constitutions and they enjoy in this city equal, if not superior, health to what they have experienced in any part of the continent.
>
> Signed in behalf of the inhabitants of the City of Washington and at their request, August 12, 1793.
>
> JAMES HOBAN,
COLLEN WILLIAMSON,
ELISHA O. WILLIAMS

In December 1793, Hoban was requested by the Commissioners to build a house to be used as a temporary hospital, on part of some public grounds convenient to a good spring.

In 1796 Congress passed a loan guarantee law, requiring semiannual reports from the Commissioners on the progress of the work and expenditures therefor. Hoban's original reports for May and December of 1796 and 1797 have been located in the National Archives. The official reports from the Secretary of the Treasury begin May 18, 1796, and continue to November 18, 1801.

Before the first report of May 18, 1796, the masonry walls and partitions for the basement and first story were essentially complete, and the second story was about 4 feet high; windows, doors, and trim were made and waiting to be installed. The roof was about half finished; most of the timbers were prepared and ready to be set. Window architraves and sills and the entablature were cut, and three of the engaged columns and sixteen pilaster capitals were carved.

By November 1796 the exterior walls of the second story were 14 feet high and the interior walls 16 feet, the full height. All the engaged columns had been raised and awaited capitals. Twenty-six pilasters were set, six with capitals. The joiners' work for the basement was finished (doors, windows, and trim) and was seasoning. Window frames and sash for the first and second stories were complete and shutters were being made. The roof had not advanced significantly since the previous report.

The following spring the west side of the building was up to the roof line, and the

whole was to be raised to that level in one month. Hoban intended to install the roof during the summer. The chimneys were above the roof line, and all brickwork would be complete in the coming season. The ornamental stone, "except some that cannot be got at until the scaffolds are struck," was done. The architrave and frieze extended halfway around the building, and would be finished in one month. The cornice was "three-fourths finished," and the balustrade begun. Plumbers were to begin casting the gutters within a week of May 25.

In the final report for 1797, Hoban reported all stonework complete including the entablature, and the stonecutters were then employed on the balustrade which would finish the building. The roof had been raised and boarded, ready to receive the slate, and covered with a coat of composition to protect the inside from the weather. Lead gutters and drains, weighing about 33,000 pounds, were installed, with about 5,000 pounds more to complete the system. Doors for the two principal stories were framed and some paneled. The inside trim was progressing rapidly.

At the same time, Hoban prepared an estimate for completing the building.

> Basement Story: Tiling the floor and plastering walls and ceiling, glazing the windows
> First and Second Stories: Flooring, 23 doors and 34 windows each, plastering, ornamental trim, glazing the windows, installing chimney-pieces, 3 staircases, and "frontispieces to doors and entrance to Staircase," painting and hardware.

In the fall of 1798, Hoban reported that the exterior was completed and workmen were "cleaning down and painting the wall of the building and striking the scaffolds." This seems to have been about all that was accomplished during the year, as an estimate of the remaining work, dated September 10, 1799, lists other parts of the building essentially as they were in November 1797. The 1798 report does show that the walls were painted white at the outset, long before the stains of the fire of 1814.

The practice of painting Virginia sandstone was probably owing to technical rather than aesthetic reasons. Sealing the porous rock prevented disintegration caused by rains and frost. Mills's Treasury Building, built in the 1830s, was faced

Fig. 71 Basement window, the White House.
Fig. 72 Hoban excelled in graceful detail, as these window brackets show.

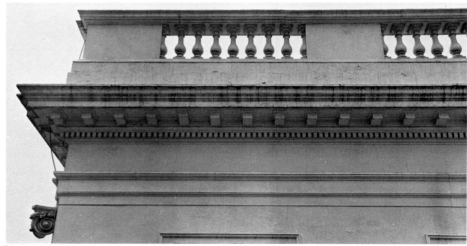

74

with the same stone, and was immediately treated upon completion with a mixture of linseed oil and whiting.

Maryland had made another loan of $100,000 in December 1797 to finish the public buildings, and the greater effort was now concentrated on the Capitol. It became quickly apparent that Maryland's loan would not be adequate for all the remaining work, and a $100,000 loan from the federal government was approved by Congress, thus reaching the ceiling the Commissioners were allowed to borrow.

As his second term ended it no doubt gratified the President to find that opposition to the new capital had now practically disappeared. The federal loan passed by an overwhelming margin. However, this money was intended to cover the cost of two new administrative buildings located "like wings" at either side of the President's House, and frugality at the President's House was still necessary.

Hoban's estimate of September 10, 1799, for finishing the President's House showed that none of the rooms had yet been plastered, windows were still without glass, no staircases existed, and the flooring was not laid. A thousand details remained to be completed. The newly elected president, John Adams, intended to occupy the house in the fall of 1800, but lack of money frustrated attempts to finish the building on time. When the President arrived on November 1, only six rooms were reasonably habitable. There was a flurry of activity to provide basic comforts, such as the "necessary" (10 feet by 4 feet—a three-holer) in the back yard, and the service bells. President and Mrs. Adams brought the old furniture bought by Washington for his rented house in Philadelphia, augmented by some of their own belongings from Bush Hill, a residence just outside Philadelphia rented by the Vice President. Since they were destined to be in the Federal City only a few months, practically no new furnishings were acquired by the Adamses for the President's House.

Because of divisions in the Federalist party and the momentum of the populist Republican movement, Adams was defeated in the election of 1800; Jefferson became President, and Aaron Burr, Vice President. Adams left the President's House early in the morning of March 4, 1801. Jefferson, later that day, was sworn in as

Fig. 73 The original entablature of the President's House. This northeast corner remained standing after the fire of 1814.

Fig. 74 George Hadfield's design for the Treasury Building, erected in 1797 east of the President's House. It was duplicated on the west for the War and State Departments.

President in the south chamber of the new Capitol, and then returned to his boarding house. He did not move to the President's House until March 19.

In the interval worn-out furniture from Philadelphia was replaced and Hoban attempted to complete more of the interior. Still, the main staircase was not built, and the East Room and some of the rooms on the second floor were not plastered.

In the summer of 1800 a stable for the President's use was built at 14th and G Streets over the protests of the neighborhood. Some stables were added in 1806 to the President's House by Jefferson.

On March 13, 1801, the Commissioners, coming near the end of their responsibilities, wrote Hoban that he was desired to execute the work to the directions given by the President of the United States.

In May, the Commissioners asked for and got Jefferson's permission to establish a market between 7th and 9th Streets on Pennsylvania Avenue. The old market was in sheds located in the President's Square, and the President was probably relieved to see it go; he asked for graveling of the square the following summer. Hoban was requested to remove the old buildings and reerect them at the new site, giving rise to the tradition that he "designed" a building for the public market. No doubt he did, but it was of the simplest kind.

Jefferson seemed satisfied for the moment with the accommodations at the President's House. Either he was biding his time, awaiting an opportunity to reexamine the building himself, or he may not have enjoyed working with the man who surpassed him in the competition for the President's House. No correspondence whatever from Jefferson to Hoban has been found, although there is evidence that they conferred.

On June 1, Hoban's principal work was transferred by the Commissioners to the still unfinished Capitol. He was asked to prepare plans and estimates for the House of Representatives, who were overcrowded in their temporary quarters. Hoban prepared three different plans, one of which Jefferson modified and adopted, calling for an elliptical chamber one story high, later known as "the Oven." It was built by Hoban in a few months, and used until replaced by a more suitable room by Latrobe.

A year later the Commissioners formally turned over their records to the custody of Thomas Munroe, and their supervision of the city ceased. Jefferson appointed Robert Brent as mayor to replace them in the civil aspects of their administration.

On June 23, 1801, Hoban wrote to the Commissioners requesting his usual salary, and enclosed a rather lengthy memorandum of work done by him since the previous October 24. In a letter of June 26, Thomas Munroe, acting for the Commissioners, notified Hoban that "his services as Superintendent was abolished on the first day of the present month," when the Board of Commissioners was abolished.

Still later, on July 13, 1802, Alexander White, one of the former Commissioners, wrote a curious letter to Jefferson:

> I am much surprised at Hobans conduct—; his agreement with the late Commissioners, as entered in their Journal, ought perhaps to have been more explicit—but I believe it does not express that he should continue in pay till the buildings should be finished. A stipulation which I should have considered so improper, would hardly have escaped my recollection, but we need not depend on memory, the writing will speak for itself. Some years ago

both my Colleagues were desirous of getting Hoban out of the way; and amazing exertions were made to find something in his conduct which would justify them in dismissing him. I believe he would then have disputed their right, but I did not understand, either on that occasion, or on a subsequent one, which I am about to mention that he expected to receive his salary after the works should cease. Towards the close of the year 1800 it was proposed to notify him that his services would not be required after a certain day, upon a supposition that there would be nothing further done towards carrying on the building till Congress should take order therein. He made no objection to this in conversation with me but the shortness of the notice—the time was then prolonged; and a letter written to him amounting to a discontinuance, and there the matter rested till after you came into office, and ordered the works to be proceeded on. After which we continued his salary by an order, implying according to my remembrance, that it had been discontinued, but the minutes will show how far I am accurate. I made no note of this transaction.

Jefferson took the position that the office Hoban held expired with the terms of the Commissioners; but he himself had, as White pointed out, asked Hoban to work on the Capitol. The Oven was finished in November 1801; it is likely that Hoban was at liberty shortly thereafter. He had worked nine years on the President's House, four years at the Capitol, supervised the building of the Treasury and War Department Buildings, built two hotels, the public market, and some private dwellings, with a minimum of wrangling, at least in public; and his public service was only at the halfway mark. His record was not to be equaled, in quantity, for a generation. It was never approached in historic importance by any other single architect in the development of the city.

From 1802 until 1814, Hoban was not involved with the federal buildings. There is slim evidence that he may have returned briefly to Charleston during this period. A small wax portrait, now hanging in the library of the White House, is believed to be by John Christian Rauschner, who advertised in the Charleston newspapers in 1810. (See Plate 11.) The William Seabrook house built at this time on Edisto Island, southwest of Charleston, has been attributed to Hoban.

Fig. 75 Entrance hall of the William Seabrook house, Edisto Island, South Carolina. Tradition ascribes this 1810 design to James Hoban.

Nine

Jefferson to Jackson: 1803–1832

Benjamin Henry Latrobe, born 1764 in Leeds, England, of an Irish father and an American mother, came to America 30 years later. He established himself in Philadelphia after a desultory career in Virginia. By 1800 he had built the city's waterworks and a building for the Bank of Pennsylvania in the Greek Revival style.

Jefferson shared Latrobe's admiration for the "models of antiquity which have had the approbation of thousands of years," and respected his ability as an engineer. In 1802 the President invited Latrobe to Washington to design a dry dock, with a roof built according to the system of laminated braced ribs invented by Philbert de l'Orme, "like that of the Halle au Blé in Paris." Latrobe produced an excellent scheme for a building 165 feet wide and 800 feet long, but Congress failed to appropriate funds.

However, Jefferson did obtain $50,000 toward the completion of the Capitol and President's House, and for improving the avenue connecting the two buildings. Latrobe was offered the job of Superintendent of Public Buildings on March 3, 1803.

The Commissioners had already cleared the carriage road and footpaths on Pennsylvania Avenue, and planted a row of fast-growing Lombardy poplars bordering the walks. Jefferson added another row along the edge of the roadway. Willow oaks and elms were intended as permanent planting in-between, but the money never became available during Jefferson's term, and the poplars were cut down when the avenue was later widened and paved.

Jefferson determined that the Capitol was to have the higher priority. For the next few years, only necessary repairs and minor improvements were made at the President's House. The great weight of Hoban's slate roof and lead gutters had caused the upper portions of the front and rear walls to spread, weakened as they were by a decision of the Commissioners to build the second story of brick faced with stone. Latrobe pulled them back in place with iron tie-rods, and lightened the load 82 tons by replacing the slate and lead with painted sheet iron. A bedroom was finished, a well was dug to replace the now contaminated water supply from a nearby brook, and a ground drain to carry rainwater away from the house to the Tiber was enlarged.

At the beginning of his second term, Jefferson initiated a more extensive building program. He never lived in a house without altering it, and the President's House was no exception.

In April 1805 Jefferson asked Latrobe to return the "only sketches I had" of the designs for a low range of household offices extending from the sides of the building, so that he could "recollect his views. . . ." On May 3 Latrobe sent him carefully made copies, as, he said, the originals were badly smudged.

At the same time Latrobe prepared drawings of the fireproof vault for the Treasury, to be located near the terminus of the eastern wing. See Plate 8. To embellish the long straight line of the wings, central pavilions were planned by Jefferson and Latrobe, but these were never constructed. A colonnade along the south front masked the utilitarian structures and provided loggias leading to the Executive office buildings.

Latrobe never liked the wings that Jefferson planned. In a letter to John Lenthall, May 3, 1805, he said,

> I am sorry I am cramped in this design by his prejudices in favor of the old French books, out of which he fishes everything—but it is a small sacrifice to my personal attachment to him to humour him, and the less so, because the style of the colonnade he proposes is exactly consistent with Hoban's pile—a litter of pigs worthy of the great sow it surrounds, & of the wild Irish boar, the father of her . . .

One can imagine Lenthall's feelings when this sarcastic letter arrived, from the President himself, with the following note:

> Th Jefferson presents his compliments to Mr. Lenthall and sends him a letter this moment received inclosed from Mr. Latrobe—being handed him among his own he broke it open without looking at the superscription; but seeing Mr. Lenthall's name at the head he closed it instantly and assures him on his honor he did not read one other word in it.

The President seems to be protesting a little too much, but the gesture was gallant.

The Treasury and War offices were not at the same grade level as the President's House, and the connections presented problems. Jefferson specified that the terrace roof meet the first floor exactly. Latrobe, in a freehand sketch dated May 5, 1805, proposed to adjust the roof in steps, and screen the complicated construction with a "blocking course" meeting the windowsills. This solution resolved all difficulties. Short lengths of the wings were built in 1805, containing the "meathouse, cellars for liquors, coal and wood, and privies." In 1806 the household offices were completed, including a stable, yet still without the colonnades, as funds were again exhausted. But within a year the "covered ways" were built. The grounds around the President's House were leveled to provide a better view of the Potomac, and the excess earth was heaped in two ornamental mounds which still exist. Jefferson proposed the location and configuration of a wall enclosing the grounds in a letter to Latrobe on May 27, 1807; about half the wall was put up that year.

The President then turned his attention to the appearance of the house itself.

Hoban had planned a verandah across the entire south front on his original competition drawing. The competition program called for elevations of both fronts, so Jefferson would have seen a view of Hoban's proposal in 1792. This portico was considerably wider than the version eventually erected. On the Hoban plan, now at the Massachusetts Historical Society, a very light semicircle is sketched in pencil, about the scale of the present South Portico, with circles indicating columns at the precise locations where they are now built. Kimball attributed this pencil addition to Jefferson. A comparison of pencil sketches for columns on his own first plan for the President's House does show a similar touch and style.

In 1807 Latrobe prepared a side view of the President's House, showing the attachment of the new east wing in section, a curved south portico following the pencil modification of Hoban's plan, and a new north portico. See Plate 9.

In letters to the President, Latrobe often said he was proud to be the instrument for decorating the capital to President Jefferson's wishes, and to have executed designs under his orders. This is certainly true of the terrace buildings and the South Portico of the President's House, as shown by other documents. If Latrobe's sweeping attribution is accepted at face value, Jefferson suggested the design of the North Portico as well. It is a logical conclusion, considering his passion for porticos, and his intense admiration for the Maison Carrée, the Pantheon, and La Rotonda. It is also consistent with his schemes for Monticello and the "AZ" design, where a plain rectangle is made more interesting by cruciform extensions.

In one of his preliminary drawings for the capitol at Richmond, Jefferson proposed a portico with two columns between the building and the front row under the pediment, modeled after his favorite temple, the Maison Carrée at Nîmes. At the President's House, the extra depth of such a portico would conveniently span the air well servicing the basement windows and provide the comfort of a porte-cochère in Washington's rainy weather.

This porte-cochère is unique, both in size and in the spacing of the side columns. The scale was determined by the original engaged columns and pediment designed by Hoban. The spacing and indeed the structural need for two side columns was determined by its three functional divisions: the platform in front of the entrance, crossing the light well; a short flight of steps to ground level; and the carriageway. In Latrobe's design, the carriageway rises to the platform level; a short flight of steps then descends to the ground. In this scheme, the side columns are necessarily widely separated in the center, to accommodate the carriageway. In Hoban's later, more practical design, the platform bridges the air well, descends a short flight of steps, and then widens to provide for the carriageway. This eliminated the necessity for extra supports for the first set of columns in the air well and simplified the whole structure. Since the porch extends 40 feet from the building it is aesthetically necessary to have two columns on the side to maintain the rhythm of the existing engaged columns on the wall and the new set of four at the front.

In 1793 Jefferson had described the classical principles which govern the spacing and number of such columns. Madison had written in May to ask if there were any "fixt rule" for the interval between the columns and the side of the house, or the distance which the pediment ought to project. Jefferson replied on June 29:

> A Portico may be from five to ten diameters of the column deep, or projected from the building. If of more than five diameters there must be a column in

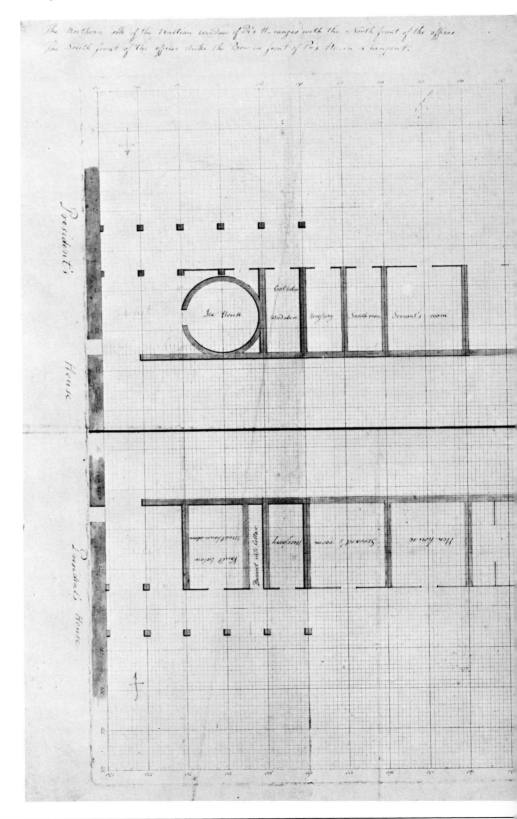

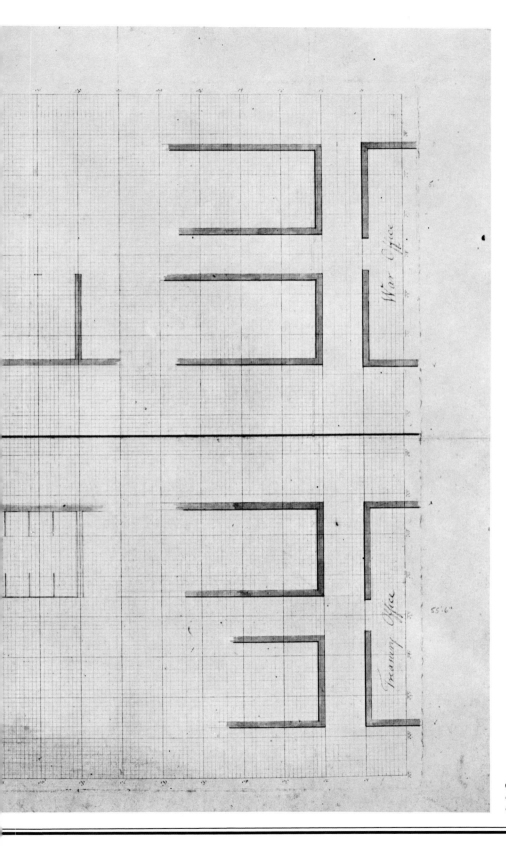

Fig. 76 Jefferson's design for household offices for the President's House. This drawing is a copy by B. H. Latrobe.

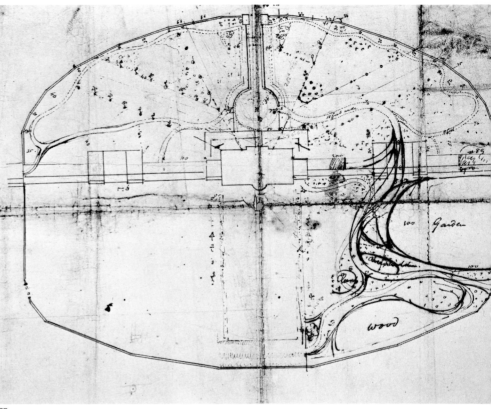

77

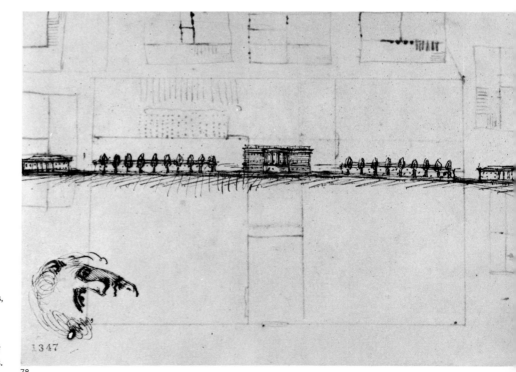

Fig. 77 Plan of the grounds and wall around the President's House in 1807.

Fig. 78 In this sketch of unknown date, trees hide two low buildings, similar to Jefferson's wings, between the President's House and the Treasury and War Department. The drawing is among the papers of William Thornton.

Fig. 79 "Cross" and "Lengthwise" sections of Jefferson's terrace buildings for household offices.

1347

78

the floor of the house is on a level with the enriched band.

enriched band	9
Story	11 - 5.5
Plinth	8.
	12 - 10.5

Terras floor		1.5		
sheet iron & sheeting		1.		
ridge joist in the middle		1 - 0.		+ 9
		1 - 2.5		1 - 2.5
Cornice 43½ =(say) 11				
Frize 26½ (say) 6.6				
Architrave 35	8.8		2 - 2.4	
1 - 45				
column 7. diam. &		8 - 9.6	11 - 0	÷7 = 15.0057
subplinth = plinth of house		8		
		12 - 10.5		

intercolonnation. 6. diam. =	7 - 6.3	
1. diam.	1 - 3.1	
cent. to cent. of column 7. diam.	8 - 9.6	

A section across the Western offices.

level of the floor of President's house

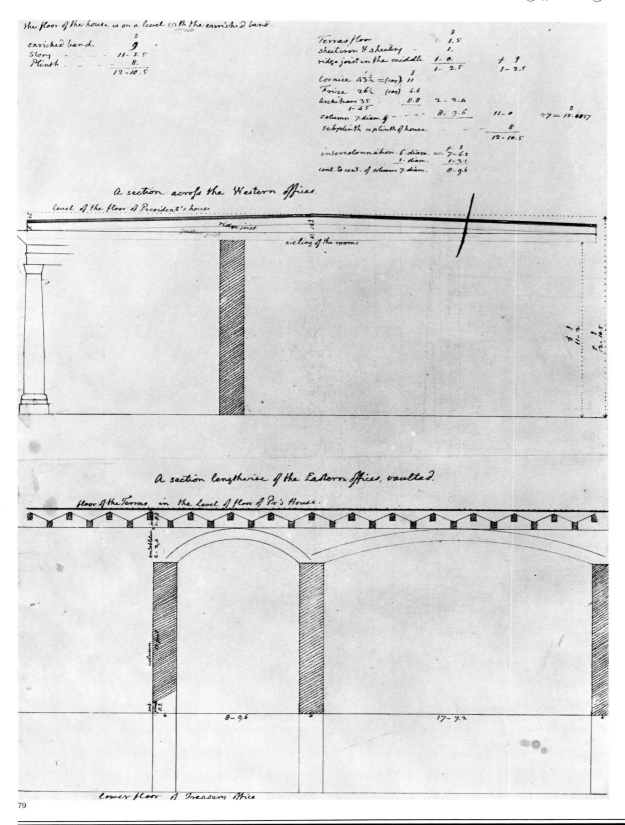

ridge joist

cieling of the rooms

A section lengthwise of the Eastern offices, vaulted.

floor of the Terras, in the level of floor of Pr's House.

8 - 9.6   17 - 7.2

lower floor of Treasury office

79

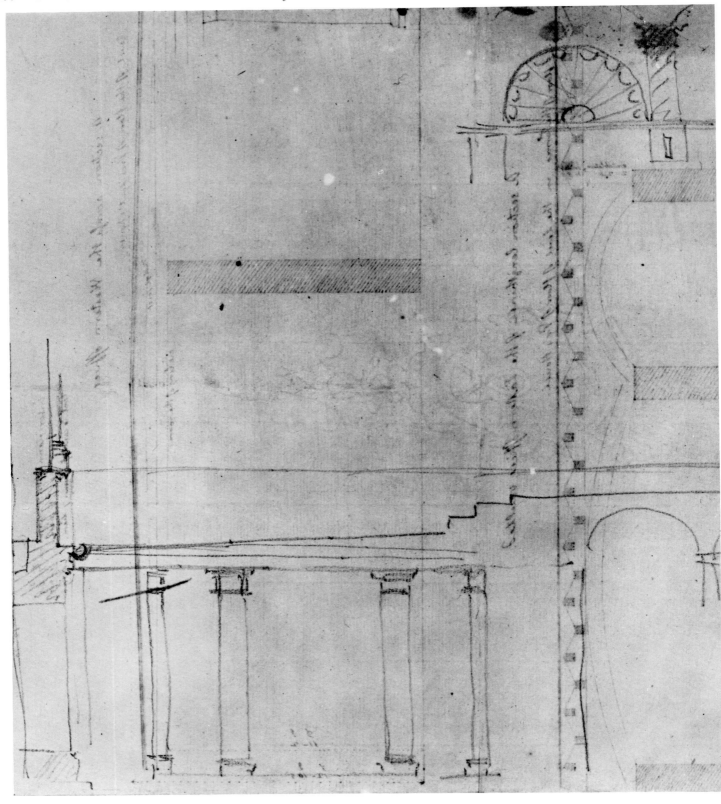

Fig. 80 Connecting the terrace to the President's House. Sketch by B. H. Latrobe.

Fig. 81 West front of the White House. The wings were constructed as Latrobe suggested.

82

the middle of each flank, since it must never be more than five diameters from centre to centre of column. The Portico of the maison quarée is three intercolonnations deep. I never saw as much to a private house.

In 1807 Latrobe prescribed a new plan for the interior. He disliked Hoban's design, considering it "a Polypus—all mouth." In the revision, the large entrance hall and transverse corridor are cut into numerous passages.

The gaping mouth is reduced in size by a new set of teeth in the form of two rows of columns. All this may have moderated the gusts of cold air that plagued the entrance hall in winter, but it did not improve the circulation very much. The plan was attached to a December 21, 1808, report of the committee appointed to ascertain the expenditures and probable estimates in relation to the public buildings. Nothing else has been found referring to it. Its low-key introduction was linked to the uproar in Congress over the cost of work on the public buildings in 1807, which exceeded the previous appropriation by over $50,000. Latrobe tried to explain this as having been caused by necessary emergency work, direct orders from the President, old bills carried over—everything but bad management on his part. Jefferson acknowledged that he urged Latrobe to employ a greater number of workmen, but did it on the ground that "it would cost no more to employ 100 hands 50 days than 50 hands 100 days."

In another letter, Jefferson gave Latrobe very specific instructions for the work to be done in 1808:

President's House. Let the other half of the wall be immediately begun, & be raised one foot higher than what is already done, & that which is already done be raised one foot higher, & the capping then to be put on as far as it is already prepared. no Gate or lodge to be attempted till we see the state of our funds at the finishing of the wall so far. when this is done so far, let us begin the stone steps, & when they are finished, and money enough put by for planting the grounds we will consider how best to employ what may remain on capping & Gates. so that the order of this part of the work is to be 1st the wall completed and raised—2. the steps—3. planting—4. capping,

Fig. 82 Jefferson's mounds, on the south side of the White House, in 1976.

Fig. 83 A proposal to revise the first floor of the President's House, B. Henry Latrobe, 1807.

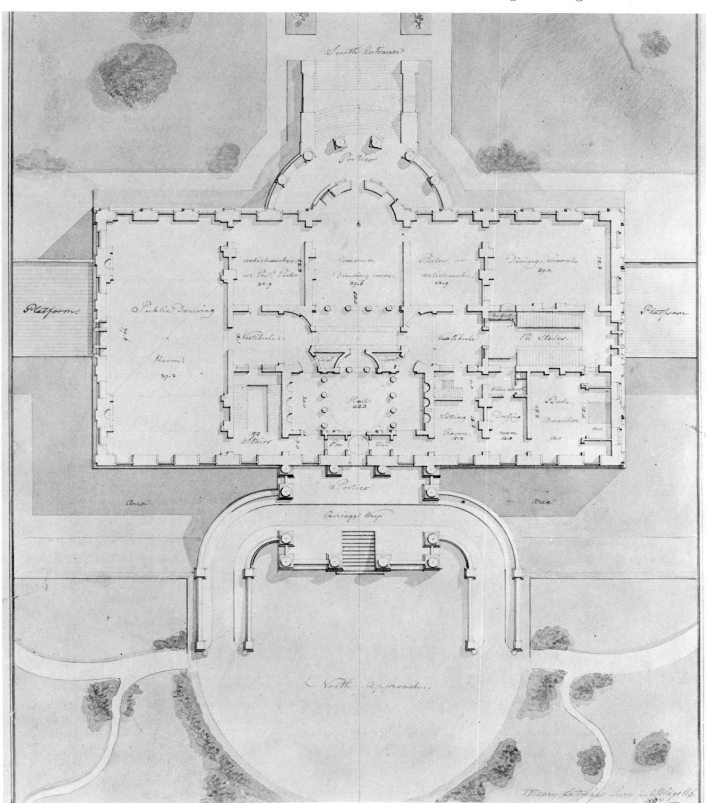

Gates, Porter's lodge, doing one thing at a time, finishing, settling & paying off one article before we begin another.

He ended with a friendly warning:

You see, my Dear Sir, that the object of this cautious proceeding is to prevent the possibility of a deficit of a single Dollar this year. The lesson of the last year has been a serious one, it has done you great injury, & has been much felt by myself. it was so contrary to the principles of our Government, which make the representatives of the people the sole arbitors of the public expense, and do not permit any work to be forced on them on a larger scale than their judgment deems adapted to the circumstances of the Nation.

By the spring of 1808, any large program for redesigning the President's House seems to have been shelved. Latrobe planned a stone flight of stairs to replace the wooden ones at the entrance to the President's House. On May 23, 1808, he reported to Jefferson:

I have made all the drawings necessary for the North steps of the house. The scheme of a Quadrant Arch I have necessarily abandoned. From the bottom of the Area to the level of the Ground floor is only 13 feet, while the area is more than 20 feet wide at the bottom and 30 feet at the top. Therefore, if a Quadrant Arch . . . were employ[ed], half the area . . . would be filled up with useless work & materials, & render much light lost to the kitchen. I have therefore thrown a flat segment arch across the Area of 20 feet span, & thus saved all the unnecessary materials, making the whole work as little expensive & light in appearance as possible.

A small cellar serving the kitchen was concealed under the stairs. The structure is dimensioned so that it could in the future serve as the center section of Latrobe's intended porte-cochère.

At the same time, Latrobe proposed to complete the stone wall, 6½ feet high and nearly 3,500 feet long, to enclose the house and grounds, at a cost of about $11,000. As part of this enclosure of the grounds at the President's House, Latrobe built an entrance gateway, at the end of Pennsylvania Avenue, in the form of a small triumphal arch. Two pencil sketches of this entrance were drawn by the Baroness Hyde de Neuville in 1818 and 1821. It also appears in the bottom center of an 1839 engraving of a view from the roof of the South Portico.

Dr. William Thornton, architect of the Capitol and the target of sarcastic criticism by Latrobe, savagely attacked this gateway and its designer in a public letter to the editor of the *Washington Federalist,* April 26, 1808. The letter complains:

The next object of taste is the wall around the president's square!—Every ten steps we are reminded of point-no-point! To emphasize the whole he has put up a Gateway, that instead of being adapted to the termination of a grand Avenue, and leading to the Gardens of a palace, is scarcely fit for the entrance of a Stable Yard. Though in humble imitation of a triumphal Arch, it looks so naked, and disproportioned, that it is more like a monument than a Gateway: but no man now or hereafter will ever mistake it for a monument of taste.

Latrobe sued Thornton for libel for this and other scathing remarks, and after five years in court was awarded one cent in damages and costs.

Fig. 84 Section of the stone stairs erected at the north entrance.

Fig. 85 Flank of the stone stairs at the north entrance.

Section looking West

84

85

86a

86b

87

By 1809, the enclosure and the stone entrance were complete. Latrobe planned a new gate in the wall opposite the President's square, and a carriage house, the old stable on F Street being inconveniently distant. A winding drive led from the gateway to the north entrance. The finished gate surmounted by eagles can be seen in a drawing of 1811.

Jefferson's second term ended March 4, 1809. Latrobe's last official act was the presentation of an inventory of the government property in the President's House, which seems to have been compiled by Jefferson himself, due to some internecine political maneuvering by his staff.

While the major beautification projects of 1807 were not attempted in Jefferson's administration, the President's House was now structurally complete and reasonably well furnished.

Latrobe had no difficulty retaining his post in the new administration, as Mrs. Latrobe was an intimate friend of the President's wife, and the Madisons and the Latrobes had belonged to the same social circle in Philadelphia. During the remaining three years of his tenure, Latrobe acted primarily as an interior decorator to the President and Mrs. Madison, who planned to refurbish the building in a manner befitting the residence of the Chief Executive.

Fig. 86a 1818 pencil sketch of Latrobe's entrance to the grounds from Pennsylvania Avenue by the Baroness Hyde de Neuville.

Fig. 86b A view through the gateway toward Pennsylvania Avenue. The previous sketch is on a more realistic scale than the huge structure in this 1821 drawing by the Baroness Hyde de Neuville.

Fig. 87 The Capitol, from the roof of the South Portico of the President's House in 1839. Latrobe's gateway stands in the shady foreground.

Fig. 88 North front of the President's House in 1811, after completion of the wall, stairs, and entrance piers as planned by Jefferson and Latrobe.

The Capitol was functionally complete in 1811, and Congress refused to appropriate funds for any further decoration or rebuilding of temporary work. Latrobe was shocked to find himself discharged as Surveyor of Public Buildings by means of a few words in an appropriation bill. Congress seems never to have liked or appreciated Latrobe as an individual or as an architect, and no thanks were extended to him for his decade of service.

The actions of Congress were wiser than it knew. Angered by interference with American shipping by Great Britain in her colossal conflict with Napoleon, the United States declared war in 1812. Jefferson had almost dismantled the Navy, and so the initial American strategy was to prevent Canada from support of harassing Indian raids on settlers in the Northwest Territory. The first expedition was disastrous, but in the second campaign military stores and government buildings at York (now Toronto), the capital of Lower Canada, were burned or blown up. Partly in retaliation for this, and partly to divert American attention from Canada, the British sent Admiral Cockburn and Major General Ross on an expedition to Chesapeake Bay. In August 1814 an operation was proposed, the first object being to neutralize the small fleet of Commodore Barney, holed up in the Patuxent River, and then to proceed to Washington.

Barney realized the futility of an engagement, and so he removed his cannon and men and blew up his ships as the British advanced. At Bladensburg, British troops, though fighting unaccustomed to 100-degree heat, overcame the poorly prepared and poorly organized Americans and marched the remaining five miles to Washington, arriving at sunset. By 10 P.M. August 24, the Capitol was ablaze.

Earlier that day Mrs. Madison had gathered the President's papers and as many cabinet papers as she could pack into her carriage. Velvet curtains from the Oval Saloon, a few books, silver, and some clothing also were taken away. She had succeeded in getting the portrait of George Washington off the wall, but it lay on the floor of the dining room. Two gentlemen from New York, Robert G. L. de Peyster and Jacob Barker, stopped by, and the portrait was entrusted to them. Mrs. Madison asked them to destroy it rather than let it fall into British hands. (See Plate 17.) The massive canvas was taken in a carriage to a farmhouse beyond Georgetown, where it was hidden for several weeks. The portrait is the only surviving object saved by Dolley Madison from the President's House. However, after Mrs. Madison left, a mob which had surrounded the house earlier after hearing reports of the President's removal entered the building and took whatever they could lay their hands on before they were driven away by soldiers. Some of these articles may still survive, unrecognized.

When Cockburn arrived later, he, too, pocketed some mementos, as did the soldiers with him. One "exchanged his dirty underclothes for fresh garments belonging to the President of the United States." (See Plate 19.) Few small items were left in the house; the remaining furniture, curtains, and pictures were piled in the drawing room. The President's wine and food were consumed while Ross sent for glowing coals from a nearby tavern. Between eleven and twelve o'clock the sailors, "artists at their work," applied torches to everything combustible. In a few hours, the result of twenty years of work by Hoban, Latrobe, and countless unsung stone-sawyers, joiners, and laborers, "literally went up in smoke." See Plate 18.

The building still stands today only by the sudden intervention of a "mighty cataract" of rain, accompanied by winds of hurricane intensity. The fires were dampened before the walls could be disintegrated, although the stone of the upper story was badly cracked. The storm continued over two hours; roofs of other buildings were ripped off; two cannon were thrown several yards. The British, already nervous about the possible arrival of Maryland and Virginia troops and terrified by the hurricane, left the city in the dark that night.

The operation, though a tactical success, was a strategic nightmare. The humiliated Americans were aroused as never before. Ross lost nearly a quarter of his men from death on the battlefield, infected wounds, the heat, or desertion. The remainder suffered intensely from dysentery. He had gained for his trouble a good supply of powder, a cannon, and cartridges, and revenge for the insult at York. The English people, on the whole, were more revolted than pleased by the magnitude of the retaliation, although the London *Times* gloated in satisfaction.

The President moved quickly to restore the damaged capital city. Inventories of the public records showed that surprisingly few important papers were lost. A timely warning by James Monroe had allowed most to be taken to safety.

Congress was housed temporarily at Blodget's old hotel, then the Patent Office. Dr. Thornton, Commissioner of Patents, had defended it on August 24 on the ground that models of inventions, its principal contents, were private property, and Cockburn spared the building.

Executive offices were reinstalled in houses throughout the city. The President took temporary living quarters at the Tayloe's Octagon House from October 1814 to August 1815. The Madisons then moved to one of the Seven Buildings on Pennsylvania Avenue at 19th Street, where they remained until the end of the President's second term.

Congress was dilatory in appropriating funds for restoration of the government

89

Fig. 89 The Seven Buildings, Pennsylvania Avenue. The Madisons moved to the corner building in 1815.

Fig. 90 Second-floor framing of 1816, exposed in the demolition of 1949.

Fig. 91 Lath under the plaster applied in 1817.

buildings. There was a real question whether the location of Washington was safe enough from the possibility of future raids. Offers to move elsewhere poured in. Whether to rebuild the damaged buildings or start anew was a second major concern. Finally, mindful of the controversy which accompanied the selection of the national district and the time consumed in determining building designs and locations, the House of Representatives decided to restore the old buildings, authorizing the necessary funds in October 1814. The Senate did not concur until February 3, 1815.

On March 3, 1815, a committee consisting of John P. Van Ness, Tench Ringgold, and Richard B. Lee, who called themselves the "Commissioners for the Public Buildings," was appointed to organize and supervise the reconstruction. James Hoban was engaged to rebuild the President's House and the Executive office buildings. B. Henry Latrobe applied for the job of restoring the Capitol, and was recalled through the good offices of the President.

As usual, costs were grossly underestimated. The total for all the buildings had been set at $550,000 by Thomas Munroe, after consulting several contractors. How Munroe managed this feat of legerdemain is not revealed. An estimate of October 13, 1814, from George Hadfield put a price of $292,000 on the restoration of the President's House alone.

When contracts were let the old complaints of extravagance and inefficiency began all over again. Latrobe bore the brunt of this, partly because of his previous problems and partly because the Capitol was by its nature the most costly project.

By April 15, 1815, the Commissioners had received a first installment of

$100,000 to begin operations. Hoban was requested a week later to make a full report on the repair of the President's House and the fireproof building adjoining the Treasury.

The old freestone quarries had been exhausted, and Hoban and Blagden were sent to look for a new source. Both they and Latrobe were successful in locating adequate quarries, not only of sandstone but of marble, near the mouth of the Seneca.

Priority was given to the Executive Offices, and by early 1816 both the Treasury and the War Office were reoccupied.

During 1815 at the President's House Hoban was primarily concerned with the removal of damaged walls and the preservation of good structure.

Strickland's engraving of the building immediately after the fire (Plate 10) shows the walls still standing to the entablature. In Latrobe's drawing of St. John's Church in 1816 (Plate 13), the President's House in the background has a huge gaping hole on the west where cracked sandstone had been removed.

The damage was worse than the contemporary drawings show. In his report of December 19, 1816, Hoban stated that the walls of the north and south fronts were taken down on the west side to the level of the first floor, and on the east to the second floor. On the east and west fronts the center section containing the Venetian windows had to be removed to the basement floor and rebuilt. Most of the present walls date from 1817, therefore, as only a small part of the shell was worth saving.

While repairing and cutting stone for the exterior, Hoban had a prodigious joinery project underway. All the wood had to be cut and fitted and allowed to season before being installed. Thousands of board feet of mahogany for the interior trim and "best yellow pine" for the structure were ordered.

90

91

Fig. 92 Ionic capitals and entablature of the South Portico.

On May 18, 1816, Hoban prepared an important, probably final, report to the three Commissioners. President Madison had abolished the Committee on May 1, and replaced its members with a single Commissioner of Public Buildings, Colonel Samuel Lane. In the May report Hoban listed the optimum number of workmen at the President's House:

30 stonecutters
40 carpenters
 4 stone setters
 6 bricklayers
50 laborers
 2 stone carriers
 2 pair of sawyers

The report also mentions for the first time the beginning of construction of the South Portico: "Agreeably to an estimate made of the Portico to the South front of the President's House, it will require to complete it, the sum of Twenty one Thousand Dollars." Appended to the report is the estimate, which begins, "Of the South Portico, The foundation is laid and the arcade of the basement is nearly ready to set." This is followed by a list of stone, brick, marble, and "6 columns and capitals—Ionic order."

Foundations and arcades in the condition described would have been constructed in the previous year, as the wet spring season was not a good time for putting down foundations. It has been suggested that the foundations were laid during Jefferson's administration, but the reports during that period by the Surveyor of Public Buildings, then B. Henry Latrobe, do not mention any such project.

The South Portico as built by Hoban is quite different in structure from the design illustrated in drawings of Latrobe in 1807. While the curved colonnade is the same, it would hardly be anything else, since it continues the entablature of the building, and the columns are cylindrical versions of the old pilasters. The substructure is more open and airy. Latrobe blocked off the first two arches on either side and placed a grand staircase in the center, equal in width to the bulge of the oval room. Arches under the staircase provided access to the basement. In Hoban's version, two smaller flying staircases led from the principal floor to the ground level, leaving the center open for a direct entrance to the basement. This entrance now leads to the Diplomatic Reception Room, a possibility not foreseen by either architect, but more dignified in Hoban's version. The only other significant difference was the substitution of a light iron railing for Latrobe's low stone wall around the porch.

Hoban reported later that his version of the portico was built in the "style of the building." Latrobe had tried to impose his own characteristic style. His stairway sacrificed convenience for grandeur.

Since Hoban had the South Portico under construction in late 1815 or early 1816, the decision to build it, and the North Portico as well, must have been made still earlier. Work could not have begun without the approval of President Madison.

In January 1817 a drawing by Latrobe of the south elevation appeared, with the caption "Elevation of the President's House, copied from the design as proposed to be altered in 1807. Jan. 1817 B H Latrobe." The drawing may have been one of those mentioned by Latrobe in a letter to William Lee dated March 22, 1817, but the subject of the letter is the interior arrangement.

Handsome as it is, the elevation served no useful purpose at this date except to bolster Latrobe's ego by showing that he "originated" the design of the South Portico at the suggestion of Jefferson, several years earlier.

Hoban's conception of the South Portico is shown for the first time in the lower left-hand corner of a map of the city published by W. Cooper from a survey by Robert King, Jr., the City Surveyor, in March 1818. The elevation is titled "South Front of The President's House as designed and executed by James Hoban." This drawing may have been made by Peter Bonanni, who was paid $100 on May 13, 1818, for six drawings of the President's House.

Colonel Lane reported to the President on February 10, 1818, that $109,180.78 was spent on the President's House during 1817. The report of James Hoban for completing the building shows that the South Portico has only slightly advanced; the arcade is now nearly "ready to be set." The North Portico also had an official budget, estimated at $26,689.35. In the spring of 1818, the south arcades were in place, but the emphasis in building suddenly shifted.

Additional executive offices were needed, and Hoban was given the responsibility for designing and supervising their construction. Work at the President's House consisted of interior finish and decoration and similar details to make the building comfortable and the grounds attractive. By 1819, the cost of improvements to the residence shrank to $8,000. Attention languished for two more years, as pressure was also exerted to finish the center section of the Capitol. By 1823, the possible disintegration of the unfinished South Portico was noted by Hoban and its comple-

Fig. 93 South elevation showing a proposal for the portico, B. Henry Latrobe, 1817.

94

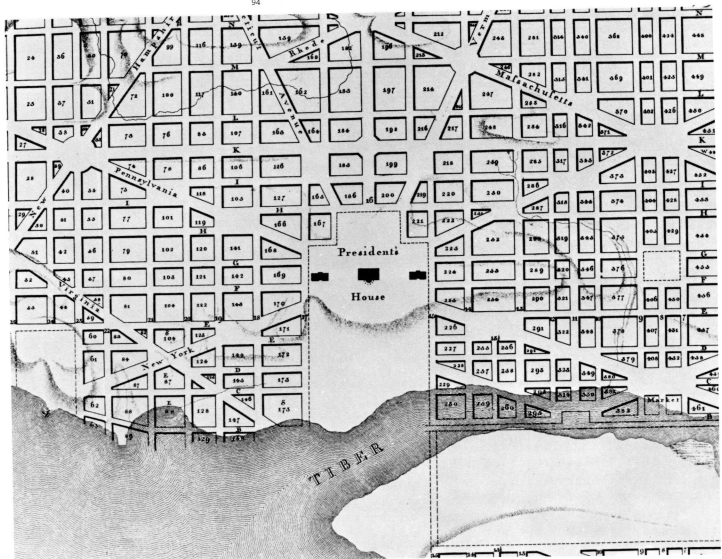

95

96

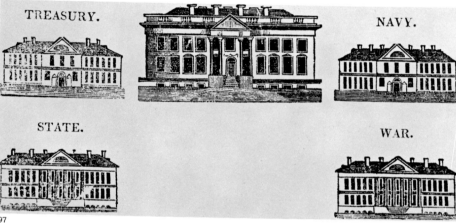

97

98

Fig. 94 James Hoban's design for the South Portico; from the map drawn by Robert King, Jr., published in 1818.

Fig. 95 Location of the President's House and the rebuilt executive office buildings, Robert King map, 1818.

Fig. 96 The Department of State, designed and built by James Hoban in 1818. The War Department was housed in an identical structure.

Fig. 97 The four executive office buildings around the President's House are shown in Peter Force's *National Calendar,* 1820.

Fig. 98 South front of the President's House in 1823. The portico is erected, but the stairs are not yet built.

Fig. 99　The North Portico was completed in 1829. American roses in full bloom decorate the four sides of each Ionic capital, complementing the garland over the entrance.

tion was strongly urged. Funds were appropriated, and the colonnade was finished early in 1824. See Plates 15 and 16.

In 1825 Charles Bulfinch provided a plan for grading, walls, and beautification of the President's Square. The work was done under Hoban's supervision over the next three years. Finally in the second session of the Twentieth Congress funds were made available for the North Portico, which was completed in 1829.

The year 1830 marked a fundamental change in the cultural and political history of the English-speaking world. In Great Britain the Georgian period ended with the death of George IV, and with it the dominance of the Tory party. The roots of a new economic society based on industry had already been planted, and the arts of a mechanical age began to evolve. The effects of this eventually crossed the Atlantic and would be seen and felt in the decoration of the President's House.

In America, nearly all the founders of the nation had passed on. Madison alone was living at the end of 1831. A remarkable era of government by the elite, with the consent of the people, succumbed to pure populism. In the city of Washington, the first wave of building was over. Bulfinch was dismissed in 1829. Latrobe died in 1820, of yellow fever; L'Enfant died in 1825, Hoban in 1831. See Plate 12.

In 1836, Robert Mills, who had been trained by Hoban, Latrobe, and Jefferson, was appointed Architect of the Treasury. The architectural quality of the government buildings was secure in his hands until 1851.

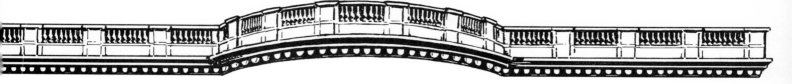

Ten

Early Interior Decoration: 1800–1830

Few of the contents and none of the inside walls of the President's House survived the fire of 1814. No engravings or sketches of the original rooms have been found. There are tantalizing interior details in the drawings of Hoban and Latrobe, but not enough to show the decoration of any complete room. The general style of the interior can only be deduced from requisitions, correspondence, and occasional descriptions by visitors.

Hoban's competition floor plan of 1792 and Latrobe's plan of 1803 differ slightly. The window reveals, originally splayed, in 1803 are shown as rectangular. The proposed grand stairs are reversed end for end. The vestibule is narrower, making the porter's lodge and the service stairway larger. The niches in the wall of the hall in the later drawing are rounded, and the arched entrances to the East Room and the Grand Stair Hall wider. The staircase itself is altered to bring the bearing walls into a continuous line across the building. These changes were not made in 1803, of course, but merely show the subtle refinements Hoban introduced into his working drawings in 1792 and 1793.

All the main rooms had a wood dado, with an applied baseboard and a bold chair rail. The dado can be seen on either side of the fireplace in Latrobe's "looking-glass" drawing for the Oval Room. Cornices in rooms on both the first and second floors extended from 6 inches to 1 foot from the wall at the ceiling. A border of fancy wallpaper from 9 to 11 inches wide, imitating a frieze, was pasted below the cornice. The plaster walls seem to have been painted, in flat pastel colors.

Doors were made of San Domingo mahogany, with matched burl panels and straight-grained rails and stiles, in what is commonly but erroneously known as the "Christian" door pattern. They were set in painted door frames, much the same as they are in the White House today. Hardware in the State Rooms was cast of heavy brass; some of the doorknobs weighed 5 pounds each. Chimneypieces of American marble enriched the principal rooms. In the more utilitarian chambers, mantels of carved local stone were used. All of the windows had inside shutters concealed in the reveals, divided into upper and lower sections to provide either privacy or shade.

The great house became a home on November 16, 1800, when Mrs. Adams arrived from Braintree. Of the six usable but unfinished rooms, two were taken for the President's office and an anteroom for his secretary. Two more on the first floor became a parlor and a levee-room. The second-floor oval room served as a drawing room, and the last of the six must have been the Adams's bedroom. Apparently neither dining room was yet ready for use.

John Briesler, who had served the Adams family for many years in Braintree, was the motive force for dozens of small improvements that made the President's House tolerable for its first occupants. Minor deficiencies were sometimes the most irritating. Water closets had been ordered but none were to be found. The expert bell-hanger in Baltimore hired to install the servants' callbells died unexpectedly. Another was located in Philadelphia four months later, through the efforts of William Blodget, but by that time the former President and Mrs. Adams had returned to Braintree.

Old furniture from the house rented by Washington in Philadelphia was made to do. Mrs. Adams put the best furniture, covered in crimson damask, in the oval room on the second floor. "It is a very handsome room now," she said, "but when completed, it will be beautiful." A substantial part of the appropriation made to Adams for furnishing was never spent, and it provided a tidy nest egg for his successor.

In March 1801 Thomas Jefferson returned to his boarding house after the inauguration, not to move in to the President's House until minimal improvements were made. Just what these were is something of a mystery. One was the water closet, not yet arrived. The contractor hired to do a number of projects thoughtlessly occupied himself with minutiae, and received a sharp note from the Commissioners about the most essential work not "compleated for the President's accomodation. He returned yesterday and is put to the greatest inconvenience not having any necessary."

Jefferson had put Hoban to work on the House of Representatives; no architect attended to the President's House except Jefferson himself until Latrobe was appointed in 1803. Jefferson seemed to be waiting to get the feel of the place, and then, as he did so often, put his imprimatur on the whole design.

Jefferson conducted his social events very informally, which greatly upset the British minister, Mr. Merry, and his wife. Consequently, when Thomas Moore visited Washington in 1803 and was presented to the President by Merry, Jefferson received them in stony silence. Moore, though an outspoken partisan for England in the growing Anglo-French controversies as Jefferson was for France, happened to be the innocent bystander in this local feud. He was sufficiently outraged by Jefferson's conduct to compose a poem, "To Thomas Hume, Esq. M.D. from the City of Washington." "Where nought but woods and J-------n they see/Where streets should run and sages *ought* to be," was one of the milder couplets. In a footnote Moore said,

> The President's house, a very noble structure, is by no means suited to the philosophical humility of its present possessor, who inhabits but a corner of the mansion himself, and abandons the rest to a state of uncleanly desolation, which those who are not philosophers cannot look at without regret. This grand edifice is encircled by a very rude paling, through which a common rustic stile introduces the visiters of the first man in America. With

respect to all that is within the house, I shall imitate the prudent forbearance of Herodotus. . . .

In 1803, Jefferson commissioned Robert Mills, then living at Monticello, to draw a revision of his La Rotonda plan for a house, incorporating a variant of the central theme of the Hotel de Langeac. This design was a much more livable scheme than the more literal Palladianism of the anonymous entry in the President's House competition. Fiske Kimball suggested that it was a study for the rebuilding of Shadwell, then changed his mind. More recently it has been thought that Jefferson may have intended to revive his proposal for a Presidential residence, leaving Hoban's building for offices. Washington was still a city of open fields, and a convenient new site could easily have been found.

Mills made the drawings while living at Monticello as Jefferson's guest. He mentions that he drafted some plans and elevations of the mansion at Monticello, and he also taught Cornelia Jefferson Randolph architectural drawing. Neither Jefferson nor Mills gave any hint that the Rotonda design might have been a new President's House.

Whatever the reason, there was a period of architectural uncertainty during the first three years of Jefferson's administration. The die was finally cast when the President drew plans for the colonnaded service wings in 1804.

Because so few specifics have been found respecting the inside of the house, there is an impression that Jefferson made no changes in the interior. Actually, he made more extensive alterations than any other President in the century. It was pointless, in the beginning of his first term, to improve the interior while the heavy roof and overflowing, leaky drains cracked walls and brought down the ceilings. As these problems were corrected, it became feasible to improve the convenience of the house.

In 1800, the second-floor plan resembled the first floor very closely, with the exception of the east side. There the cross-corridor had been extended to the outside wall, breaking the area over the East Room into two large bedrooms. The ceiling of the East Room was 2 feet higher than the ceilings in other rooms on the first floor; consequently, a flight of three steps connected the east section of the corridor with the central section.

Comparing this layout of the house (confirmed by Latrobe's 1803 plan and Hoban's 1799 tabulation) with the list of rooms on the inventory presented to Latrobe by Jefferson in 1809, it appears that nine additional rooms were created. Jefferson dramatically altered Hoban's huge bedrooms into sets of small bedrooms with adjoining dressing rooms, a direct effect of his delight in the prevailing French style he had enjoyed at the Hotel de Langeac. Marie Kimball has noted the absence of tall pieces—highboys and chests of drawers—among Jefferson's furniture. In the remodeling, closets had replaced most of them, but the locations are not recorded.

Margaret Bayard Smith said that "too often the practical was sacrificed to the fanciful" by the President, but in this case a bedroom consisting of only a single bay was about 12 feet by 28 feet, ample for the accommodation of all but visiting royalty.

On the first floor, the partitioning seems to have remained almost the same. Latrobe's proposed floor plan of 1807 was never used. The south end of the unfinished East Room was partitioned off to provide an office and bedroom for the

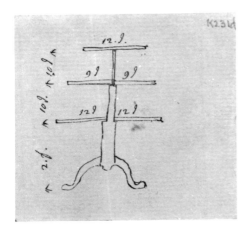

Fig. 100 Jefferson's design for a dumbwaiter. These stands with rotating shelves were invented in England about 1755.

President's secretary. The secretary's office was later used by Madison as a "cabinet" (private office).

Elbridge Gerry, son of Madison's Vice President, described that part of the President's House in 1813:

> Next to the drawing room [the Oval Room] is the President's sitting room [the Green Room] which has no connection with the former and opens to the hall. . . . This opens to his cabinet which I did not see. The cabinet is divided by a temporary partition from the grand audience chamber [the rest of the East Room] which runs the whole breadth of the house and is more than twice the breadth of common halls. This room is unfinished.

Besides the increase in bedrooms and dressing rooms, probably intended to encourage Jefferson's married daughters and their families to visit him as well as to accommodate his many guests, the President made some of his "fanciful" improvements on the first floor. Latrobe had designed in 1804 sets of revolving shelves to service the dining room and drawing room of the Worthington House, Adena, at Chillicothe, Ohio, to provide privacy for the owner and his guests. In 1807, his proposed floor plan for the President's House shows such a device as part of the buffet closet in the stair hall.

Margaret Bayard Smith mentioned that revolving shelves like these were indeed installed in the dining room wall, so that confidential matters could be discussed without speaking in whispers, as the diplomats of the time were accustomed to do.

Jefferson also designed small dumbwaiters which were placed at the side of each guest with the entire meal on the several shelves. Mrs. Smith said that he never had more than four guests at his private dinners, and the inventory of 1809 shows only four dumbwaiters in the small dining room. A fifth large dumbwaiter enabled the host to serve the main dishes.

A striking innovation made by Jefferson was the use of copper-plate-printed chintz and dimity, light and cheerful materials, instead of conventional heavy damask and velvet draperies. Of the twenty-seven rooms listed, only one has damask curtains, and these are probably the old crimson set brought by Adams from Philadelphia. Two other rooms have "elegant" curtains, of an unspecified material.

Heavily used public areas, such as the vestibule and dining room, had green-painted canvas floor coverings. Brussels carpets were used elsewhere.

Jefferson left a presentable, comfortable home for his friend, James Madison, who took up residence in March 1809. Since their architect-predecessor had done everything structurally necessary, the fashionable Madisons decided to improve the plain interior that Jefferson preferred. The new President immediately informed Latrobe that he would receive instructions from Mrs. Madison on all domestic arrangements, and was to render accounts to her.

The first result of this collaboration was a drawing room (now called the Red Room), fitted with yellow damask draperies, Sheraton furniture, and a new carpet. It was on view for the first weekly "drawing room," May 31, 1809.

The redecoration of the Blue Room had begun about the same time, but the project was more ambitious. New furniture designed by Latrobe in the Greek style, probably based on drawings in Thomas Hope's *Household Furniture and Interior Decoration,* was made by John and Hugh Finlay of Baltimore. (See Plate 20.) John

Rea of Philadelphia found enough crimson velvet not only for the five sets of curtains covering the three windows and the two alcoves, but for the upholstery of two sofas, four settees, and thirty-six chairs.

Latrobe also designed an immense overmantel looking-glass frame for the Blue Room, but the glass was broken in transit. (See Plate 21.) Two smaller mirrors were substituted. The frame of the fireplace in Latrobe's drawing is the first use in the President's House of the familiar Greek Revival pattern of fluted or molded rails and stiles terminating in square corner bosses. Hoban took up this new fashion after the fire of 1814, and most of the original or reconstructed door and window frames of the White House today are made in this manner.

Expenses of the undeclared war with Great Britain in 1811 cut off nonessential funds. Latrobe was dismissed, and Mrs. Madison's program came to a halt.

"Every article of the former furniture was totally destroyed when the house was burnt" in Cockburn's ruthless foray of 1814. The rebuilding of the structure itself was to be essentially completed in late 1817, and plans for redecoration and furnishing began again in the spring of that year.

On April 2, 1817, Colonel Lane requested James Hoban to furnish a list of the "paints and oils, also wallpaper, etc." for the President's House. Hoban responded on April 4, estimating the quantities of linseed oil, white lead, and whiting needed to cover the stains of fire and signs of repair on the exterior. He also asked for:

Rolls or pieces of Paper for walls of Principal Story—

Eliptic Room	B	30 Rolls each roll 11 yards long
Room East of Eliptic	B	25 Rolls D°
West of Eliptic	B	26 D° D°
South East Room	B	30 D° D°
North West Room	B	27 B° D°
Hall or Vestibule	B	60 D° D°

—2nd Story—

Eliptic Room	B	25 Rolls
East of Eliptic Room		21 D°
West of Eliptic Room		21 D°
South east chamber & Dress.g		30 D°
North West Chamber & D°		30 D°
Two chambers over the Hall		42 D°

N.B. Those marked B are the principal apartments, and the usual proportion of Border to match the paper will be necessary.

Congress had ordered that the President's House be restored to the same condition it was before the fire, and this list shows that Hoban obeyed the instruction quite literally. Jefferson's dressing rooms, as well as the partitioning of the large room over the entrance hall, were faithfully reproduced. Twelve additional fireplaces were also added to the original number, to provide warmth for the newly created rooms.

On December 11, 1817, Stephen P. Franklin was paid $314.16 for "Hanging 238 pieces of wallpaper and 86 pieces of border."

In a report submitted in February 1818 covering the remaining work to be done in the President's House, Hoban included some changes:

990 yards	plain Painting on Walls and Ceiling of Hall & Eliptic @ 20 cts		$198.00
270 "	Painting walls and Ceiling Eliptic Room Compartments @ 2.00		540.00
720 "	Painting walls and Ceiling of Hall in Compartments @ 2.00		1,440.00

Of the Drawing Room 40 × 80 feet Twenty feet six inches elevation between the floor and Ceiling and not included in former estimate—

810 yards Painting on walls plain	25	202.50
615 yards Painting on wood work	20	122.80
810 yard Painting walls and Ceilings in Compartments	2.00	1,620.00

According to various bids received for painting during this period, the standard charge was 5 cents per (square) yard per coat. It was the practice to apply three coats for good uniformity and coverage. An additional 5 cents was added for ordinary tints, and a further charge of 5 cents for flattening, which was the mode for plaster walls. Doors and woodwork were left with the natural gloss. A 20-cent per yard charge for paint on plaster implied plain white, flattened. A 25-cent charge meant that the paint was both tinted and flattened. For freehand fancy decorative painting, the rate was $2 per yard.

The final result was, then, that the walls of the vestibule, the oval room, and the East Room were hand-decorated, in a pattern of "Compartments." It is possible that these compartments contained panels of ornamental paper. These usually depicted an allegorical subject, a copy of a painting, trompe-l'oeil drapery, or flowers.

The remaining rooms on Hoban's list of April 1817 were papered. The wallpaper was repaired by C. Alexander in 1820 for $35.38. Because pieces were used, the paper was probably English, as both French and American manufacturers had then largely converted to rolls made by pasting twenty-four sheets together before printing. The English lagged for political reasons—a tax of a shilling per square was levied during the Napoleonic Wars, and the government was loath to lose this revenue. None of these early papers were scenic. A scenic paper, "Views of North America" by Jean Zuber, first sold in 1834, is now beautifully displayed in the oval Diplomatic Reception Room, where the continuous curved wall is a perfect setting for the diorama.

After the fire, the President's House had but one article of "furniture"—the large portrait of George Washington acquired shortly after Washington's death and placed in the President's House as a memorial.

The history of this portrait prior to its purchase in 1800 is as dramatic as Dolley Madison's rescue of it in 1814. It is a copy of the Gilbert Stuart portrait of Washington painted for William Bingham of Philadelphia. The original was signed by Stuart at Bingham's request. Almost simultaneously, Stuart made duplicates for William Constable and for Lord Lansdowne, a great admirer of Washington. The pose has been called the "teapot" Washington, as the left arm, elbow bent as he grasps his sword, resembles a handle and the right arm, outstretched, a spout. Another copy by Stuart was painted for a museum originally opened under the auspices of the Society of St. Tammany in New York. Gardner Baker, who had been a prime mover in the establishment of the Tammany museum, soon acquired and operated it as a private business, featuring the Stuart portrait. Baker died of yellow fever in Boston in

September 1798, and the painting passed to William Laing, to whom Baker has assigned it as security for a debt.

George Washington died on December 13, 1799. Soon after, a committee consisting of the Secretaries of State, War, and Navy was asked to find a suitable portrait of the late President to be placed in the President's House as a memorial. The painting owned by Laing had been sold to General Henry Lee for $800. It was bought by the Committee from him at that price, and a Treasury record shows that payment was made on July 5, 1800. Lee's role in the transaction is unclear; technically he acted as agent for Laing, the seller, although it is likely his intention was to aid the committee.

During this period William Winstanley, an English landscape and portrait painter, was living in New York, supporting himself mainly by making copies of Stuart's portraits of Washington. On January 6, 1800, Mrs. William Thornton, wife of the architect of the Capitol, wrote to Winstanley about a velvet suit belonging to the former President, which the artist wished to use in painting his portraits of him. Mrs. Thornton's detailed diary records that Winstanley arrived in Washington June 29, and stayed at the Thornton's most of the time. On July 5, his baggage arrived, including an original Stuart portrait of Washington, a small full-length copy after Stuart by Winstanley, and several other copies.

According to William Dunlap, Laing knew Winstanley as a competent painter, and asked him to supervise the packing and shipping of the Washington portrait. Mrs. Thornton said that Winstanley left her house for Alexandria, the seaport for the capital, on August 21, and did not appear again until 6 weeks later. The portrait for the President's House arrived before September 5 at the Treasury Office. Dr. Thornton went to see it, but Mrs. Thornton told her diary, "He does not like it." Dunlap says that Winstanley substituted one of his copies for the original Stuart, but does not cite any proof. Stuart himself viewed the portrait at the President's House at a later date, and denied that it was his work. Although Dunlap's histories are generally factual, some of the colorful anecdotes, like this one, raise questions regarding the veracity of Dunlap's sources. Both he and Stuart obviously disliked Winstanley.

The figure of Washington does seem somewhat awkward and disproportionate when compared to the Bingham version, but the White House portrait was restored and partially repainted by Joel N. Barlow in 1862, and perhaps at other times. In 1978, the portrait was removed from its place in the East Room of the White House for cleaning, x-ray photographs, pigment analyses, and stylistic comparison. These data, together with a search for additional documentation, may determine the identity of its painter and provide an explanation for its confusing history. In any event, the historical significance of the portrait cannot be affected by its origin or the manner by which it reached the President's House.

As Minister to France in Washington's administration and as a special minister plenipotentiary on several other occasions, James Monroe developed a taste for French furniture and objects of art. At his Virginia residence, Oak Hill, he had a substantial collection of his own, some of which he sold to the government for the President's House when he was elected President. Monroe supplemented this nucleus with new importations from France, a set of twenty-four chairs and four sofas made by William King of Georgetown, and some articles bought from the

Fig. 101 The Cabinet table used from Madison's administration to Grant's. The Emancipation Proclamation was read by Lincoln to his Cabinet at this table.

Madisons. The fine quality of most of Monroe's acquisitions has prevented their wholesale dispersal in the sweeping redecorations of Grant, Arthur, and Roosevelt. Some pieces have been sold, but the still numerous Monroe pieces are the earliest, most historic, and most valuable in the collection of authentic White House furniture. See Plate 22.

Colonel Samuel Lane, Commissioner of Public Buildings, died in 1822. An audit of his accounts initially showed a discrepancy of about $20,000, which greatly embarrassed the President. To isolate himself from gossip and innuendo, Monroe bought back furniture he had sold from his own collection at the purchase price. Later studies of Lane's books found the missing entries, and the problem disappeared. The Congressional Committee on the Public Buildings in its report of February 14, 1823, "feeling perfectly satisfied with the Commissioners management of the public interest . . . felt it their duty to express their unqualified approbation . . . ," but not before a number of "details of a very humiliating character" for President Monroe had been made public. Many pieces bought back by the President are now in the James Monroe Museum and Memorial Library housed in the brick building at Fredericksburg, Virginia, in which he first began the practice of law in 1786.

The administration of John Quincy Adams was not a happy one, either for the President or for the building in which he lived. The political tension between his supporters and those of Andrew Jackson prevented any appropriations for improvement of the President's House. About $11,000 was spent on the President's Square, but Adams dipped into his own pocket for some of the few articles bought for the house itself.

This situation was resolved by the overwhelming victory of Andrew Jackson in 1828. The Federalist party had died when Monroe was reelected by all the electoral votes but one. Now the Republicans had split into two factions: the Democrats, led by Jackson, and the Whigs, headed by Henry Clay and Daniel Webster. Jackson met Whig challenges head-on, and he barreled legislation through the Congress with all the legal powers and personal influence he could command. He wanted the President's House completed, and got not only the appropriation Hoban had long urged for the addition of the North Portico, but funds totaling $50,000 to redecorate the interior in a grand, and rather gaudy, manner.

A man from a frontier state and one close to the people, he felt that the public should be allowed to visit the President's House freely. As a consequence of this easy attitude, furniture was smashed, draperies and upholstery cut for souvenirs, and the rugs ruined by spilled food and drink. After the frugal years of John Quincy Adams, when even broken windows were left unrepaired, it was appropriate that the whole building be renewed. Jackson's refurbishing took place while the Federal style, still suited to its architecture, remained popular. For the first time, the East Room was furnished. The effect must have been overwhelming to the plain folk who came to see the President in his new "banqueting room":

> This room is eighty by forty feet, and twenty-two high; it is finished with
> handsome stucco-cornice. It has lately been fitted up in a very neat manner.
> The paper is of fine lemon-colour, with a rich cloth border. There are four
> mantels of black marble with Italian black and gold fronts, and handsome
> grates; each mantel is surmounted with a mirror, the plates of which measure

one hundred by fifty-eight inches, framed in a very beautiful style, and a pair of rich ten-light lamps, bronzed and gilt, with a row of drops around the fountain; and a pair of French cepina vases, richly gilt and painted with glass shades and flowers. There are three handsome chandeliers of eighteen lights each, of cut glass of remarkable brilliancy, in gilt mountings, with a number of gilt bracket-lights of five candles each. The carpet, which contains nearly five hundred yards, is of fine Brussels, of fawn, blue, and yellow, with red border. Under each chandelier is placed a round table, with splendid lamps on each of them. The curtains are of light blue moreen with yellow draperies, with a gilded eagle, holding up the drapery of each. On the cornices of the curtains in a line of stairs, and over the semicircle of the door, besides large gilded and ornamented rays, are twenty-four gilded stars, emblematic of the States. The sofas and chairs are covered with blue damask satin. All the furniture corresponds in colour and style.

In this blaze of glory, the President's House was at last completed, inside and out. More than forty years had passed since the cornerstone was laid.

Eleven

The Victorian Period: 1832–1902

The architectural development of the President's House rested for a while with the completion of the North Portico and the East Room. For the next seventy years, the building was often repaired and improved, but the basic structure remained unchanged. The growing nation alternated among financial panic, political discord, an ugly Civil War, and the fervor of explosive growth in industry and trade. Meanwhile, the fabric of the President's House sat in almost benign neglect, seldom getting more than cosmetic treatment.

Considerable wear and tear was caused by the comings and goings of the citizenry. In many a European palace, furniture twice as old as the White House can still be found with its original upholstery. In Washington, the incoming President was generally forced to replace or repair the furniture of his predecessor.

There were many reasons for diminished activity at the President's House. The new structure of 1817 did not need urgent attention. A panic in 1837 sharply reduced government income, curtailing everything after Jackson's last splurge. Jackson's system of patronage swelled the federal bureaucracy, and the building of new government offices took priority. The burning of the old Treasury Building in 1833, and of the Patent Office (Blodget's Hotel) underlined the necessity for fireproof construction, which was far more expensive and difficult to build. The erection of a new Treasury, Patent Office, General Post Office, jail, and insane asylum almost simultaneously was a tremendous undertaking. Robert Mills, a pupil of Hoban, protegé of Jefferson, and assistant to Latrobe, was the architect who guided this vast program and kept his eye on the President's House as well.

The improvements made at the President's House during this period were primarily due to advances in technology. Additional fireplaces installed in 1817 helped alleviate the winter cold in the new rooms, but did not make the house truly comfortable. President Jackson complained that hell itself couldn't heat the northwest corner. In 1837, the first central heating system, circulating hot air, was installed to warm the drafty corridors and the vast new East Room. To contain the precious heat Mills designed and erected wooden screens in the arcades between the entrance hall and the main corridor, with simple sash and glass. A vestibule of wood was also built inside the north entrance. The great corridor became a gloomy cavern.

The Whigs captured the White House in 1841 with "Tippecanoe and Tyler too," but popular General Harrison died exactly a month after his inauguration. His lesser known running mate had little success with either the Executive or the Congressional establishment. The interior of the President's House reached its nadir during the administration of John Tyler.

A great change came in the mid-1840s, and with it a more expansive mood in the Congress. A series of landmark inventions—vulcanized rubber, the reaper, sewing machine, power loom, telegraph, rotary printing press, and the discovery of safe anaesthesia—was accelerating the pace of the industrial revolution. Immigration was on the increase, providing workers to exploit these new wonders, to build the railroads and canals, and settle the new lands to the west.

In 1845, the new President James K. Polk found no difficulty in obtaining an appropriation to improve the shabby interior of the Executive Mansion. The rudimentary heating plant was rebuilt and four additional furnaces added by Haywood Fox & Co. Central heat was extended to all the first-floor rooms and some on the second story, twelve in all. The "valves" for controlling the flow were silver plate in the East Room, brass in other State Rooms, and japanned iron in the working quarters. Polk also acquired a "refregerator" for $25, an amenity for the steamy Washington summers.

Hoban had paved the basement with tiles. For some reason a plank floor was preferred in the nineteenth century, but the wood rotted rapidly and had to be replaced every few years. In the interim, partially decayed boards provided a home for mold, damp, and vermin. The basement was at this date partitioned into eleven rooms, including servants' bedrooms. It was extremely unhealthful, and had intolerably bad ventilation in the summer. Efforts to freshen the air included keeping stoves going the year around to create a draft. From 1842 to 1850 improvements were continued until the service rooms were reasonably sanitary.

An 1845 sketch of the furnace locations shows two innovations on the ground floor: a butler's pantry, which may have been included in the rebuilding of 1817, and doors in the archway separating the main corridor of the first floor from the private stairs. A later plan of the second floor shows a similar partition separating the corridor serving the family living quarters from that leading to the President's offices.

The double circles that are shown on the sketch between the entrance hall and the corridor are not Hoban's columns; they are most likely ducts for the heating system.

In 1848, the Washington Gas Light Company, an offshoot of the Philadelphia company, connected mains at the Capitol to a new line down Pennsylvania Avenue. At the President's House, a pipe ran in the basement passage to a point near the center of the building. Not only was the lighting in the house greatly improved, but eighty new gas lamps on the avenue and around the government buildings replaced the old oil lamps.

Mrs. Polk, apprehensive about an adequate supply of fuel for the new system and its reliability, asked that one chandelier be left with candles. At the first reception

Fig. 102 A sketch of furnace locations by Haywood Fox & Co., 1845.

Fig. 103 The first known photograph of the President's House, a daguerrotype taken by John Plumbe about 1846. The image is reversed left to right.

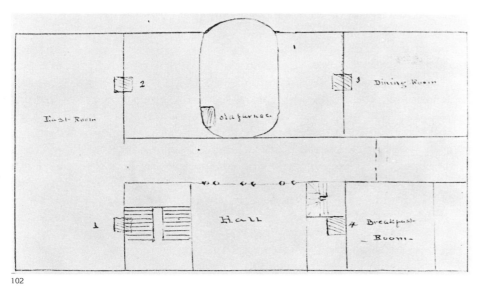

102

103

given after the new installation, the gas supply gave out; the evening ended illuminated by candlelight.

The grounds south of the President's House were a disgrace; "gullied, dilapidated and filthy with rubbish." In the following year, an effort was made to create a more parklike appearance by grading and draining. The old stable for the President's House on 14th Street was sold in 1849 to a local group for use as a school.

The next President, Zachary Taylor, spent only a year in the President's House before dying of an illness then diagnosed as cholera. Millard Fillmore, a Whig facing an overwhelmingly Democratic Congress, astutely engineered the Compromise of 1850. At the White House he is remembered primarily for having installed a new kitchen stove, replacing the open fireplaces used for cooking since 1817. Mrs. Fillmore, a former schoolteacher, obtained enough money to start a small library, the first government-owned collection of books in the President's House.

Furnishings changed, and conveniences multiplied. During the administration of Franklin Pierce, Thomas U. Walter was commissioned to modernize the interior. Walter removed Mills's old partition in the entrance hall and substituted an iron-framed screen with ground-glass panels, greatly improving the light in the corridor. A similar iron-and-glass enclosure replaced the small wooden vestibule at the front door. "New, modern mantels" took the place of the "very, very old-fashioned" ones Hoban had put there. All the State Rooms were redecorated to Walter's direction. Structural changes were minimal; only the fireplaces seem to have been rebuilt. Pierce was the first President to have a modern bathroom, with both water closet and tub.

Fig. 104 The vestibule, fitted with a new iron and ground-glass partition, by T. U. Walter.

105

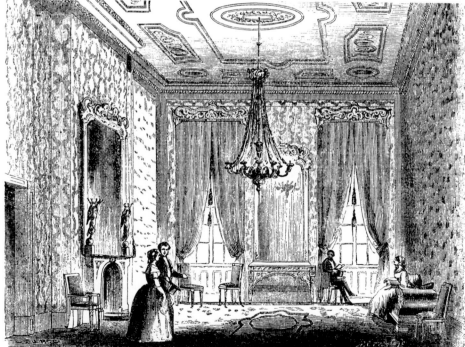

107

106

Fig. 105 In the East Room, Walter added a white-and-gilt frieze.

Fig. 106 Hoban's wood-burning fireplaces were replaced by coal grates with new mantelpieces.

Fig. 107 Green was first used in this room by Jefferson. Later Presidents elaborated on the color scheme, and Walter continued the tradition.

109

108

Fig. 108 Monochrome color schemes were used by Walter in the other two central reception rooms. The Red Room was papered, carpeted, and upholstered in deep crimson.

Fig. 109 The President received official visitors in the Blue Room.

Fig. 110 The Cabinet met in a room on the second floor, now the Lincoln Bedroom.

110

President Buchanan and his niece, Harriet Lane, ordered to be erected "an elegant coach-house and stable," but unfortunately they chose "a very injudicious site," according to the *National Intelligencer.* East of the mansion and somewhat forward, it obstructed the view of the President's House from Pennsylvania Avenue. A conservatory designed by Edward Clark, assistant architect to Thomas U. Walter, was added in 1857, the first of seemingly endless glasshouses and propagating rooms which spread like a giant fungus to the west for the next forty years. The conservatory, which stood on top of Jefferson's service wing, was decorated with twelve stained-glass picture windows made by P. Klaus of Baltimore. The structure can be seen, extended, in an 1869 *Harper's Weekly* view.

The iron-framed glass screen in the entrance hall and the new conservatory were built only a few years after the Great Exhibition in London, 1851. It was housed in the Crystal Palace, a joint conception of Prince Albert and architect Joseph Paxton. The building itself was so spectacular that in 1854 it was moved from Hyde Park to the outskirts of London, where it remained a popular attraction for many years. The glass dome of the Halle au Blé in Paris had inspired Jefferson's plans for a dry dock, a ceiling for the House of Representatives, his "AZ" entry in the President's House competition, and an amphitheater that was proposed by Samuel Blodget in 1797. The Crystal Palace may have begun the new wave of enthusiasm for glass structures in the 1850s.

Fig. 111 A reception in the East Room for the Prince of Wales, 1860.

Fig. 112 By 1869, conservatories nearly covered the west wing. The Navy Department building (right) and War Department building (left) had been raised 1-1/2 stories.

Fig. 113 The earliest known photograph of the East Room, 1861.

President Lincoln would not allow substantial funds to be spent on his house while the nation was at war. The only change he made was a private passage through the reception room to his office, a reflection of his frequent periods of melancholy, during which he withdrew from contact with his staff and the public as much as possible. When Willie Lincoln died, Mrs. Lincoln also became deeply depressed, and later, eccentric. She spent money lavishly for furniture, piling up bills unknown to the President. Some of her acquisitions are in the Lincoln Bedroom today. Like Jackson, President Lincoln allowed public access to the house at almost any time, and the ravages of souvenir-hunters ruined the draperies and upholstery. The President's compassion for the common soldier was so great that troops guarding the capital city were sometimes quartered in the East Room.

After Lincoln's assassination, the Johnsons moved into an almost derelict house. Fortunately, the new President's daughter, Martha, was strong-willed and industrious. Diligent cleaning and modest redecorating made the interior presentable again. In 1867 a fire destroyed one-third of the greenhouses, including many valuable plants, some of which had been collected by Washington.

The new Treasury Building, completed in 1869, made Latrobe's fireproof rooms in the east range of the White House offices unnecessary. The entire wing, built in Jefferson's time, was demolished. Alfred B. Mullett, Assistant Supervising Architect for the Treasury Department, designed a new portico that was appropriate and attractive. The single and paired columns of the portico responded beautifully to the vertical elements of the first floor. It was very similar to the entrances of the State, War, and Navy Building designed by Mullett two years later.

All of the area east of the White House was regraded by Mullett and a walk laid out connecting the central wing of the Treasury to the new entrance. East Executive Avenue was also built at this time.

Fig. 114 The White House stables were a constant annoyance to the neighborhood. An 1869 view.

Fig. 115 A portico at ground-floor level, landscaped walks, and East Executive Avenue were created simultaneously by Alfred B. Mullett in 1869.

During the 1860s, the term "White House" began to appear commonly both in the popular press and in government documents. One of the first official references is in a letter of the Commissioner of Public Buildings, April 2, 1861, to Doremus and Nixon, telling them that "Mrs. Lincoln is not furnishing the White House." Before that the building was known formally as the Executive Mansion and popularly as the President's House.

From the earliest days of its occupancy, the White House was regarded as unhealthful in warm weather because of the nearby flats of the Tiber. From late spring to the first frost, carrier mosquitos came out of the swamps when darkness fell. A miasma often enveloped the President's House on summer nights. Many Presidents felt safe during working hours, but prudently moved to higher or drier ground after dusk. Adams spent the summer in Braintree; Jefferson returned to Monticello. Later Presidents spent the hot months on farms beyond Georgetown, on the heights above Kalorama, in rented homes in the vicinity of Massachusetts Avenue, or, in the case of the bachelor President Buchanan, at the Soldiers' Home. Channelizing of the Tiber into the "Washington Canal" dried up some of the worst swamps, but the area was not considered reasonably safe until the early 1870s when "Boss" Shepherd sanitized the city. He built sewers, paved all the streets in the area between and around the Capitol and the White House, laid a culvert in the bed of the Washington Canal, and covered it over.

Shepherd's wild spending and grandiose improvements were symptoms of the overblown reaction to the tragedies of the Civil War, Lincoln's assassination, and Johnson's impeachment. The ebullient spirit of the time was evident in the general renovation of the White House carried out during the Grant administration.

The President's secretary, Orville Babcock, became Commissioner of Public Buildings and Grounds in 1871. He reported the building to be in deplorable condition. Beams were decayed, the heating system required an overhaul, and replacement of floors and repair of ceilings were necessary. The East Room needed redecoration. Gigantic crystal chandeliers were ordered from Germany for it, and two new beams were installed under the second-floor partitions to ensure that the total weight did not bring the whole ceiling down. These beams were supported by columns at each end. The decorative frieze of the room as designed by Walter was extended along the sides of the beams, in white and gilt. Although the "Greek" design was retained, the sheer quantity of this ornamentation overpowered the sense of structure. Fireplace mantels and overmantel mirrors were mounted in new, more elaborate frames. These repairs and decorative projects were completed in 1873. The following year, another sash screen was added to the entrance hall, cutting it in two unequal portions. Visitors to the family entered the smaller area, and visitors to the President's offices the larger. The screen was designed so that it could be taken down for great public receptions. Babcock's program included a substantial new brick stable, built in a corner of the park opposite where the Corcoran Art Gallery now stands.

The major legacy of the Hayes administration was another greenhouse, the Rose House, added in 1879 to the already formidable warren on the west. Nearly 100 feet long and 26 feet wide, it rivaled the East Room in area. From the State Dining Room, the visitor could pass into the Palm House, through the camelia, fern, and primrose house, and into the Rose House. These buildings completely covered the

Jefferson wing. A grapery, built in 1869, and an orchid house were other major attractions.

The unexpected Presidency of Chester Arthur following Garfield's assassination brought a new phase in the interior design of the President's House. Arthur hired Louis Comfort Tiffany, now best known for his work in stained glass, to redecorate the building in a less garish fashion. The fastidious President refused to live in the White House until it was cleared of the clutter left by the two previous administrations. He lived nearby with a friend while Tiffany worked. When Congress questioned the $15,000 cost, Arthur said he would pay it himself if necessary, but Congress eventually voted the money.

Tiffany was to his immediate American predecessors as William Morris was to Sir Charles Eastlake in England: a purifier and innovator of style. A trend toward the "colonial" had been developing as a consequence of the American Centennial in 1876. Tiffany pointed out in a later ghostwritten biography that admirers of chaste white Grecian temples and statues had forgotten that the ages washed away their lively polychrome decoration. For the White House, he mixed American eagles, bas-reliefs, flowers, and foliage with scrolls and curlicues in a style rather like the "Pompeian" wall painting of the late eighteenth century.

Tiffany left the white and gilt of the East Room as it was, but decorated the ceiling with patterns in silver and ivory. The marble columns of the vestibule remained unpainted, but Walter's iron and ground-glass screen was replaced in part with new panels and doors containing stained glass. This may have been the greatest area of Tiffany glass executed in the United States. It was later surpassed by the spectacular 22-ton glass curtain he created for the Palacio de Bellas Artes in Mexico City.

Fig. 116 In Grant's renovation, beams supported by columns were installed in the East Room under the second-floor partitions. This 1890 photograph shows Hoban's entrance to the room, Thomas U. Walter's decorative frieze, and the 1873 additions.

More practical achievements of the 1882 renovation were the installation of two new bathrooms on the second floor and an elevator. Needless to say, Arthur also enlarged and improved the greenhouses. The surplus furnishings acquired by Arthur's predecessors were sold at a great auction held April 15, 1882, when no less than 24 wagonloads were dispersed. More than 5,000 people attended, making it the most popular White House sale ever held.

The modest private rooms of the White House were adequate for Chester Arthur, a widower with two small children. His successor, Grover Cleveland, was married there during his first term.

117

118

Fig. 117 The Blue Room with principal decoration by L. C. Tiffany. Photographed during the Harrison administration.

Fig. 118 Tiffany's stained-glass screen was installed in the vestibule in 1882. By 1891, the white marble columns were painted and the ceilings and walls completely redone by Mrs. Harrison.

Fig. 119 This 1882 first-floor plan is marked with the carpet requirements for each room.

Fig. 120 Second-floor plan, 1882. Chester Arthur's new elevator and bathtubs are shown.

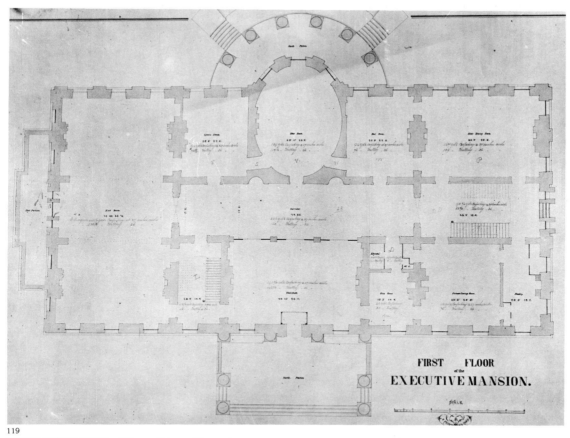

119

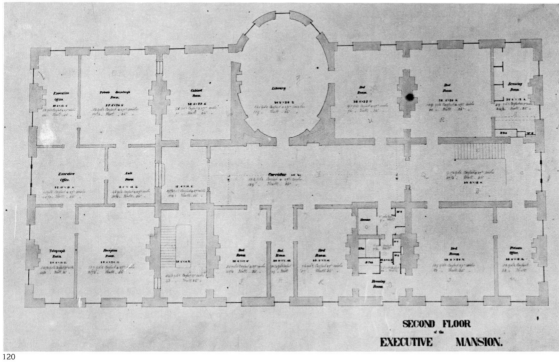

120

Fig. 121 The maze of greenhouses was nearly complete in 1885.

President and Mrs. Harrison, however, found the mixture of offices and bedrooms an impossible combination for their large family; an average of nine relatives stayed with them most of the time. Determined to solve the problem by the building's centennial, October 13, 1892, Mrs. Harrison arranged for architect Fred D. Owen of the Office of Public Buildings and Grounds to prepare three proposals. Owen first planned a separate President's House to be built on nearby 16th Street; his second effort called for a modest enlargement of the existing building. The third was a grandiose scheme, which went far beyond the immediate needs of the family. It involved an absurd and ostentatious waste of space in reception areas, galleries, a statuary hall, and a historical museum. At the end of the large U-shaped structure, closing the "Private Court," was to be an enormous series of greenhouses and conservatories. A bill to approve the last proposal actually reached the floor of the House, but was not passed for political reasons, quite apart from the lack of merit in the plan. A redeeming aspect of this monster scheme was that it provided a dignified view of an appropriate part of the whole for each of the four radiating avenues. L'Enfant planned his President's House so that the two facades would provide visual focuses for the main approaches. Hoban's smaller house was located properly on the north, but did not fill the space to the south. The huge Treasury Building further interfered with the view from the Capitol. Mrs. Harrison's buildings were consciously located to be seen as L'Enfant intended.

The space problem persisted. Large receptions were chaotic affairs; guests still left the building through the stair-hall window, as they had for 90 years. The returning President, Grover Cleveland, had a new plan prepared that was less extravagant and more in keeping with the existing building. T-shaped wings on each side, almost as large as the old building, were to be added: one for social functions and the other for offices. At last the original building could become the President's almost-private residence. Each bay of the extension was an exact duplicate of a bay of the original building. The result was an acceptable functional solution, but visually monotonous. Fortunately, the new scheme did not get past Congress. The President's House was spared mediocrity, but the problems remained unsolved.

By now the reversion from Victorian Gothic and Romanesque to Renaissance styles was fully underway. The influence of the Beaux-Arts school and the World's

Fig. 122 President Harrison's office.

Fig. 123 Harrison slept in the famous bed bought by Mary Lincoln. It is not likely that President Lincoln ever used it.

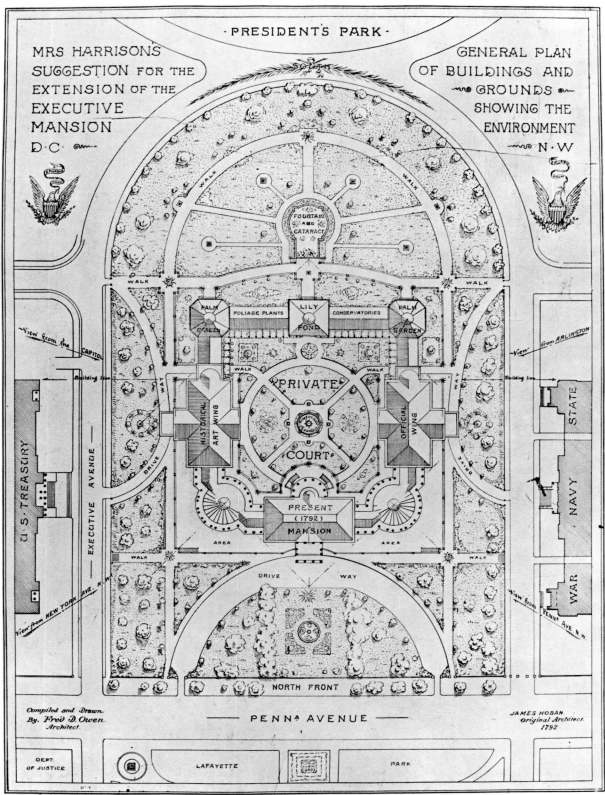

- PRESIDENT'S PARK -

MRS HARRISON'S SUGGESTION FOR THE EXTENSION OF THE EXECUTIVE MANSION D·C·

GENERAL PLAN OF BUILDINGS AND GROUNDS SHOWING THE ENVIRONMENT N·W

SOUTH

FOUNTAIN AND CATARACT

PALM GARDEN   FOLIAGE PLANTS   LILY POND   CONSERVATORIES   PALM GARDEN

WALK   WALK

PRIVATE

HISTORICAL ART WING   OFFICIAL WING

COURT

View from the CAPITOL

Building line

U.S. TREASURY

EXECUTIVE AVENUE

DRIVE

View from ARLINGTON

Building line

STATE

NAVY

WAR

View from PENNᴬ AVE. N.W.

PRESENT (1792) MANSION

AREA   AREA

WALK   WALK

DRIVE   WAY

NORTH FRONT

View from NEW YORK AVE. N.W.

Compiled and Drawn. By Fred D. Owen. Architect.

— PENNᴬ AVENUE —

JAMES HOBAN. Original Architect. 1792

DEPT. OF JUSTICE

LAFAYETTE   PARK

·VIEW·FROM·THE·SOUTH·
·OF·THE·RESIDENCE·WINGS·
·CONSERVATORY·AND·COURT·

Official Wing
WEST

National Wing
EAST

F.D.Owen
Archt.

125

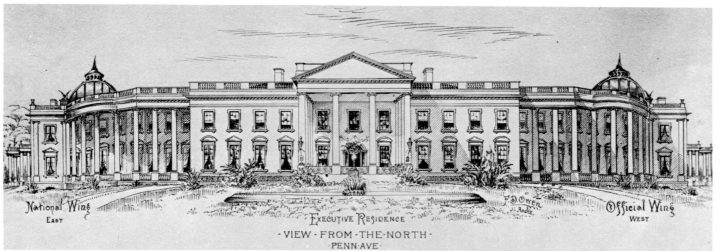

National Wing
EAST

EXECUTIVE RESIDENCE
·VIEW·FROM·THE·NORTH·
PENN·AVE·

Official Wing
WEST

F.D.Owen
Archt.

126

127

Fig. 124 Mrs. Harrison's "suggested" plan for extending the White House.

Fig. 125 Fred D. Owen's rendering of Mrs. Harrison's concept, as seen from the south.

Fig. 126 The north elevation of Mrs. Harrison's extended building.

Fig. 127 A plan for expanding the White House proposed in Cleveland's second administration.

128

Columbian Exposition held at Chicago in 1893 was felt in Washington. The new Corcoran Art Gallery, the Library of Congress, the Central Library, the Union Station, and a number of private mansions were designed in the latest fashion. Washington was tinged with Paris.

Both the Chicago Exposition, planned by Daniel H. Burnham and executed by a number of architects under the overall supervision of Charles F. McKim, and the Paris Exposition of 1900 showed what breathtaking effects could be accomplished by a proper master plan. In 1897 Colonel Theodore A. Bingham assumed charge of the Office of Public Buildings and Grounds. Bingham was an organizer, and he took his responsibilities seriously. He first surveyed the need for better planning of the city park system. At the request of the Senate, he then reviewed the history of property rights to lots in the city, thereby sparking a renewed interest in L'Enfant's plan.

At the direction of Congress, Bingham and landscape architect Samuel Parsons of New York prepared a new plan for the mall and its adjoining areas. Bingham sent the indefatigable Fred D. Owen back to the drafting table to produce a more modest version of Mrs. Harrison's plan for expanding the White House, omitting from the plan everything except the two rotundas, which were redesigned in more classical form.

129

130

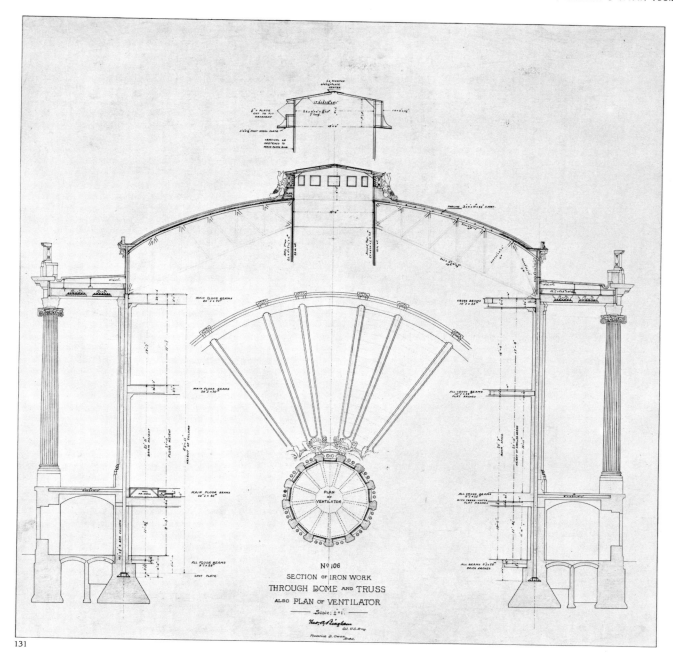

N⁰ 106

SECTION OF IRON WORK
THROUGH DOME AND TRUSS
ALSO PLAN OF VENTILATOR

Scale: ¼" = 1'

131

On the north front, the great wings were stepped back one bay, so that the central block dominated the composition. But on the south, the rotundas overwhelmed the original structure, which now appeared as a mere connecting link between them. Because the ground sloped away, the staircases at the south ceremonial entrances were very grand, quite out of scale with Hoban's design.

A single circular room occupied the first floor of each wing. On the west a new State Dining Room was created, and on the east a general reception area augmented the adjacent East Room.

Fig. 128 Erecting the marquee at the stair-hall window for departing guests, a scheme used since 1800. Mrs. Russell Harrison and children are in the foreground.

Fig. 129 Col. Theodore Bingham resurrected part of the Harrison scheme in more classical style, 1900. The south front of a model.

Fig. 130 The north front of Bingham's model of 1900.

Fig. 131 A structural section of the rotundas.

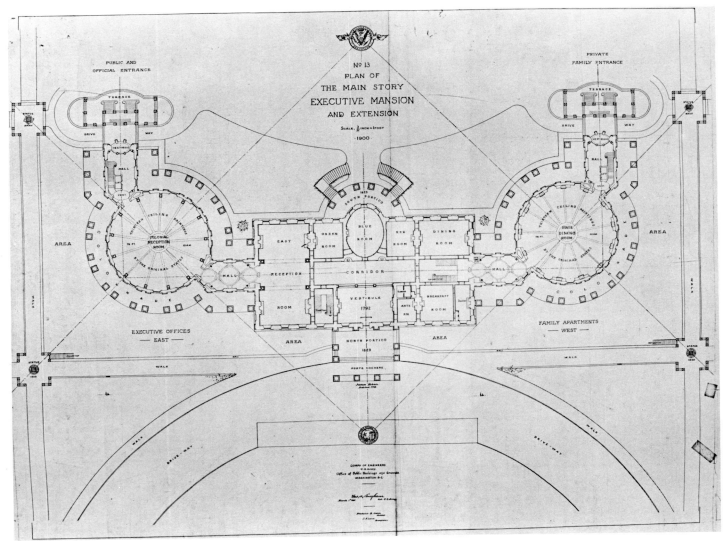

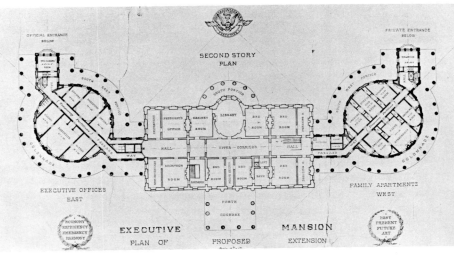

Fig. 132 The first floor of Bingham's addition was largely ceremonial.

Fig. 133 Second-floor plan, Bingham's proposed extension of the White House.

The upper floor of the East Rotunda was a suite of executive offices; that of the West Rotunda, additional bedrooms. The existing offices in the White House were to be retained. Thus the principal relief provided the President's family from the tangled functions was a separate stair and entrance to the offices.

The centennial of the removal of the government to the city of Washington was celebrated on December 12, 1900. One of the many commemorative events was the convention of the American Institute of Architects which began the following day.

The Bingham plans were strongly condemned by the Institute. Out of this welter of good intentions and bad plans, Senator McMillan, Chairman of the District Committee of the Senate, brought order by the appointment of Daniel A. Burnham, Frederick L. Olmsted, Jr., Charles F. McKim, and Charles Moore to restudy the whole question and report their findings by December 1901.

The McMillan Commission enthusiastically undertook a photographic and topographic survey of the city, visited other planned American cities, such as Annapolis and Williamsburg, and made a grand tour of French, English, and Italian sites to visualize possible treatment of the Mall. The work of the Commission was of great interest to the public and gradually developed a constituency in Congress, persuaded by the influential and skillful Senator McMillan. The time was ripe to broach an expansion of the White House, and Charles F. McKim, an energetic member of the McMillan Commission, had the confidence of the legislators.

In September 1901 President McKinley was assassinated, and Theodore Roosevelt succeeded him. The new President had six children, and the pinch of private space in the White House became a serious problem. When he resolved on a removal of the offices to provide more bedrooms, the work of the McMillan Commission had created a background of goodwill and a receptive attitude on the part of Congress. The extension of the White House was incorporated into the McMillan plan.

Fig. 134 By the turn of the century, the White House had a serene and settled appearance.

Fig. 135 The north entrance about 1890. The swag contains American roses; griffins guard the central ornament in the garland below. The stained-glass fanlight and door panels probably date from 1882.

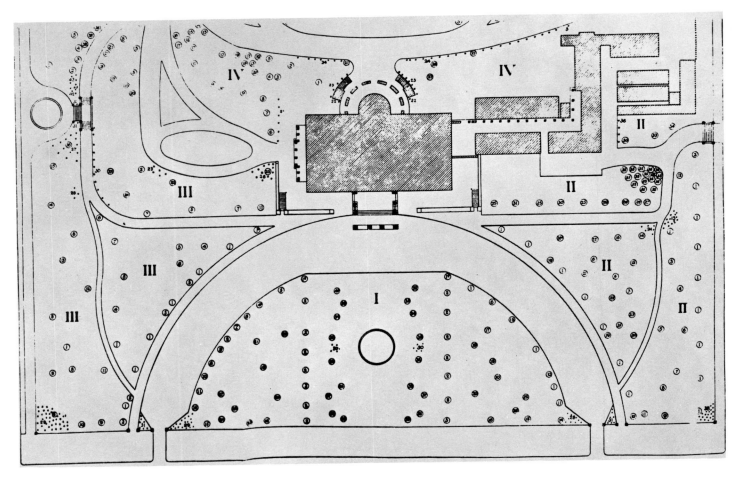

Fig. 136 Plan of the White House grounds just before the modifications of 1902.

A survey of the vacated offices, which were to be remodeled for family use, showed that the 1817 structure was now in poor condition. Radical rebuilding was necessary to relieve the beams from the overload imposed on them. The original house, McKim said, was built simply, but well built. The many alterations over the years had introduced a hodgepodge of structural change and decoration of little permanent value. It would not be feasible to redo a portion of the house; the necessities of electric power, plumbing, and additional bathrooms, and the desirability of harmony in architectural style required that the entire house be treated as a single problem. Consequently, an additional appropriation of $343,945 was obtained to overhaul the existing building. Refurnishing was estimated at $131,500.

A Sundry Civil Act passed June 28, 1902, provided funds for the necessary additions and for renovation of the vacated portion of the White House. The President moved to a house owned by Mary S. Townsend at 22 Lafayette Place, and removal of the furnishings began.

The President insisted on an unbelievably short schedule, allowing only 4 months for the offices and slightly longer for the house itself. In a letter to Colonel Bingham on June 27, McKim outlined his proposed strategy. The architectural work, based on plans prepared by McKim, Mead & White, would be supervised by the partners or by Mr. C. W. Kaiser of their office. Glenn Brown of Washington would have general oversight of the plans and the work. Construction was the responsibility of Norcross Brothers Co. of Worcester, Massachusetts, represented by Mr. French. Although Congress had appropriated specific sums for the several categories of the work, any money saved on one part might be used for another, provided the expenditures did not exceed the total appropriation.

Much to his credit, Colonel Bingham had a survey made of all original Hoban work in the building before renovations began. Fred D. Owen was also charged with keeping a diary of the project, making sketches where necessary.

The President had stipulated that none of the essential features of the White House should be sacrificed in the restoration and that the State Rooms should continue to be known by the names made familiar by long usage. McKim noted that "these limitations were welcomed, because among no class of the people was the feeling for the historic White House stronger than among the members of the profession of architecture. The first aim, therefore, was to discover the design and intention of the original builders, and to adhere strictly thereto in so far as the public or state portions of the house were concerned." These sentiments were carefully respected on the exterior, but somehow were largely swept aside in the execution of the interior decoration.

As McKim later reported, the initial step was to find a new site for the Executive Offices.

> Every suggestion for the location of a permanent office building was open to some objection that seemed insuperable. No location outside the White House grounds could be decided upon and secured in the short time available. To construct within those grounds a building sufficiently large and imposing to stand as permanent offices would be to detract from the White House itself so seriously as to be absolutely out of the question. The one possible solution, therefore, was to occupy the only available space with a temporary building, which should be comfortable within and inconspicuous in appearance.

The available space was then occupied by a number of small greenhouses, at the end of Jefferson's west range of offices, which still existed under the conservatories.

Fig. 137 Greenhouses on the site of the future Executive Office Building. Jefferson's wing can be seen beneath the conservatories.

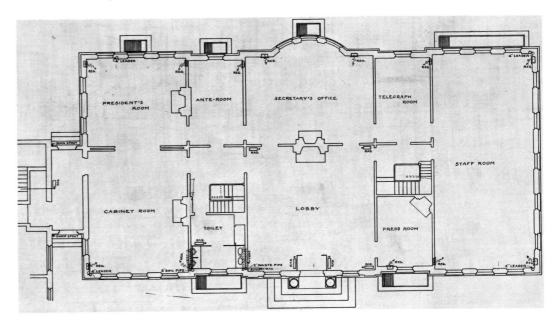

Fig. 138 Plan of the Executive Offices as built.

Although Congress stipulated in the enabling legislation that the walls of the Executive Offices should be constructed to support a future second story, McKim recommended against an increase in height that might injure the appearance of the White House.

A curious legend has arisen about the collection of greenhouses that had to be removed to make room for the new building. "Smash the glass houses!" Roosevelt is reported to have said. Letters among Mrs. Roosevelt, the President, Colonel Bingham, and Charles McKim show, however, a more gentle concern. On June 28, 1902, the President wrote to Colonel Bingham:

> I think you ought to show Pfister's letter to Mr. McKim and also read to him the following extract from a letter from Mrs. Roosevelt:
>
> "I thought of course they would make provision for these valuable plants, and though the green houses in my [opinion] were no pleasure, it is absolutely essential that they should exist for the sake of the decorations. You can realize how expensive they would be to buy, while it would be impossible to do without them. I cannot submit to the architects spending every penny on the house until such a point as this has been met."
>
> Please tell Mr. McKim that this is absolutely essential. The green house *must* be provided for. It is in this, as in other matters, the first requisite that we shall have comfort and conveniences in the needs of our life in the White House. If the architectural business cannot be made to subserve these, then it must be sacrificed without a moment's hesitation. Please take this up at once. The green houses must not be torn down, unless provision as above outlined can be made. We do not need anything like the present amount of room in green houses, but we want good green houses with ample provisions for plants sufficient to decorate the mansion. I have no doubt that we can do with a fifth of the space now occupied; but that fifth is essential.
>
> Sincerely yours,
> Theodore Roosevelt
>
> I desire the present green houses kept unless the needed provision can be made. [Handwritten postscript.]

The impasse eventually was solved by McKim, who had one of the most modern of the existing greenhouses carefully taken down and reerected at the propagating grounds of the Botanic Gardens. He also withheld $6,000 from the expenditures during this process, so that if a catastrophe occurred, a new greenhouse of suitable size could be provided.

The east terrace erected by Jefferson had been removed in 1869. Excavation revealed that its foundations were buried under Alfred Mullett's regrading. Still strong, they served as the base for an arcade connecting the White House to a new public entrance at the basement level. The pavilion at the end consisted of a porte-cochère, a large vestibule, and a guardroom. In this new wing more than 500 people could be accommodated.

Fig. 139 The old west terrace revealed after the conservatories were removed, 1902.

Fig. 140 The east portico erected in 1902 on the 1805 foundations.

An inspired innovation of the architects was the use of some of the basement for reception rooms. The removal of dozens of utility pipes from the ceiling of the long hall revealed once more the fine groined vaulting designed by Hoban. New service lines were buried under the cellar floor. More than half the basement on the east side was made available for the use of guests. Dressing rooms with toilets were installed, and the oval room opening at ground level on the south was made into a reception area for distinguished visitors. The displaced household service rooms were relocated in the west terrace.

By July 24, the old first-floor interiors of the White House had been removed, and the heavy beams which had supported the first floor since 1816 were hauled off to the city dump. New masonry and steel replaced them.

All the rooms on the first floor had to be rebuilt. McKim expressly stated that "the [new] work should represent the period to which the house belongs architecturally" and that "a return to the original design . . . will serve every use intended for many years to come." In carrying out the project, however, entirely different decorative schemes were introduced. Before 1902, most of the structure and woodwork dated from 1817. It seems inconsistent to have replaced almost everything with designs fifty to a hundred years older than the house itself, but the architects felt impelled to "improve" on the original, contrary to their stated objective.

The State Dining Room was enlarged by extending it into the main corridor, eliminating the grand staircase and a partition. Since a bedroom on the upper floor was supported by this partition, an ingenious bridge-truss was hung inside the wall to suspend the second floor.

The enlarged State Dining Room was decorated in a mixture of English styles from 1660 to 1750, hardly ever seen in America. With its dark oak paneling and silver chandelier and sconces, it reflected the taste of Charles II.

The two original fireplaces were considered too small for the scale of the new larger room. They were relocated in the Red and Green Rooms, where similar 1817 mantelpieces had been removed by 1853.

The new East Room, stripped of Grant's beams and columns, was designed in a later eighteenth-century style; the doorways hint of the Chinese motif made popular by William Chambers.

McKim's entrance hall would have been exactly right for a prosperous bank of 1900, although this area should have been the easiest to restore to Hoban's original design. His Ionic columns, arched doorways, and niches were still intact. So was some original egg-and-dart molding around the ceiling. But the whole was changed from delicate Ionic to ponderous Doric: the graceful, simple arches were replaced by a heavy, straight entablature with decorated metopes, and a puzzling substitution of paired columns for Hoban's single set was made.

The Blue Room was provided with a new fireplace of early nineteenth-century design; the supports for its mantelshelf consisted of bundled arrows in white and gilt marble.

The Family Dining Room, redecorated with a cross-vaulted ceiling and new paneling in plaster above wood wainscoting, was remarkably similar to a room at Lucan, the Irish house which probably inspired Hoban's oval room.

After making the old elevator shaft fireproof, a new car was installed. Some of its oak woodwork was carved from roof beams of the Old South Meeting House in

Fig. 141 The enlarged State Dining Room, 1902.

Fig. 142 State Dining Room mantelpiece.

Fig. 143 McKim, Mead & White's East Room.

141

142

143

145

144

Fig. 144 The robust Georgian ceiling design for the East Room, 1902.

Fig. 145 An East Room fireplace, 1904.

Boston, beneath which the Boston Tea Party was plotted. This was an ironic gesture, considering that several wagonloads of equally historic timbers from the White House itself had just been thrown away.

The project was a masterpiece of organization, coordination, and execution, although some of the hurried decisions and compromises made as the work progressed probably contributed to the difficulties found in 1948. The executive offices were completed September 30, well under the President's deadline. The family floor was finished on November 4, and a Cabinet dinner was held in the State Dining Room on the first floor on December 18. Staring down on the admiring

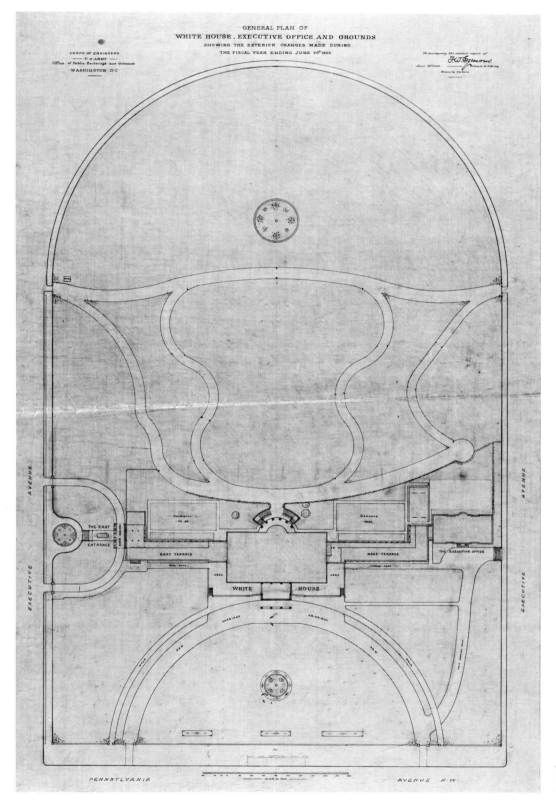

Fig. 146 Plan of the White House grounds after the extensions of 1902.

assembly were the glass eyes of heads of game, bought from a New York taxidermist for $2,000. In later times, it was assumed that Roosevelt had bagged the animals himself.

Norcross Brothers had done the structural work; Herter Bros. and L. Marcotte & Co., both of New York, made and installed the woodwork and basic interior decoration. The latter also furnished the East Room and the Blue Room. A. H. Davenport Co. of New York and Boston supplied furniture for the Executive Offices, the State Dining Room, Family Dining Room, and the four bedrooms created from the old offices over the East Room. Many others supplied chimneypieces, rugs, chandeliers, and hundreds of other small items.

After the work was complete, the meticulous McKim sent a note to Colonel Bingham recommending that "one or two men, two or three times per month, clean, wax and polish the wood floors. The new stone floor in the hall will show dust unless it receives careful attention on the part of the house servants." Only a man who would write such a note could have performed more than the contract called for, completed most of the work a month earlier than expected, and brought the project to a close for less than the budget allowed.

In his report to Congress in 1903, President Roosevelt said:

> Through a wise provision of the Congress at its last session the White House, which had become disfigured by incongruous additions and changes, has now been restored to what it was planned to be by Washington. In making the restorations the utmost care has been exercised to come as near as possible to the early plans and to supplement these plans by a careful study of such buildings as that of the University of Virginia, which was built by Jefferson. The White House is the property of the nation, and so far as is compatible with living therein it should be kept as it originally was, for the same reasons that we keep Mount Vernon as it originally was. The stately simplicity of its architecture is an expression of the character of the period in which it was built, and is in accord with the purposes it was designed to serve. It is a good thing to preserve such buildings as historic monuments which keep alive our sense of continuity with the nation's past.

The principle stated by the President in 1903 served as a manifesto for the major restoration programs at the White House from that time forward. Unfortunately, this noble objective was not always carried out with the "utmost care" that Roosevelt intended.

Twelve

Twentieth-Century Renascence

After the completion of the renovation of 1902, government storehouses were filled with the great mass of interior ornament and furniture removed from the White House. With the President's permission, the old building materials and fixtures were sold at public auction, by C. G. Sloan & Co., on January 21, 1903. This sale of 28 wagonloads of White House property was the largest of its kind ever held, exceeding Chester Arthur's disposal of 24 wagonloads. Included were six glass doors and iron parts of T. U. Walter's entrance-hall screen of 1853, which were found in the attic; the entire Tiffany screen of stained glass which replaced it in 1882; the four East Room fireplaces and mirrors and the four columns which held up the beams installed there in the Grant redecoration of 1873; three window grilles from the Blue Room, chosen by Mrs. Harrison; and a vast quantity of furniture, lighting fixtures, and miscellany. The Tiffany screen was sold to Turner A. Wickersham, for $275, the highest price of the sale. Mr. Wickersham, a real estate agent for the Chesapeake Beach Railway, developer of a resort 30 miles east of Washington, was determined to get it and had been willing to pay any price necessary. The Tiffany screen probably ended its days in the Belvedere Hotel at Chesapeake Beach, Maryland; the building burned to the ground in 1923. Everything else sold for ridiculously low prices and the sale netted only $2,641.88 for the government.

In 1905, a sale of White House office furniture was held. Many pieces were bought directly by former Cabinet members and other officials because of sentimental association with the offices they had occupied.

President Taft, in 1909, took the first step toward making the "temporary" offices permanent. The west pavilion was nearly doubled in size, according to plans prepared by Nathan C. Wyeth. The new addition, like the original wing, had a curved bay in the center of the south front echoing the appearance of the White House; but in the later plan, the curve contained a new "oval office" for the President.

During the following administration, Mrs. Wilson made the first tentative intrusion of the family quarters into the large attic, then used only for storage. A few additional bedrooms were built there.

147

Upon assuming the Presidency in 1923 after the death of Harding, Calvin Coolidge received a report from the Office of Public Parks and Buildings that the White House roof was unsound. He brushed off the possible danger, saying that there were plenty of others willing to take the risk of living beneath it. By 1927, however, further studies had made replacement clearly mandatory, and the Coolidges moved to a house on Dupont Circle while repairs went on.

Since the basic structure had to be replaced, it was an exceptional opportunity to expand the still modest Presidential living quarters by converting the attic to a penthouse, nearly doubling private living space. William A. Delano, a New York architect, advised on the project. After a temporary arched roof was built over the entire area, the old roof and the attic floor were removed. Steel beams and trusses resting on the masonry walls and bearing partitions were installed to support the second-floor ceiling and the new third floor, containing bedrooms, baths, a solarium, and numerous rooms for service and housekeeping. The new addition could hardly be detected from the ground, but it extended the President's quarters by eighteen rooms.

Fire damaged the Executive Offices in 1929. President Hoover operated from the White House and the State, War, and Navy Building while repairs were made.

Mrs. Coolidge persuaded Congress to permit the White House to accept gifts of appropriate furnishings. Later, Mrs. Hoover and Mrs. Eisenhower encouraged such donations, and several pieces of antique furniture were added to the White House collection.

The New Deal policies of Franklin D. Roosevelt automatically increased the Executive Office staff; in 1934, the west wing was again enlarged. Office space was developed in the basement, and that floor was also extended to the south under the lawn. See Plate 23. To provide light, West Executive Avenue was lowered, and a light well opened in the center of the underground area. The Oval Office was relocated to a more favored view, at the southeast corner of the expanded building. A low penthouse completed the additions, heeding the admonition of Charles F.

Fig. 147 Aerial view of the White House in the 1930s. The rooflines show Taft's doubling of the Executive Office Building, and the 1927 third floor on the White House.

148

149

150

Fig. 148 A temporary arched roof covered the White House while the third floor was under construction in 1927.

Fig. 149 The 1927 third floor in a 1949 photograph.

Fig. 150 President Roosevelt's enlargement of the Executive Offices, 1934.

McKim not to add height to the offices which would detract from the dominance of the White House.

In the last month of 1941, the United States declared war on Germany and Japan. Almost immediately, partly for security reasons, White House architect Lorenzo W. Winslow greatly enlarged the east portico. The lengthened pavilion provided a reception room in addition to the vestibule, larger quarters for the security staff, a bomb shelter, and an extended porte-cochère to accommodate six to eight cars, rather than only three. Office space was provided in a second floor above, giving Eleanor Roosevelt, a very active First Lady, sufficient room for her staff.

Each successive architect of the east portico seems to have been impelled to alter the exact order of coupled and single columns used by his predecessor, while retaining a general resemblance to the earlier version. A comparison of the 1869, 1902, and 1942 variations shows that the next architect will be hard put to find a new combination.

When Harry S Truman became President he felt that the White House staff, greatly expanded by the war, was again overcrowded. In early 1946 Lorenzo W. Winslow presented plans for another enlargement of the Executive Office wing. The new scheme not only proposed a long extension to the south, but added another story to the existing building. Congress refused approval, primarily because of its $1,650,000 cost. Thus the White House narrowly escaped an appendage potentially as ugly as the old conservatories. Two years later the President announced plans to build a balcony on the South Portico, to which the Commission of Fine Arts voiced strong objection. Since its opinion was advisory and not binding, the President decided to proceed anyway. The $15,000 cost did not require an appropriation, so that Congress was also helpless, in spite of general public opposition. *The New York Times* noted that the White House was a national shrine, temporarily held in trust by the President and occupied on sufferance. Truman was urged to take second thought on an alteration of such historic significance. The construction of the balcony was justified not because the President would like to sit on it, but because Jefferson's colonnade was disproportionate. Besides, the balcony would support neat wooden-slat awnings to cool the Blue Room, instead of the conventional canvas variety.

The President's record for backing down never was extensive, and the balcony remains today. W. A. Delano's plain slab is tightly crowded between the pediments of the first-floor windows and the console brackets of those above.

In June 1946 signs appeared that the structure of the White House was rapidly weakening. The first floor was safe enough, having been set on steel and concrete by McKim, Mead & White in 1902. The third floor was suspended by steel framing in the 1927 reconstruction. The second floor, however, was still supported on wooden beams set in place by James Hoban in 1816. Utilities added to the building over the years had been installed at times by thoughtless workmen; beams were cut into as much as 5 inches, and outside walls were channeled with little regard to the effects on their load-bearing capacity. The President became aware of this when a hole in the second-floor corridor was being repaired. He wrote to his mother that it looked like they intended to hang a murderer in the White House hallway.

Margaret Truman has observed that her father saw an East Room chandelier swinging as a color guard marched across the floor. Later he felt vibrations and swaying of the floor in his study.

Plate 23 Exterior of the Oval Office.

Plate 24 The entrance hall was rebuilt in a simplified version of Charles McKim's design of 1902.

26

27

28

Plate 25 The Green Room was magnificently redecorated in 1971.

Plate 26 Early nineteenth-century wallpaper, "Scenic America," was donated for the Diplomatic Reception Room, 1961.

Plate 27 A pier table by Bellangé of Paris was retrieved from storage and returned to the Blue Room.

Plate 28 A private dining room was created on the second floor during the Kennedy administration.

Plate 29 In 1972, a mantelpiece with herm columns, similar to those in the Red and Green Rooms, was acquired for the Blue Room. The chandelier was previously hung in the Yellow Oval Room.

Plate 30 This Italian marble mantelpiece is one of a pair installed after the fire of 1814 in the old State Dining Room. In 1902, it was moved to the Green Room.

Plate 31 An outstanding collection of Empire furniture by Charles Honoré Lannuier has been assembled for the Red Room.

Plate 32 The bow windows of the Blue Room form one of the most beautiful architectural features of the White House.

Plate 33 The State Dining Room.

Plate 34 The Family Dining Room was given its present appearance by McKim, Mead & White in 1902. A French mantel was added in 1962.

29

31

30

32

33

34

35

Plate 35 The Yellow Oval Room is the focal point of the second-floor living area.

Plate 36 The East Room: McKim's elaborate Georgian detail was subdued in Winslow's redesign of 1952.

36

Plate 37 The Lincoln Sitting Room. James Hoban's desk stands before the window.

Plate 38 The Queens' Bedroom has been occupied by several reigning Queens, but Winston Churchill and V. M. Molotov also stayed here.

Plate 39 The Lincoln Bedroom is decorated in mid-Victorian style. Much of the furniture was bought by Mrs. Lincoln.

37

38

39

40

Plate 40 President Carter has chosen the *Resolute* desk for his Oval Office.

151

152

Fig. 151 The enlarged east portico designed by Lorenzo W. Winslow in 1942.

Fig. 152 Model of a rejected extension of the Executive Offices, 1946.

Fig. 153 The South Portico with President Truman's balcony.

153

Fig. 154 Beams carelessly cut caused much of the weakness found in the White House in 1948.

The President asked the Commissioner of Public Buildings to investigate these incidents. His office found suspiciously cracked plaster and sagging ceilings and recommended an exploratory study. In February 1948 a committee of distinguished engineers was formed, with an appropriation of $50,000 to make a thorough structural survey. By September, the experts concluded that problems were not confined to the second floor; the fundamental cause was the settling of the interior brick bearing partitions. Their footings stood on a clay base containing small amounts of organic matter, permitting long-term slow compression. The heavy third-floor structure put an overload on the outside walls as well. The committee recommended that the interior of the building should be supported on an independent frame, standing on a safe sand-and-gravel stratum 20 feet beneath the clay.

The report raised serious questions as to the President's safety. For a while, the First Family lived among a forest of temporary supports. One of the legs of Margaret Truman's piano broke through the floor in the summer of 1948. By November, the White House architect and the engineers had closed the East Room and advised the President to move out.

Of several alternatives, it was decided to retain the exterior walls, with new underpinnings, and reconstruct the entire interior. The President moved to Blair House, across the street. The Commissioner of Public Buildings presented a detailed report on February 7, 1949, estimating the cost of reconstruction at $5,412,000. Funds were promptly made available to the Federal Works Agency, but the President, noting the magnitude of the undertaking, preferred that a Commission on the Renovation of the Executive Mansion oversee the project, to ensure that all its aspects—historical, aesthetic, and sentimental, as well as engineering and architectural—be adequately protected. On April 14, 1949, the Commission was established by Congress, comprising two senators appointed by the President of the Senate; two representatives appointed by the Speaker of the House; and two other members. The President requested Richard E. Dougherty, president of the American Society of Civil Engineers, and Douglas W. Orr, president of the American Institute of Architects, to serve as the public members. Distinguished consultants advising the Commission included William A. Delano, architect, the consultant for the third-floor reconstruction of 1927, and engineers Emil H. Praeger and Ernest E. Howard.

In the meantime, Lorenzo W. Winslow and his associates made measured drawings of the interior, showing the house as it appeared prior to reconstruction. Abbie Rowe, the White House photographer, also took pictures of every part of the building. Photographs of the empty White House show that mixed with and underneath later decoration much of the 1817 material remained. A wealth of historical information clung to the surfaces, awaiting recognition, but retention of samples for future study was minimal. A small amount of material was left with the White House staff; and surplus mantelpieces and some ornamental plaster were offered to a selected list of museums, but few accepted. Some of the best of the work which was removed and replaced, including a section of the East Room, is now installed in the First Ladies Hall at the Smithsonian Institution. Original White House furniture, fixtures, rugs, and ornaments decorate the room settings. Small pieces of wallcoverings and fabrics found beneath the current layers are also on display there.

155

156

157

Fig. 155 Abbie Rowe photographed the entire exterior from this crane in 1949.

Fig. 156 Looking down on the South Portico from the crane.

Fig. 157 In the empty White House, the beauty of its woodwork could be appreciated. The State Dining Room, 1949.

158

159

160

161

Fig. 158 Hoban's second-floor window frame and decorative brackets.

Fig. 159 The center window of the East Room opened upon the terrace built in 1902.

Fig. 160 Double doors separated the kitchen and service rooms from the reception areas in the restored ground-floor corridor of 1902. A 1949 photograph.

Fig. 161 The Green Room walls had been covered in fabric since the 1890s. Beneath were remnants of frescos applied in the mid-nineteenth century.

164

162

163

165

Fig. 162 In the Family Dining Room, 1817 shutters and window trim were still in place in 1949.

Fig. 163 The Grand Staircase of the White House closely resembled its counterpart at Leinster House, Dublin.

Fig. 164 Demolition of McKim's entrance hall revealed Hoban's original cornice with an egg-and-dart molding.

Fig. 165 The second-floor center hall. A legend on the wall reads: "Note: 1817 cornice left in place at time of 1902 remodelling. 1902 maple floor laid over original floor const."

When work began on December 12, 1949, the first phase was to secure the outer walls. As the interior was removed, temporary steel bracing was immediately installed, stabilizing the remaining structure and supporting the roof. To run footings to a depth more than 20 feet below the old foundations, the clay substrate was excavated in 4-foot sections. New footings constructed under the existing wall were extended for a new steel frame. This process was repeated 126 times until the whole wall was standing on its new, lower foundation. The depth of the new footings became a distinct advantage; the entire area inside the house could now be lowered 20 feet, providing two levels of subbasement for heating, air conditioning, plumbing, electric wiring, communications, and other equipment. Excavation was also extended under the North Portico and the front lawn for air conditioning compressors and shops.

By February 17, 1950, the interior had been dismantled. Woodwork and ornament intended for reinstallation was carefully removed and stored. Material not being reused was sent to Fort Myer, Virginia, for temporary storage.

Erection of the permanent frame was begun in May and completed by December. A complex system of utilities was installed, and new partitions were constructed, duplicating those of 1817. Some of the structure of the 1927 third floor, being of sound fireproof material, was retained, but the interior was entirely renovated.

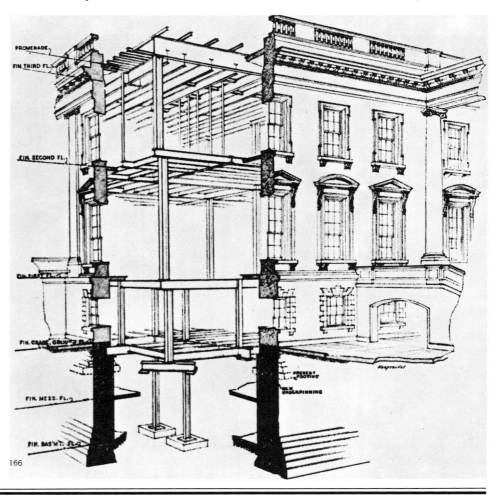

166

167

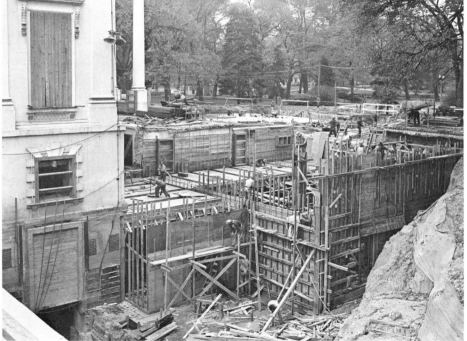

168

Fig. 166 Underpinning and steel frame system, 1950 renovation.

Fig. 167 A forest of temporary steel supported the walls as the basement was lowered 20 feet.

Fig. 168 The new, deeper basement extended under the north driveway and lawn. This area contained air conditioning equipment.

War in Korea had begun in June 1950; the effect of military priorities and an escalation of prices increased the estimates and lengthened the schedule. It was clear that the original appropriation would no longer cover the costs. The budget was twice revised, bringing the total to $5,761,000.

In March 1951 the general plan of interior decoration was approved. Some changes, such as the decision to paint the State Dining Room, were made later, but the detail work now proceeded according to drawings prepared by Lorenzo W. Winslow and his staff. The Commission of Fine Arts visited the building on July 19, and unanimously approved the architectural plans. On August 17 another meeting of the Commission was held to consider the interior decoration proposed by B. Altman & Co., which was also approved. A severe shortage of trained floor-layers had developed because of the war, and several months passed before the flooring, much of it parquet, was installed satisfactorily.

169

170

Fig. 169 The redesign of the third floor provided a broad promenade around the building.

Fig. 170 The solarium, 1951. The roofs of the Oval Office and the Executive Office Building appear in the background.

Fig. 171 Ground-floor plan after rebuilding, 1952. The "restored" kitchen was used as a broadcasting room.

Fig. 172 The first-floor plan brought the stairway into the entrance hall instead of the corridor.

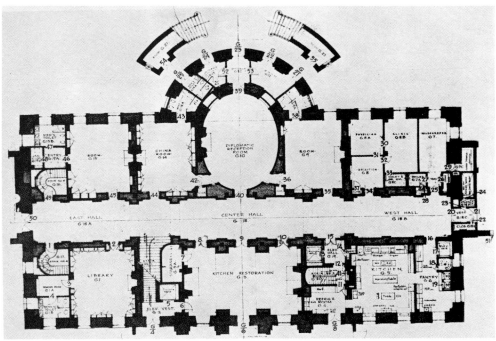

171

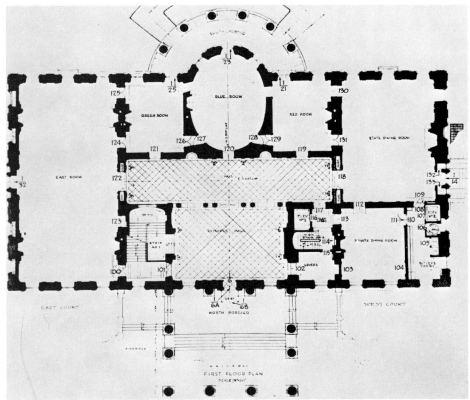

172

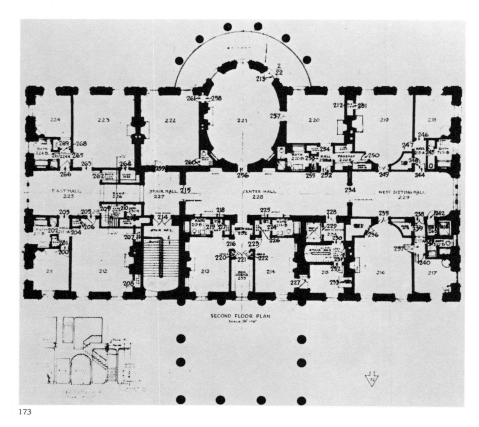

173

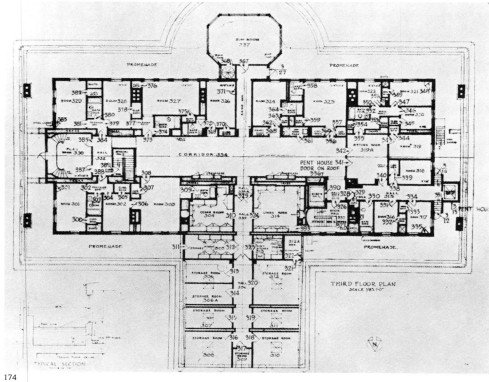

174

175

176

Fig. 173 Second-floor plan, 1952. In 1961, room 216 became the private dining room. Room 222 is now the Treaty Room.

Fig. 174 The remodeled third floor. In addition to new family bedrooms and sitting rooms, there is a large storage area.

Fig. 175 Decorator's sketch of the second-floor sitting room, 1951.

Fig. 176 Proposed refurnishing of the Red Room.

Fig. 177 The Green Room, as reconstructed and furnished, 1952.

The patient President was consulted from time to time, and in January 1952 asked that work be completed by April 1. The Commission, headed by Senator McKellar, was greatly pleased to advise the President on March 27 that the building was again ready for occupancy.

Periodic readings of reference marks on the walls showed that throughout the project the settling of the building on its new foundation had amounted to less than one-third of an inch.

While not every feature of the renovated White House met with the approval of all historians, preservationists, and architects, the engineering, with all the limitations imposed, was performed almost perfectly. There are reports by later administrations of the independent spirit the air conditioning system seems to have, but at least the structure is safe and nearly indestructible.

The replacement of the wooden frame by steel and concrete should have solved another problem that had persisted since 1800—recurring infestation by rats and mice. It was thought, in Jefferson's day, that the rats came from the stables. Through the years there are frequent letters, contracts, and purchases to rid the building of them. Mrs. Harrison's campaign, which involved complete renovation of the basement, was probably the most successful, but the persistent creatures continued to make "news" as late as 1977.

In 1902, one of the Washington papers carried a small story about the rat problem; no doubt the reconstruction stirred them up. Papers in other cities repeated the story, and soon suggestions from the whole country landed on Colonel Bingham's desk. A man in Beverly, Massachusetts, shipped six cats, each with a name of a former Beverly mayor on white ribbon around its neck. Massachusetts cats, he said, were especially good at that sort of job. A company offered its patented "Smithereen" Exterminator. While Colonel Bingham's responses were calm and understated, apparently the problem was serious. Finally, a man with ferrets and dogs was hired for $25 a night; it took only two nights to relieve the situation.

When the Trumans moved into the White House, Mrs. Roosevelt tactfully told Mrs. Truman about mice strolling along railings and up the draperies, while guests at tea tried to look at something else. In 1977, the pesky creatures were even seen in the Oval Office. The President urgently requested the General Services Administration to do something, and an exterminator was put to work. The population diminished, but one or more had the poor taste to expire in the wall of the President's office. The President once more asked for action, but the GSA declined, as its responsibility ended at the inside wall. The Park Service said its ended on the outside wall. The President expressed his opinion in no uncertain terms, after which appropriate services were performed. The mice are probably amused that architectural improvements actually facilitate their ability to move about. In the old building, sleepers on the basement floor and lack of masonry firestopping gave them literally the run of the house. Now, the multiplicity of ducts, conduits, and pipes in a steel and concrete building makes communication just as easy.

The architects and decorators of 1951–1952 were no doubt well-intentioned and sincere in their intent to create "faithful architectural reproductions of the original rooms as to finishes, details and arrangement," but the operative word seems to be "reproduction." Two Italian mantelpieces of 1817 are in the Red and Green Rooms, and one is in a bedroom; all the other mantels were replaced.

McKim's East Room was subjected to "a detailed redesign, the spirit being retained . . . a certain gentle simplification of its former bold high-relief having been worked out." The chandeliers were shortened in this process.

The Green and Red Rooms were given cornices of "original Hoban design to which has been added a delicate Greek fret." Over the Red Room fireplace hung a portrait of Theodore Roosevelt, "by Sargeant." The Blue Room retained the mantel bought by Stanford White in 1902. The walls were covered with blue and gold silk.

Oak paneling of the State Dining Room was painted pale green, giving the room (which can seat 130 people) "intimacy somewhat lacking before."

The Family Dining Room was carefully restored to the appearance of the 1902 McKim design. It contained "an actual chandelier in that it is not wired for electricity but furnishes light by means of candles."

The quotations, from the *Report of the Commission on the Renovation of the Executive Mansion* (1952), show that a "basic concept" of the renovation was conscientiously observed: "Due consideration will be given . . . to the elemination of present minor features the natures or general motifs of which are inconsistent with the periodicity or general motifs of the rooms in which they appear." It seems the interiors were now to be as bland as possible.

The walls of 1817 still stood in 1952, but the project was not a restoration in any sense. While the structural replacement was an outstanding engineering success, from a preservationist's viewpoint the rebuilding was the greatest calamity to befall the President's House since the fire of 1814. The lack of attention to archaeological and historical analysis and the callous disposal of important architectural elements is difficult to excuse.

By 1948, Colonial Williamsburg had been essentially completed, establishing precedents and techniques for careful documentation, research, and restoration. Regional preservation groups were very active. Monticello, Mount Vernon, and other great national shrines had received sensitive and sympathetic treatment. A scholarly and accurate restoration of the principal rooms, at least, could have been easily achieved. They had been engraved, photographed, and described hundreds of times during the nineteenth century. Instead, redesign of the 1902 interiors and almost total replacement of the original wood trim and plasterwork was considered more appropriate.

The "restorers" seemed determined to obliterate the remains of the original house. Bricks, doors, and flooring sent to Fort Myer were reused there. Other material went to Fort Belvoir for "training purposes." Old metal was reused for the District of Columbia jails, and 95,000 bricks were given to Mount Vernon.

Ornamental plaster and woodwork, sections of wall, bricks, innumerable details of hardware, and beams were cut into small pieces for "souvenir kits," which netted only $10,000 to the Treasury. Combustible material was burned, and the balance mixed with other rubble so that "its identity is no longer determinable." So the last of the old interiors ended, in dismemberment, cremation, and final burial in a potter's field.

The Eisenhowers inherited a brand-new house. See Plate 24. Completeness of the rebuilding and furnishing a year earlier left little to do. In 1956 an incomparable collection of vermeil was bequeathed to the White House by Margaret Thompson Biddle. It is displayed in one of the ground-floor rooms otherwise used only during large receptions. The Diplomatic Reception Room opening on the south lawn was appropriately redecorated four years later as a gift to the White House. (See Plate 25.)

The contributions of the Kennedy administration began even before the inauguration, with an announcement of Mrs. Kennedy's hope to improve and extend the quality and quantity of works of art at the White House. This idea, once the family had moved in, expanded to a far greater program.

Because of the constant change of administrations, the White House lacked a permanent collection of the amenities for comfortable living. Fine art, good furniture, a library, and countless small things that a good home acquires over a lifetime were absent. The building had many historic pieces, and some gifts of fine antique furniture, but it looked like, and in a sense was, a hotel for distinguished transients. The Eisenhowers ate private meals in the center hall of the second floor from trays brought from below, rather than face the cold formality of dining alone in one of the great rooms. Mrs. Kennedy planned to change this impersonal and impermanent feeling.

The recent renovation had made no attempt to recreate the decorative effect intended by our early Presidents, all of whom were perceptive and knowledgeable in the arts. In 1960, the decor was "American Presidential," replete with eagles, patterns of the seal of the United States, and other symbolic paraphernalia on walls, cornices, draperies, and upholstery. Mrs. Kennedy believed the appearance of the interior should reflect the history of the house—each room an example of a period of good taste and interesting style in its evolution.

At the close of the Truman administration the White House contained many reproductions of period furniture, supplied by L. Marcotte & Co., A. H. Davenport,

W. & J. Sloane, and W. B. Moses & Sons in 1902, and B. Altman & Co. in 1952. Except in areas where public use was too great for antique furniture, most of these would be replaced with original pieces typical of the earlier furnishings. Only a few dozen items of 1817 to 1830 White House furniture still existed. Actual restoration of the rooms was now quite impossible. Besides, scholarly analysis of period rooms has shown that their arrangement is not compatible with modern usage. A re-creation of the spirit of the time, using antique pieces arranged for today's social patterns, is a better compromise for a house that is both a museum and a home.

To implement Mrs. Kennedy's plan a curator was obviously necessary, but there was no provision for such a position at the White House. Mrs. John N. Pearce, the first curator, was therefore employed by the Smithsonian, but assigned to the White House. She undertook the formidable task of cataloging the furniture and other articles not only in the rooms, but in the attic, basement, and warehouses, to locate pieces of historic and artistic value. The best, such as the Bellangé pier table acquired by Monroe, were repaired and used. (See Plate 27.) An effort was made to trace items sold by indifferent administrations prior to the conservation restrictions; some of these were found and returned to the White House by loan, gift, or purchase.

A $100,000 congressional appropriation was available for a redecoration. Mrs. Henry Parish of New York was an early advisor to Mrs. Kennedy on the selection of color schemes, drapery design, and the many other details needed to transform the rooms to their desired appearance. Existing furniture, pictures, and chandeliers, augmented by some early gifts, were regrouped while a final plan was being developed.

It was evident that the scale of this project would require resources far beyond the limits of the White House staff and budget. Shortly after the inauguration, a Fine Arts Committee for the White House had been organized. Henry F. Dupont of Winterthur agreed to become chairman. Twelve knowledgeable people, some amateur and some professional, also served as members. Subcommittees were formed for special purposes: one on paintings, another for the selection of books for a White House library.

The National Park Service, responsible for the care of the White House, is authorized to establish nonprofit cooperating associations for the sale or free dissemination of educational material at national parks, historic sites, and national monuments. Since President Kennedy did not feel that the White House should be declared a National Monument, with all the impediments that status involved, special legislation was passed defining the museum-like character of parts of the building and linking these areas to administration by the Park Service. The Act permitted the White House Historical Association to be organized, November 3, 1961, primarily to publish and sell guidebooks to benefit the restoration programs. This it has done most successfully.

In early days, Presidents ate privately in the Family Dining Room on the first floor, in effect meeting the food halfway on its long trip from the basement kitchen. After trying the Eisenhower's tray system upstairs, President and Mrs. Kennedy felt that an intimate dining room with a small kitchen attached should be part of the private quarters on the second floor. A bedroom was converted for the purpose, and the bathroom next to it became the new kitchen. (See Plate 28.)

Gradually, with the help of many experts and many generous donations, the process of re-creating or improving the State Rooms and the family quarters was completed. In a second-floor room where Cabinet meetings were held in the late nineteenth century, Grant's Cabinet table and other Grant furniture and late Victorian furnishings were assembled. A chandelier bought by Grant for the East Room was retrieved from a Capitol corridor adjacent the Senate. Framed facsimiles of treaties were placed on the walls, which were covered with green-velvet flocked paper and a geometric border. The "Treaty Room" now serves as a private meeting room for the President or the First Lady.

Mrs. Pearce served as curator from March 1961 to the summer of 1962, when she retired to private life. During her tenure, she prepared the text of the first edition of *The White House: An Historic Guide.* William Elder succeeded Mrs. Pearce, but resigned a year later to accept another position. James R. Ketchum, then registrar for the White House, replaced Elder as curator. Mr. Ketchum became curator of the Senate in 1970.

On November 2, 1963, Mrs. Kennedy wrote to Clark Clifford, "—the White House is as it should be—it is all I ever dreamed for it—," a fitting stopping point for a most imaginative and appropriate rehabilitation and re-creation of the White House interior. Little architectural alteration had been attempted, but the decoration was superior to any since the days of James Monroe. Valuable furniture and fine art of museum quality had been acquired by gift or purchase, yet no funds except the routine appropriation came from the government. At Mrs. Kennedy's invitation, hundreds of interested people had contributed talent, time, and money to ensure the success of the project. The organizational basis for a continuing program completed this personal gift to the house and to the nation.

After the tragedy in Dallas, the Johnsons, like the Eisenhowers, came to a newly finished house. Only a few administrative loose ends of the Kennedy program remained undone. During her first few weeks in the White House, Mrs. Johnson discussed these technical matters with Clark Clifford, a distinguished Washington lawyer. Some of the Kennedy committees had no legal authorization for a continued existence; only the White House Historical Association was a duly constituted nonprofit organization. Mrs. Johnson felt that other safeguards should assure the permanence of the curator's position, and the continuity of outside advice on the arts.

Clifford suggested that the President issue an Executive Order to create a Committee on the Preservation of the White House, and the office of Curator of the White House. Some of Mrs. Kennedy's earlier groups, having completed their work, would be allowed to lapse. The new committee would have a broad cross section of representation and expert opinion. Its members would include a designated officer of the Commission of Fine Arts, National Gallery of Art, National Park Service, Smithsonian Institution, the White House (represented by the First Lady, the Curator, the Chief Usher), and several public members. The President approved these recommendations and issued an Executive Order in 1964 implementing them.

Mrs. Paul Mellon had in 1962 redesigned nondescript areas south of the two arcades into delightful gardens, which were completed a few years later. Mrs. Johnson named the garden to the east for Jacqueline Kennedy in 1965. It is used as an informal outdoor reception area by the First Lady in the same way that the Rose Garden is used by the President.

In 1965, a portable stage for the East Room was contributed by a generous donor. The reddish marble mantelpieces and baseboards in the same room, considered incompatible with the white and gold color scheme, had been painted off-white during the Kennedy administration. Mrs. Johnson hoped to replace the red marble with white, but the hope was never realized.

No longer do guests of the White House cut off draperies or slit panels of upholstery from the chairs and sofas as souvenirs, but the principal rooms are still subject to unbelievable wear. In addition to the thousands who attend official functions each year, the 1,500,000 sightseeing visitors add to the burden of maintenance. After a Presidential term, a general renovation is required, and it has been the custom for Congress to provide an appropriation for this purpose to each new administration. When President and Mrs. Nixon occupied the house in 1969, the regular renewal was begun.

In 1970, Clement E. Conger, deputy chief of protocol, chairman of the fine arts committee of the Department of State, and curator of the Diplomatic Reception Rooms, was asked to take the responsibility for the White House as well. Mrs. Nixon, Mr. Conger, and the other members of the Committee for the Preservation of the White House developed a long-range plan to make the public areas protected by the Act of 1961 a living museum of American period furniture and fine art. The fundamental purpose of this project was to make unnecessary any extensive restoration in the future. By a day-to-day program of maintenance and repair, the furnishings are kept in excellent condition. An emergency supply of high-quality antique chairs, tables, and other objects is available to replace those accidentally damaged, or undergoing reupholstering and refinishing.

The architectural detail installed in the period 1950–1952 has been restudied. Cornices, dadoes, plaster ornamentation, mantelpieces, and other elements dating from the Truman rebuilding have been replaced in several rooms according to authentic period designs. Wherever possible examples of the local idiom have been used, from mansions of the same age as the White House in the District of Columbia, nearby Virginia, or Maryland.

The permanent collection of fine art in the White House is modest in quantity, but of excellent quality. It is slowly being augmented by purchases and gifts as suitable pictures, and the money to buy them, become available. A special effort to find missing items in incomplete series, such as portraits of the First Ladies, has been initiated. Eight wives of the Presidents and four nineteenth-century Presidents are still not represented in the collection of life portraits.

The success of the present system can be measured by the relative ease and serenity of transition in the last two administrations. It is expected that the interests of the President and his family should be accommodated in the personal quarters and the Presidential offices, and for both President and Mrs. Ford and President and Mrs. Carter these changes were provided. In the public areas no significant alterations were either necessary or desired.

During the 1970s several major rooms, including the reception and museum rooms on the ground floor, all the State Rooms on the first floor, and the principal rooms of the living quarters above, have been redecorated and to some extent redesigned to clarify their architectural and decorative integrity.

In 1925 the Green Room has been decorated in the American Federal style for the first time since Jackson's administration, using modern reproductions. It was the first area of the White House to receive the attention of the Kennedy Fine Arts Committee in 1961, when original Federal period furniture was secured for the room. Green damask hung on the walls in 1952 was allowed to remain until 1962, when it was replaced with moss-green watered silk. The rug, bought in 1927, was the last item designed for the White House by the Tiffany Studios. Redecoration of the Green Room in 1971 included the addition of several pieces of furniture by Duncan Phyfe and elegant green and coral draperies under wood cornices of coral and gilt, each surmounted by an eagle. The drapery design is based on a document of approximately 1815. (See Plates 26 and 30.)

The Red Room was decorated in 1961–1962 in the Empire style. The French and American furniture includes some excellent examples of work by Charles Honoré Lannuier. The walls were covered in cerise silk and the same color was used for the upholstery. In the 1972 refurbishing, the collection of Empire furniture was substantially enlarged. The wallcovering was changed to the shade of red shown on the back of the chair in Mrs. Madison's portrait by Gilbert Stuart. The portrait, on loan from the Pennsylvania Academy of Fine Arts, now hangs in the room. (See Plate 31.)

After the rebuilding of 1952, the Blue Room was still furnished with the armchairs, footstools, and shield-back side chairs designed in 1902 by Stanford White. Though inspired by the Bellangé furniture, White's motifs were chosen to harmonize with the fireplace he had selected for the room. Mrs. Kennedy had the extant Bellangé furniture repaired and replaced in the room in 1961, together with copies of the missing pieces, donated by a member of the Adams family. The following year the walls were covered in cream-colored striped satin.

In 1972, architectural changes were made in the Blue Room to agree more closely with local fashion during the administration of James Monroe. Additional furniture in the French Empire style now supplements the Monroe purchases, and a French gilded-wood and crystal chandelier is a spectacular centerpiece. A few more of the dispersed Bellangé chairs have been reacquired. The walls are now papered, as most of the main rooms were, in a French pattern of 1800. The silk-screened borders below the cornice and above the chair rail are so skillfully done that they may well resemble the "fancy painting" which graced the walls in 1817. Elaborate blue and gold draperies in an authentic French pattern frame the windows. (See Plates 29 and 32.)

The design of McKim, Mead & White still prevails in the State Dining Room, but the dark oak paneling is now painted ivory. Mrs. Kennedy had the silver chandelier and sconces gilded to match the Monroe plateau. This bronze-doré centerpiece was made by Denière et Matelin of Paris, about 1817. The draperies are gold damask. In the 1948–1952 rebuilding the McKim mantelpiece was removed and is now in the Truman Library at Independence, Missouri. The Kennedy Fine Arts Committee had the plain bolection molding of 1952 replaced with a replica of the 1902 mantel for sentimental reasons. The older mantel bore an inscription composed by John Adams during his second night in the President's House:

I Pray Heaven to Bestow the Best of Blessings on this House and on All that shall hereafter Inhabit it. May none but Honest and Wise Men ever rule under This Roof.

Furniture in the State Dining Room is largely that designed by Stanford White in 1902, as more fragile antique furniture would be exposed to the danger of accidental breakage. This is the only State Room in the White House where the design has remained essentially intact. (See Plate 33.)

Now used only for small official dinners, the Family Dining Room was originally the larger and more formal of the two provided by Hoban. Prior to 1845, it was reduced in size by the creation of a butler's pantry on the west. The cross-vaulted ceiling and cornice designed and installed in 1902 were reused in 1952. The room was redecorated and refurnished ten years later, when the present mantelpiece was acquired. Most of the furniture, donated during the Kennedy administration, is American Sheraton. (See Plate 34.)

The East Room retains the basic design of McKim, Mead & White as "simplified" by Winslow in 1950. See Plate 36. The furnishings are sparse, consisting principally of benches, torchères, and a Steinway piano presented by the firm in 1938. The 100,000th Steinway piano was given to the room in 1902; it is now in the Smithsonian.

Several rooms on the second floor are noteworthy, although simpler than those on the floor below. The oval sitting room has always been considered one of the most attractive and comfortable in the house. It is the only room for which Abigail Adams had a kind word, and it is still the social center of the President's private quarters. The room is decorated in shades of yellow, with coral and white accents. The marble fireplace and trim are early nineteenth century in style, but the furniture is Louis XVI, a concession to variety and comfort. In 1889 the first White House Christmas tree stood here.

Two guest bedrooms for distinguished visitors are located on the east side of the second floor. Each has a small sitting room. For several decades prior to 1902, this area was used for the President's offices. The Lincoln Bedroom on the south contains many pieces ordered by Mary Lincoln. The bed originally had an elaborate canopy. In the Lincoln Sitting Room is a small desk made by James Hoban from short lengths of mahogany during the construction of the White House. It was used by Hoban during his lifetime and presented a few years ago to the White House by his descendants. In the Queen's Bedroom and Sitting Room on the north side, the furniture is primarily of the late Federal period. The overmantel mirror and still life in a gilded frame was presented to the White House by Princess Elizabeth of England, on behalf of the King, during her visit in 1951. (See Plates 37 to 39.)

The President's office (Plate 40) is always decorated according to the personal wishes of the Chief Executive. President Carter has chosen the carved oak desk bearing a plaque inscribed with its history:

> H.M.S. "RESOLUTE" forming part of the expedition sent in search of SIR JOHN FRANKLIN IN 1852, was abandoned in latitude 75° 41' N. Longitude 101" 22' W. on 15th May 1854. She was discovered and extricated in September 1855, in latitude 67° N. by Captain Buddington of the United States whaler "George Henry." The ship was purchased, fitted out and sent to England, as a gift to her Majesty Queen Victoria by the President and People of the United States, as a token of goodwill & friendship. This table was made from her timbers when she was broken up, and is presented by the QUEEN of GREAT BRITAIN & IRELAND TO THE PRESIDENT OF THE UNITED STATES, as a memorial of the courtesy and loving Kindness which dictated the offer of the gift of the "RESOLUTE."

Although more than twelve hundred objects of art, furniture, rugs, and chandeliers have been acquired over the past nine years, several hundred additional items are needed to decorate the building in a manner befitting the residence of the President. Suitable pieces are now borrowed from museums, art galleries, and private owners.

Mrs. Carter presided at the first formal meeting of the Committee for the Preservation of the White House under the Carter administration, on October 20, 1978. Mr. Conger announced that a drive to raise a $20,000,000 endowment would be undertaken by the White House Historical Association, to provide funds for accessions and conservation. The income from the endowment, together with other earnings of the Association and continued generous gifts, should make this already fine museum of early nineteenth-century arts the preeminent collection in America.

Enough time has now passed so that the Competition entries of 1792—"the pile of trash presented as designs," George Hadfield called them—can be reassessed to see how clear, or how cloudy, the vision of their creators really was. It is all too easy to judge the proposals by modern academic and professional standards, and to overlook their historical significance, their novelty and merit for their own time, as Kimball and Bennett said 60 years ago. But by comparing the tentative sketches of 1792 with the White House as it stands and functions today, we can perceive something of the degree of insight these artisans and amateurs had.

Hoban, of course, rightly deserves the greatest credit; his general plan endures, and he built the building twice under most difficult circumstances. But the modifications of 1793 drastically altered his original elevations, and of the competition drawings, Jacob Small's eleven-bay elevation most nearly approximates the size, shape, and proportions of the White House as it was actually built. Eventually Hoban's three-story design has been vindicated; first in 1927, and again in 1952, the third story was inconspicuously restored so that functionally the building is about what Hoban envisioned.

The extension of the White House to the east and west has long been attributed to Jefferson, but his competition drawing had no hint of such a possibility. The idea was first proposed in the drawings of Jacob Small and James Diamond, and to them should go the credit for conceiving the only prudent method for expansion of the building.

Andrew Mayfield Carshore suggested a feature not incorporated until 160 years later. His roof plan called for a broad promenade around the perimeter inside the balustrade, and the rebuilt third floor of 1952 provides a promenade much as Carshore imagined it.

While it is Hoban's oval room that was built and is so much admired, Jacob Small deserves recognition for selecting an oval room for the same location in his eleven-bay design. Although the alcove bedroom is no longer in style, James Diamond's plan for a bedroom with a curved end wall concealing closets was duplicated in the 1952 rebuilding of the White House. Diamond also antedated Jefferson's dressing rooms for each bedroom by twelve or more years.

Thomas Jefferson's love for porticos, so amply expressed in his competition design, led to the addition of the north portico, a noble feature of the present structure.

Thus, no architect who entered the competition of 1792 fully anticipated all of the elements that make the White House the remarkable and handsome building it has become, but it is also true that every entrant we know of originated one or more unique features that have since been used to solve a problem, contribute to convenience, or add dignity to its appearance.

The White House has always had a special place in the affections of the American people. It was the first great building of a new nation. Some of our country's noblest moments occurred there, and some of its greatest men lived there. The shell and the form of the building selected by George Washington stand as a symbol of the resilient strength of the new concept of government so skillfully devised by the founding fathers.

A generation ago the structure was made safe and secure for centuries to come. Through the dedication and generosity of a great many people, in recent years that structure has become a very beautiful house. As a residence of a Chief of State, it has few peers anywhere. But the existence of the White House has often been threatened. By its nature, the building cannot be a mere period piece; evolution is an element of its purpose and its destiny. Age will surely enhance its great tradition, but the challenges of the future will add to its vitality, beauty, and variety only if there is a continued insistence on excellence.

Bibliography and Sources

I. BIBLIOGRAPHY

Adams, William Howard, editor: *The Eye of Thomas Jefferson,* National Gallery of Art, Washington, 1976.

Bernhardt, Duke of Saxe-Weimar-Eisenach: *Reise Sr. Hoheit des Herzogs Bernhard zu Sachsen-Weimar-Eisenach durch Nord-Amerika in den Jahren 1825 und 1826,* Heinrich Luden, Weimar, 1828. Also published in English by Carey, Lea & Carey, Philadelphia, 1828.

Berry, Henry F.: *A History of the Royal Dublin Society,* Longmans, Green & Co., London and New York, 1915.

Breton, Ernest: "Halle au Blé de Paris," in Jules Gailhabaud, *Monuments Anciens et Modernes: Tome Quatrieme, Periode Moderne,* Didot Freres, Fils et Cie., Paris, 1865.

Bryan, John Morrill: *Robert Mills, Architect, 1781–1855,* The Columbia Museum of Art, Columbia, S.C., 1976.

Bryan, Wilhelmus Bogart: *A History of the National Capital,* Macmillan Company, New York, 1914.

Busey, Samuel C.: *Pictures of the City of Washington in the Past,* Wm. Ballantyne & Sons, Washington, 1898.

Butler, Jeanne F.: "Competition 1792: Designing a Nation's Capitol," *Capitol Studies,* vol. 4, no. 1, U.S. Capitol Historical Society, Washington, 1976.

Caemmerer, H. Paul: *The Life of Pierre Charles L'Enfant, Planner of the City Beautiful, the City of Washington,* National Republic Publishing Company, Washington, 1950.

Caemmerer, H. Paul: *A Manual on the Origin and Development of Washington,* Senate Document No. 178, 75th Congress, 3rd Session, U.S. Government Printing Office, Washington, 1939.

Carter, Edward C., editor, and Thomas E. Jeffrey, microfiche editor: *The Papers of Benjamin Henry Latrobe,* published for the Maryland Historical Society by James T. White & Company, Clifton, N.J., 1977.

Columbia Historical Society: *Records,* (March 1894–) Washington, 1897–.
Vol. 10: Mrs. Thornton's Diary for the year 1800
Vol. 11: John Sessford Annals
Vol. 17: Writings of George Washington Relating to the National Capital

Colvin, Howard Montagu: *A Biographical Dictionary of English Architects, 1660–1840,* Harvard University Press, Cambridge, 1954.

Craig, Maurice: *Dublin 1660–1860,* Hodges, Figgis. 1952; Allen Figgis Ltd, Dublin, 1969.

Dunlap, William: *History of the Rise and Progress of the Arts of Design in the United States,* George P. Scott & Co., New York, 1834; Dover Publications, New York, 1969.

Fant, Christie Zimmermann: *The State House of South Carolina: An Illustrated Historic Guide,* R. L Bryan Company, Columbia, S.C., 1970.

The First Ladies Hall, National Museum of History and Technology, Smithsonian Institution, Smithsonian Institution Press, Washington, 1976.

Force, Peter: *National Calendar for 1820,* Davis and Force, Washington, 1820.

The Formation of the Union, National Archives Publication No. 70-13, General Services Administration, Washington, 1970.

Granger, Alfred Hoyt: *Charles Follen McKim, A Study of His Life and Work,* Houghton Mifflin, Boston, 1913.

Green, Constance McLaughlin: *Washington: Village and Capital, 1800–1878,* Princeton University Press, Princeton, N.J., 1962.

Griffin, Martin I. J.: "James Hoban, The Architect and Builder of the White House and the Superintendent of the Building of the Capitol at Washington," *American Catholic Historical Researches,* January 1907.

Guinness, Desmond, and William Ryan: *Irish Houses & Castles,* Thames & Hudson, London; Viking Press, New York, 1971.

Hamlin, Sarah H. J. Simpson: "Some Articles of Architectural Interest Published in American Periodicals Prior to 1851," Appendix B, in Talbot Hamlin, *Greek Revival Architecture in America,* Oxford University Press, New York, 1944; Dover Publications, New York, 1964.

Hamlin, Talbot: *Benjamin Henry Latrobe,* Oxford University Press, New York, 1955.

Harris, Ray Baker: "James Hoban (1762–1831) Architect, Builder, and Master Mason," *The New Age,* May 1959, Supreme Council 33° Ancient & Accepted Scottish Rite of Freemasonry Southern Jurisdiction United States of America.

——— : *The Laying of Cornerstones,* Supreme Council 33° Ancient & Accepted Scottish Rite, 1961.

Horsman, Reginald: *The War of 1812,* Alfred A. Knopf, New York, 1969. Chapter 8, The Burning of Washington, pp. 194–214.

Jefferson, Thomas: *Papers,* Julian P. Boyd, editor, Princeton University Press, Princeton, N.J., 1950–.

——— : *Writings,* Andrew A. Lipscomb, editor, The Thomas Jefferson Memorial Association, Washington, 1903.

Johnson, Lady Bird: *A White House Diary,* Rinehart and Winston, New York, 1970.

Johnston, Frances Benjamin: "The White House," *Demorest's Family Magazine,* vol. 27, no. 7, May 1890, pp. 385–391, and no. 8, June 1890, pp. 451–458.

Kimball, Fiske, and Wells Bennett: "Competition for the Federal Buildings, 1792–93," *Journal of the American Institute of Architects,* vol. 7, no. 1, January 1919, page 8; no. 3, March 1919, page 98; no. 5, May 1919, page 202; no. 8, August 1919, page 355; no. 12, December 1919, page 521; and vol. 8, no. 3, March 1920, page 117.

Kimball, Fiske: *Domestic Architecture of the American Colonies and of the Early Republic.* Charles Scribner's Sons, New York, 1922; Dover Publications, New York, 1966.

——— : *Thomas Jefferson, Architect,* privately printed, Boston, 1916; Da Capo Press, New York, 1968.

Kite, Elizabeth S.: *L'Enfant and Washington, 1791–1792,* Institut Français de Washington and The Johns Hopkins Press, Baltimore, 1929.

Lossing, Benson J.: *Mount Vernon and its Associations,* W. A. Townsend & Company, New York, 1859; reprinted, The Fairfax Press, n.d.

——— : *Pictorial History of the War of 1812,* Harper & Brothers, New York, 1869.

Lowry, Bates, editor: *The Architecture of Washington, D.C.,* vol. 1, chapter 1, "The White House" (microfiche edition), The Dunlap Society. Washington, 1976.

Mathews, Catharine Van Cortlandt: *Andrew Ellicott: His Life and Letters,* The Grafton Press, New York, n.d.

Morris, Edward Bateman, Compiler: *Report of the Commission on the Renovation of the Executive Mansion,* U.S. Government Printing Office, Washington, 1952.

Nichols, Frederick Doveton: *Thomas Jefferson's Architectural Drawings, Compiled and with Commentary and a Check List,* The University Press of Virginia, Charlottesville, Va., 1961.

Padover, Saul K., editor: *Thomas Jefferson and the National Capital 1783–1818,* U.S. Department of the Interior, Source Book no. 4, Washington, 1946.

Palladio, Andrea: *The Four Books of Architecture,* translated and published by Isaac Ware, London, 1738; Dover Publications, New York, 1965.

Ravenel, Beatrice St. Julien: *Architects of Charleston,* 2d ed., Carolina Art Association, Charleston, S.C., 1964.

Reiff, Daniel D.: *Washington Architecture 1791–1861, Problems in Development,* U.S. Commission of Fine Arts, Washington, 1971.

Restoration of the White House: Message of the President of the United States Transmitting the Report of the Architects, Senate Document No. 197, 57th Congress, 2nd Session, 1903.

Rice, Howard C.: *L'Hotel de Langeac: Jefferson's Paris Residence,* Henry Lefebve, Paris, and the Thomas Jefferson Memorial Foundation, Monticello, N.Y., 1947.

Spreiregen, Paul D., editor: *On the Art of Designing Cities: Selected Essays of Elbert Peets,* M.I.T. Press, Cambridge, 1968.

Thayer, Mary Van Rensselaer: *Jacqueline Kennedy: The White House Years,* Little, Brown and Company, Boston, 1971.

Truman, Margaret, *Harry S. Truman,* Morrow, New York, 1973.

Washington, George: *Writings of, from the Original Manuscript Sources, 1745–1799,* George Washington Bicentennial Commission, 1931–44.

——— : *The Diaries of George Washington,* edited by John C. Fitzpatrick,

Mount Vernon Ladies Association of the Union, Houghton Mifflin, Boston and New York, 1925.

The White House; An Historic Guide, White House Historical Association, 1962, 1964, 1971, and 1977 editions.

A Winter in Washington; or, Memoirs of the Seymour Family, published anonymously by Margaret Bayard Smith, E. Bliss & E. White, New York, 1824.

Withey, Henry F., and Elsie Rathburn Withey, *Biographical Dictionary of American Architects (Deceased),* Hennessey & Ingalls, Los Angeles, 1970.

Wittkower, Rudolf: *Architectural Principles in the Age of Humanism,* Alec Tiranti, London, 1962; Academy Editions, London, 1978.

The United States Magazine, "The President's House," vol 3, no. 3, September 1856, J. M. Emerson Co., New York.

II. SOURCE MATERIAL IN THE NATIONAL ARCHIVES, WASHINGTON, D.C.

A. Civil Archives Division: Records of the Office of Public Buildings and Grounds

Records of the District of Columbia Commissioners and of the Offices Concerned with Public Buildings, 1791–1867. Microfilm M371, 27 rolls. Correspondence and proceedings.

L'Enfant, Peter Charles, Reports to the President of the United States, nos. 1, 21, 39, and 73 of the original classification, dated March 26, June 22, and August 19, 1791, and January 17, 1792, respectively.

Letters of the Presidents to the Commissioners of the District of Columbia, 1791–1869.

Schedules of Sales of Public Lots, 1791–1802. Contains reports of James Hoban on the President's House, May and November, 1796, and May and November, 1797.

Bonds, Powers of Attorney, Capitol and other Buildings, Miscellaneous Accounts from June, 1792, to March 30, 1868. Contains memoranda relating to the President's House.

Day Books, 1791–1793, 1796–1800. Names of workmen, amounts and dates of payments, items of expense.

Journals, 1791–1816. 4 vols.

Accounts and Abstracts of Expenditures, 1817–33.

Receipted Accounts, 1793–1843. Receipted Bills, 1819, 1824, 1834, 1837.

Proposals and Estimates, 1795–1840.

Contracts, 1791–1913. Some in bound volumes, others in loose files.

Other Records Pertaining to the White House, Record Group and Preliminary Inventory numbers:

Records of the Commission of Fine Arts, RG66/PI179

Records of the National Capital Planning Commission, RG328/PI175

Records of the Department of the Treasury, RG56/PI187

Records of the Commission on the Renovation of the Executive Mansion, RG220/PI117

B. Audiovisual Division, Still Pictures Branch

Photographs and prints of the White House made by government agencies. The largest collection comprises negatives by Abbie Rowe, White House photographer during the renovation of the building in 1948–1952.

C. Cartographic Division

Maps and plans of the White House grounds and buildings from 1836 to the present, including plans for extensions and alterations proposed but not adopted.

D. Washington National Records Center, Suitland, Maryland.

Wills and administration of estates in the District of Columbia, 1801–1878.

III. NATIONAL OCEANIC AND ATMOSPHERIC ADMINISTRATION, NATIONAL OCEAN SURVEY, ROCKVILLE, MARYLAND 20852

Facsimiles of the 1887 copy of L'Enfant's plan made by the Coast and Geodetic Survey, and of Ellicott's map of 1792, are obtainable from the National Ocean Survey. In 1979 the price per copy was $1.50. This agency has custody of the original plate made and used by Thackara and Vallance in 1792.

page 2: Early offers of a site for the national capital: *Papers of the Continental Congress,* Item 46, Proposals to Congress relative to locating the seat of government, March 7, 1783, pages 9–11, and June 16, 1783, page 143. National Archives, Record Group 11.

page 2: Lancaster "mutiny": *Journals of the Continental Congress,* vol. XXV, 1783, Library of Congress, 1922, pages 970–974.

page 5: Jefferson note: written in *The Anas,* about May 1790; Saul K. Padover, in *Thomas Jefferson and the National Capital,* edited the extraneous material.

page 8: Federal Hall in New York was torn down in 1812. Louis Torres, "Federal Hall Revisited," *Journal of the Society of Architectural Historians,* December 1970, pages 327–338.

page 10: Washington noted his conversations at George-town in his diary. J. C. Fitzpatrick, *Diaries of Washington,* vol. IV, page 152.

page 11: Pennsylvania passed the bill mentioned and the President's House was built on 8th Street, Philadelphia. Washington refused to occupy it, to avoid strengthening Pennsylvania's hold on the capital. The building cost $120,000 but sold for $40,000 when it became clear that the ploy had failed.

page 11: J. P. Dougherty, "Baroque and Picturesque Motifs in L'Enfant's Design for the Federal Capital," *American Quarterly,* vol. 26, March 1974.

page 12: William T. Partridge worked for McKim in the preparation of the MacMillan Plan of 1901. As a consultant to the National Capital Park and Planning Commission in 1926, he made a detailed study of L'Enfant's plan, which was published in their Annual Report, 1930.

page 12: Robert C. Dean, an architect for the Williams-burg restoration, pointed out the similarity of L-shaped plans and their proportions in a lecture at the Wayside Inn, Sudbury, Mass., 1976.

page 12: Washington to Lafayette: The letter was handed to Lafayette's son on October 26, 1797.

page 12: The texts of L'Enfant's reports and letters used here are from photographic copies of the originals in the Library of Congress.

page 15: The exchange of letters regarding L'Enfant's actions in late 1791 and early 1792 leading to his dismissal is in Padover, *Thomas Jefferson and the National Capital,* and the biographies of L'Enfant by Kite and Caemmerer.

page 17: Washington letter to David Stuart, November 20, 1791, in *Writings,* Fitzpatrick, ed.

page 20: Elbert Peets: See Spreiregen, ed., *On the Art of Designing Cities.* Excavation: The size is mentioned in a letter from the Commissioners to the President, July 19, 1792.

page 20: The "different views" are mentioned by Washington in a letter to Jefferson, received February 22, 1792. Padover, page 92.

page 20: Washington's library is catalogued in Benson J. Lossing, *Mount Vernon and Its Associations,* pages 375–394. An engraving of Washington's plan for Pohick church is also in this book, page 88.
Washington's enlargement of Mount Vernon is de-scribed in his diaries and in correspondence with Lund Washington, manager of the estate. T. T. Waterman has suggested that the designs for the extensions were by John Ariss, but the only evidence produced was a remark by a descendant of the Washington family in recent

times, which could not be substantiated. Waterman, *The Mansions of Virginia,* page 408.

page 24: Jefferson wrote to the Comtesse de Tessé on March 20, 1787. Lipscomb, *Writings,* vol. 6, page 102.

page 35: Clarendon House and its progeny are discussed in Summerson, *Architecture in Britain, 1530–1830,* pages 87–88.

page 36: Carshore, first use of perspective in an Ameri-can architectural proposal: Jeanne F. Butler, "Competi-tion: 1792," *Capitol Studies,* vol. 4, no. 1, page 17.

page 38: Collins: All that is known about John Collins of Richmond is contained in a letter from the Virginia State Librarian to Fiske Kimball, May 21, 1919, Kimball Pa-pers, Fine Arts Library, Harvard University.

page 42: All quotations of Palladio are from the Isaac Ware translation of 1738.

page 43: President's House memorandum: *District of Columbia Papers,* Department of State, vol. 6, part 2, no. 138.

page 45: Jefferson's competition drawings: *The Eye of Thomas Jefferson,* W. H. Adams, ed., pages 238–240.

page 59: Small Hoban drawing: attached to proposal to the Commissioners, August 19, 1799.

page 61: Hoban's prize money: January 5, 1793, entry in *Journal A, 1791, 92,93 for the City of Washington.*

page 62: Kimball's derivation of original scale, Hoban plan: Kimball, *Thomas Jefferson, Architect,* page 177.

page 62: Kimball's erroneous scales for Hoban plan: Kimball, *Thomas Jefferson, Architect,* page 176, draw-ing 179.

page 67: Latrobe letter to Philip Mazzei, Pisa, Italy, May 29, 1806.

page 70: Parkman houses: Kimball, *Domestic Architec-ture,* pages 152–153 and 206.

page 70: Hoban's medal: H. F. Berry, *A History of the Royal Dublin Society,* page 115. The medal is displayed in the First Ladies Hall, National Museum of History and Technology, Smithsonian Institution.

page 70: Castletown: Desmond Guinness and William Ryan, *Irish Houses & Castles,* 1971, pages 193–210.

page 71: Washington to Thornton, December 30, 1798.

page 72: Richard Castle: the Knight of Glin, "Richard Cas-tle, A Synopsis," *Quarterly Bulletin, Irish Georgian Society,* 1964, vol. 7, no. 1, pages 31–38.

page 72: Leinster House: Georgian Society, *Records of Eighteenth-Century Domestic Architecture and Decora-tion in Ireland,* 1913, vol. 4, pages 43–61.

page 72: Unequal window spacing: On the opposite fa-cade, Hoban opened another pair of windows in the wide spaces, to provide more light for the rooms adjacent to the oval room.

page 74: Thomas Milton, "A Collection of Select Views from the different Seats of the Nobility and Gentry in the Kingdom of Ireland," 1783–1793.

page 78: Lucan House: Guinness and Ryan, *Irish Houses & Castles,* pages 130–136.

page 78: John Harris, "Sir William Chambers, Friend of Charlemont," *Quarterly Bulletin, Irish Georgian Society,* 1965, vol. 8, no. 3, pages 91–97.

page 81: Elizabeth Carter, *Letters to Mrs. Montagu be-*

tween the Years 1755–1800, Chiefly upon Literary and Moral Subjects,* London, 1817.

page 83: "It's scarce worth the attention . . . ," noted by Maurice Craig, *Dublin, 1660–1860,* page 221.

page 86: The small plan is mentioned by Ellicott in his letter to the Commissioners, March 7, 1792.

page 86: "To find himself" meant that Hoban would pro-vide his own food, clothing, and shelter.

page 90: The memorandum "Expenses of the Presi-dent's House" is in *Bonds, Powers of Attorneys, Capitol and other Buildings, Miscellaneous Accounts, etc.,* in the National Archives, RG42.

page 91: Hoban as a Mason: R. B. Harris, "James Hoban, Architect, Builder and Master Mason," *The New Age,* May 1959, pages 300–306.

page 91: Census report: Martin I. J. Griffin, "James Hoban, The Architect and Builder of the White House and the Superintendent of the Building of the Capitol in Washington," *American Catholic Historical Researches,* 1907, page 40.

page 91: Hoban's reports for 1796 and 1797 are bound in error in *Schedules of Sales of Public Lots, 1791–1802,* National Archives, RG42.

page 94: White's letter to Jefferson: Padover, *Thomas Jefferson and the National Capital,* page 276.

page 95: Hoban wax portrait: private communication from James Hoban Alexander.

page 95: Seabrook House: Attribution to Hoban, S. G. Stoney, *Plantations of the Carolina Low Country,* Caro-lina Art Association, Charleston, S.C., 1938, page 78.

page 95: Oak Hill, Loudon County, Virginia, the residence of James Monroe, is believed to have been remodelled by Hoban.

page 97: Drydock: Jefferson to Latrobe, November 2, 1802. Pennsylvania Avenue: March 14, 1803, Thomas Munroe sent Jefferson sectional sketches by Nicholas King. The trees along the walks were already being planted. Jefferson replied March 21, 1803, with a sketch of his own, requesting rows of trees next to the carriageway.

page 98: Jefferson to Latrobe, April 22, 1805. The draw-ings of the wings attributed to Jefferson in the Coolidge collection, Massachusetts Historical Society, are un-doubtedly Latrobe's copies. The draftsmanship and let-tering are unusually fine. (Kimball drug. no. 175)

page 98: "Short lengths . . . built": *Report of Supt. of Public Buildings and Grounds,* December 12, 1805.

page 99: Jefferson's portico for the capitol at Richmond with two columns on the sides: Kimball drug. no. 110.

page 106: "a Polypus—all mouth": comment by B. H. Latrobe in a letter to William Lee, March 22, 1817. We thank Dr. Charles E. Brownell for bringing this important letter to our attention.

page 106: Jefferson to Latrobe, April 25, 1808.

page 112: A diorama of Mrs. Madison's frantic packing in the oval room is displayed in the First Ladies Hall, Smith-sonian Institution.

page 113: Several authors have used the irresistible ex-pression "went up in smoke"; we first saw it in Talbot Hamlin, *Benjamin Henry Latrobe,* page 304.

page 114: There are numerous reports and debates in the *Annals of Congress* for the years 1814–1817 regard-ing the rebuilding of Washington.

page 116: Hoban's May 18, 1816, report is in *Proposals and Estimates,* National Archives, RG42.

page 117: Publication of the King map was announced in the *National Intelligencer,* February 27, 1818.

page 121: Wallpaper frieze: Commissioners to Samuel Blodget, June 10, 1800; Blodget to the Commissioners, June 15, 1800.

page 123: Marie G. Kimball, "The Original Furnishings of the White House," *Antiques,* June 1929, pages 481–486, and July 1929, pages 33–37.

page 123: Margaret Bayard Smith, *The First Forty Years of Washington Society,* page 386.

page 124: A Winter in Washington, a novel published anonymously by Margaret Bayard Smith, contains many passages describing the President's House during Jefferson's occupancy.

page 124: Margaret Brown Klapthor, "Benjamin Latrobe and Dolley Madison Decorate the White House 1809–1811," Paper 49: Bulletin 241 *Contributions from the Museum of History and Technology,* Smithsonian Institution, 1965.

page 125: Every article . . . burnt: Statement of William Lee, March 9, 1818, quoted by Robert L. Raley, "Interior Designs by Benjamin Henry Latrobe for the President's House," *Antiques,* June 1959, page 571.

page 127: Mrs. Thornton's diary for the year 1800, Records of the Columbia Historical Society, vol. 10, pages 88–226.

page 127: William Winstanley: J. Hall Pleasants, *Four Late Eighteenth Century Anglo-American Landscape Painters,* Amer. Antiq. Soc., pages 117–137.

pages 128: "details of a humiliating character": John Quincy Adams, diary.

page 128: Description of East Room: William Eliot, *The Washington Guide,* 1837, pages 106–107.

page 131: Heating system and entrance hall screen: *Report of Commissioner of Public Buildings,* House Document No. 28, 25th Congress, 2nd Session, December 15, 1837, page 5.

page 132: Haywood & Fox sketch: attached to letter to the Commissioner of Public Buildings, June 14, 1845, Contracts file, National Archives, RG42.

page 140: The Baltimore *Whig* used the term "White House" in 1810, and Margaret Bayard Smith mentioned "the white-house" in an 1837 account of the fire of 1814.

page 148: Fred D. Owen, "The First Government Architect. James Hoban of Charleston, S.C.," *Architectural Record,* vol. 11, 1910, pages 581–589.

page 161: A complete list of articles sold by C. G. Sloan is in the National Archives, RG42, Letters Received 1899–1906, item 1346, part 531, dated January 21, 1903. The previous location in the White House of major articles is in an undated memorandum on the letterhead of A. E. Kennedy, in the same file. The Washington *Evening Star,* January 21, 1903, and the Washington *Post,* January 22, 1903, carried reports of the auction.

page 166: Reconstruction of the White House is well described in the *Report of the Commission on the Renovation of the Executive Mansion,* 1952. Records of the Commission are in Record Group 220, National Archives (Preliminary Inventory 117).

page 181: The description of the present appearance and contents of White House rooms is compiled from the following sources. Articles in *Antique Monthly,* Gray D. Boone, editor:

Janet Green, "Interest Focuses on White House Guest Rooms," August 1969, page 6; "Elegant New Look in White House Public Rooms," December 1970, page 14B; "Red Room Redecoration Completed," January 1972, page 1; "19th Century Decor Unveiled in Green Room," February 1972, page 1A; "White House Blue Room Redecoration Complete," July 1972, page 1; "White House Grand Hall is Refurbished," March 1973, page 1.

Mary Hubbard, "President's Bedroom Redecorated," November 1973, page 6A.

Articles in *The Connoisseur,* May 1976:

Clement E. Conger, "The White House," pages 3–10. Clement E. Conger and Betty C. Monkman, "President Monroe's Acquisitions," pages 56–63.

Margaret Brown Klapthor, "The White House Porcelain," pages 16–21. Marvin Sadik, "Paintings from the White House," pages 23–31. Marvin D. Schwartz, "Decorative Objects from the White House and the Diplomatic Reception Rooms of the State Department," pages 32–39.

Berry B. Tracy, "Federal Period Furniture," pages 11–15. *The White House: An Historic Guide,* White House Historical Association, 1962, 1964, 1975, and 1977 editions.

Picture Credits

The authors and the publisher wish to thank the following individuals and institutions for permission to reproduce illustrations appearing in this book:

James Hoban Alexander, *22, 48, 68,* plate *11*

Alderman Library, University of Virginia, *18a, 18b*

Archives de France, *Service Photographique des Archives Nationales, 17a*

James Austin, *17b*

The Bettman Archive, Inc., *98*

The Boston Athenaeum, *46, 47*

Samuel Chamberlain, *75*

Columbia Historical Society, *111, 121*

Concord (Massachusetts) Public Library (Keith Martin, photographer), *101*

Cornell University Archives, *9*

Country Life, London, *60, 61, 62*

The Dunlap Society, *97, 136, 137, 139, 152, 166, 172, 173;* Richard Cheek (photographer), *99, 151;* Frank Herrera (photographer), *71, 72, 81, 82, 92*

Eastern National Park and Monument Association, *1, 2*

Fogg Art Museum, Harvard University (Barry Donahue, photographer), *58, 59*

The Green Studios, *49, 52, 53,* plate *5*

Historic Urban Plans, Inc., *94, 112*

The Houghton Library, Harvard University (Barry Donahue, photographer), *3, 7, 34, 39, 40*

The Huntington Library, San Marino, California, plate *15*

Irish Tourist Board (Brian Lynch, photographer), *51*

Library of Congress, *4, 5, 16, 42, 69, 70, 77, 78, 83–85, 87–89, 93, 96, 103, 113–130, 134, 135, 140, 143, 145–147, 150, 177,* plates *8, 9, 10, 21*

Maryland Historical Society, *21, 23–26, 28–32, 35–38,* plates *3, 4, 20*

Massachusetts Historical Society, *19, 20b, 41, 74, 76, 79, 80, 100*

Mount Vernon Ladies' Association, *12, 13, 14*

Musee Carnavalet, Paris (Lauros-Giraudon, photographer), plate *2*

The Hon, David Nall-Cain, *27*

National Archives, Washington, *73, 90, 91, 131, 132, 133, 138, 141, 142, 144, 148, 149, 154–165, 167–170, 175, 176*

National Library of Ireland and the Irish Architectural Records Association, *60, 64*

National Gallery of Art, Washington, plate *1*

National Maritime Museum, London, plate *18*

New York Historical Society, *86a, 86b*

The New York Public Library, I. N. Phelps Stokes Collection, plates *14, 16*

Howard C. Rice, Jr., *20a*

Franklin D. Roosevelt Library, plate *19*

St. John's Church, Washington, plate *13*

Thames & Hudson Ltd, London, *50, 66*

The White House Collection, *44, 45,* plates *11, 12, 17, 22, 27*

White House Historical Association (photographs by the National Geographic Society), plates *11, 17, 22–40*

Note: Italicized page numbers indicate illustrations.